PRAISE HER WORKS

The publication of this book is made possible by
generous gifts from

Congregation Shaarei Tefillah,
Newton Centre, Massachusetts

Phyllis Hammer

Marcia Cohn Spiegel,
her daughters, Linda, Randi, and Judy,
and granddaughter, Sharon Allen

Rabbi Sue Levi Elwell
in honor of Claire Levy Levi, Hana and Mira Elwell

PRAISE
HER
WORKS

Conversations with Biblical Women

Edited by Penina Adelman

5765 ✦ 2005
The Jewish Publication Society
Philadelphia

Copyright © 2005 by Penina Adelman
First edition. All rights reserved.

No part of this book may be reproduced or transmitted in any form or by any means,
electronic or mechanical, including photocopy, recording, or any information storage or
retrieval system, except for brief passages in connection with a critical review, without
permission in writing from the publisher:

The Jewish Publication Society
2100 Arch Street, 2nd floor
Philadelphia, PA 19103
www.jewishpub.org

Composition and design by Desperate Hours Productions, Philadelphia

Manufactured in the United States of America

Library of Congress Cataloging-in-Publication Data

Praise Her Works / edited by Penina Adelman.
    p. cm.
  Includes selections from *Midrash ha-Gadol* in Hebrew and English translation.
  Includes bibliographical references.
  ISBN 0-8276-0823-3 (alk. paper)
  1. Women in the Bible. 2. *Midrash ha-Gadol*. 3. Bible. O.T. Proverbs XXXI—
Commentaries. I. Adelman, Penina V. (Penina Villenchik) II. *Midrash ha-Gadol*.
English & Hebrew Selections.
  BS575.P67 2005
  296.1'4—dc22
                    2005009307

To my mothers: Mom and Helene, z"l, and all the other righteous women in my families

P.A.

Contents

Acknowledgments

The Women's Studies Research Center at Brandeis University continues to provide me with a space of my own where I can write and think, as well as wonderful colleagues with whom I can bounce around ideas. The "22 Women" study group—including Nechama Cheses, Nurit Eini-Pindyck, Cindy Marshall, Marsha Mirkin, and Rosie Rosenzweig—has been the wise cocoon that gave me a safe place to experiment and improvise. Funding from the Hadassah-Brandeis Institute allowed this group to try out our work on the public. *B'not Esh* is there to remind me of my roots.

These individuals must be mentioned: Ellen Frankel, who shared my vision and showed patience above and beyond; Carol Hupping and Janet Potter, who guided this book into the world, and all the rest of the staff at JPS who take such care in their work; Sue Berrin, my personal editor and friend; Aviva Dautch, whose thinking widened my own; Nurit Eini-Pindyck, who took great care with the Hebrew; R. Sheila Shulman, who knew Tamar and Dinah; Irit Koren, who helped crack open the Hebrew text; R. Benjamin Samuels, who was always ready for my questions; Laura, my daughter, who was and still is my inspiration; Daniel and Gil, who feed my soul and have tolerated my attention to this work; my dad, Burt (Binyamin Lev) z"l and Steve, my *Anshei Chayil.*

Eishet Chayil

אשת חיל

PROVERBS 31:10–31

[10]What a rare find is a capable wife!	‏אֵֽשֶׁת־חַ֭יִל מִ֣י יִמְצָ֑א[10]
Her worth is far beyond that of rubies.	‏וְרָחֹ֖ק מִפְּנִינִ֣ים מִכְרָֽהּ׃
[11]Her husband puts his confidence in her,	‏בָּ֣טַח בָּ֭הּ לֵ֣ב בַּעְלָ֑הּ[11]
And lacks no good thing.	‏וְ֝שָׁלָ֗ל לֹ֣א יֶחְסָֽר׃
[12]She is good to him, never bad,	‏גְּמָלַ֣תְהוּ ט֣וֹב וְלֹא־רָ֑ע[12]
All the days of her life.	‏כֹּ֝֗ל יְמֵ֣י חַיֶּֽיהָ׃
[13]She looks for wool and flax,	‏דָּ֭רְשָׁה צֶ֣מֶר וּפִשְׁתִּ֑ים[13]
And sets her hand to them with a will.	‏וַ֝תַּ֗עַשׂ בְּחֵ֣פֶץ כַּפֶּֽיהָ׃
[14]She is like a merchant fleet,	‏הָ֭יְתָה כׇּאֳנִיּ֣וֹת סוֹחֵ֑ר[14]
Bringing her food from afar.	‏מִ֝מֶּרְחָ֗ק תָּבִ֥יא לַחְמָֽהּ׃
[15]She rises while it is still night,	‏וַתָּ֤קׇם ׀ בְּע֬וֹד לַ֗יְלָה[15]
And supplies provisions for her household,	‏וַתִּתֵּ֣ן טֶ֣רֶף לְבֵיתָ֑הּ
The daily fare of her maids.	‏וְ֝חֹ֗ק לְנַעֲרֹתֶֽיהָ׃
[16]She sets her mind on an estate and acquires it;	‏זָמְמָ֣ה שָׂ֭דֶה וַתִּקָּחֵ֑הוּ[16]
She plants a vineyard by her own labors.	‏מִפְּרִ֥י כַ֝פֶּ֗יהָ נָ֣טְעָה כָּֽרֶם׃
[17]She girds herself with strength,	‏חָֽגְרָ֣ה בְע֣וֹז מׇתְנֶ֑יהָ[17]
And performs her tasks with vigor.	‏וַ֝תְּאַמֵּ֗ץ זְרוֹעֹתֶֽיהָ׃
[18]She sees that her business thrives;	‏טָ֭עֲמָה כִּי־ט֣וֹב סַחְרָ֑הּ[18]
Her lamp never goes out at night.	‏לֹא־יִכְבֶּ֖ה בַלַּ֣יְלָה נֵרָֽהּ׃
[19]She sets her hand to the distaff;	‏יָ֭דֶיהָ שִׁלְּחָ֣ה בַכִּישׁ֑וֹר[19]
Her fingers work the spindle.	‏וְ֝כַפֶּ֗יהָ תָּ֣מְכוּ פָֽלֶךְ׃

²⁰She gives generously to the poor;   20כַּפָּהּ פָּרְשָׂה לֶעָנִי

Her hands are stretched out to the needy.   וְיָדֶיהָ שִׁלְּחָה לָאֶבְיוֹן:

²¹She is not worried for her household because of snow,   21לֹא־תִירָא לְבֵיתָהּ מִשָּׁלֶג

For her household is dressed in crimson.   כִּי כָל־בֵּיתָהּ לָבֻשׁ שָׁנִים:

²²She makes covers for herself;   22מַרְבַדִּים עָשְׂתָה־לָּהּ

Her clothing is linen and purple.   שֵׁשׁ וְאַרְגָּמָן לְבוּשָׁהּ:

²³Her husband is prominent in the gates,   23נוֹדָע בַּשְּׁעָרִים בַּעְלָהּ

As he sits among the elders of the land.   בְּשִׁבְתּוֹ עִם־זִקְנֵי־אָרֶץ:

²⁴She makes cloth and sells it,   24סָדִין עָשְׂתָה וַתִּמְכֹּר

And offers a girdle to the merchant.   וַחֲגוֹר נָתְנָה לַכְּנַעֲנִי:

²⁵She is clothed with strength and splendor;   25עֹז־וְהָדָר לְבוּשָׁהּ

She looks to the future cheerfully.   וַתִּשְׂחַק לְיוֹם אַחֲרוֹן:

²⁶Her mouth is full of wisdom,   26פִּיהָ פָּתְחָה בְחָכְמָה

Her tongue with kindly teaching.   וְתוֹרַת־חֶסֶד עַל־לְשׁוֹנָהּ:

²⁷She oversees the activities of her household   27צוֹפִיָּה הֲלִיכוֹת בֵּיתָהּ

And never eats the bread of idleness.   וְלֶחֶם עַצְלוּת לֹא תֹאכֵל:

²⁸Her children declare her happy;   28קָמוּ בָנֶיהָ וַיְאַשְּׁרוּהָ

Her husband praises her,   בַּעְלָהּ וַיְהַלְלָהּ:

²⁹"Many women have done well,   29רַבּוֹת בָּנוֹת עָשׂוּ חָיִל

But you surpass them all."   וְאַתְּ עָלִית עַל־כֻּלָּנָה:

³⁰Grace is deceptive,   30שֶׁקֶר הַחֵן

Beauty is illusory;   וְהֶבֶל הַיֹּפִי

It is for her fear of the LORD   אִשָּׁה יִרְאַת־יְהוָֹה

That a woman is to be praised.   הִיא תִתְהַלָּל:

³¹Extol her for the fruit of her hand,   31תְּנוּ־לָהּ מִפְּרִי יָדֶיהָ

And let her works praise her in the gates.   וִיהַלְלוּהָ בַשְּׁעָרִים מַעֲשֶׂיהָ:

Introduction

N ew rituals are found, not made. They are waiting to be uncovered, like the sculpture living inside the stone.

Books are often the same. *Praise Her Works* is a book inspired by a ritual, which, in turn, emerged from a text. Jewish creativity encourages interaction between tradition, text, and human being.[1]

How the Ritual Came from the Text

I saw a need for a ritual that would be held close to the time of my daughter Laura's bat mitzvah. It would be a ritual of preparation and affirmation, of gathering together and making blessings. It would have to bring together all the important women and girls in Laura's life: grandmothers, aunts, friends, and mothers of friends, as well as favorite teachers. Ultimately, it would give her the extra push up to the *bimah*, where she would read her Torah portion and give her speech. If this public ritual made her a Jewish adult before the entire community, then this preparation ritual would make her a Jewish woman.

Since this would be Laura's first time in the spotlight, she and I thought of this preparation ritual as a dress rehearsal. Also, as the mother of the bat mitzvah, I wanted Laura to shine first on her home turf with the women and girls who were her intimates. I hoped she would then be ready to cross the threshold of the synagogue where she would make her debut on that public stage.

The ritual had begun coming into focus as I prepared for another gathering of women and girls months earlier, during Sukkot. We were having our annual "Women's Night in the Sukkah," when the women of my community invite biblical ancestors and female relatives to join us. This custom is called *ushpizin* (Aramaic for "guests"). Its roots are in the Jewish mystical tradition. We renamed the custom *ushpizot* (female guests). On this particular night, we were planning to invite Elisheba, wife of Aaron, into our sukkah.

Not knowing much about Elisheba, I looked her up in that well-stocked lake of a book called *Legends of the Jews* by Louis Ginzberg. While fishing for Elisheba, I retrieved a curious item I had never known before: Elisheba was one of 22 righteous women written about in a 13th-century Yemenite collection of midrashim called *Midrash ha-Gadol* (literally, The Great Midrash).

The word "midrash" comes from the Hebrew root *dalet-resh-shin*, meaning "to seek, inquire." A midrash is part of rabbinic commentary on the text and occurs in a place where something "disturbs," as my teacher Judah Goldin used to say. This disturbance could be a misspelling, an odd grammatical usage, a contradiction in the text, or anything the commentator felt worthy of notice. Midrashic tradition continues into the present day.

My curiosity was piqued by *Midrash ha-Gadol*. Who were the other 21 women? Which qualities determined who was on the list?

After Sukkot, I resolved to find the answers to these questions. I discovered that *Midrash ha-Gadol* has not been completely translated into English, so I made my way through the Hebrew and Aramaic to learn who the 22 righteous women were. Each one of the 22 was linked to a line from the familiar poem "Eishet Chayil" (Woman of Valor) found in Proverbs 31:10–31. In Jewish lore, this poem was written by Solomon for his mother, Bath-Sheba. Some say it was really written by Abraham as a eulogy for his wife, Sarah. In traditional Jewish homes, it is sung at the Shabbat table by husband to wife. It is sung at a wedding by groom to bride, and it is recited at a woman's funeral. However, the poem has been anathema to some Jewish feminists for decades. Why? Because on its surface it described an "ideal" Jewish woman, who was trusted by her husband, considered only what was good for him and not herself, managed real estate and business, stayed up all night sewing and making clothes for her family, and spoke mostly words of Torah. She seemed to be utterly self-sacrificing to the point of being self-effacing. "Eishet Chayil" was experienced as a burden to Jewish feminists. I wondered, as a modern Orthodox Jewish feminist, was it possible this poem could have been redeemed by the Rabbis who wrote *Midrash ha-Gadol?*

Finding the list made me marvel at the Rabbis' ability to be creative and traditional at the same time. Of course the four Matriarchs were on the list, as well as Miriam, Hannah, Ruth, Naomi, Bath-Sheba, and Esther. However, I also found women I had barely heard of, such as Hatzlelponi (the mother of Samson) and someone referred to only as the wife of Obadiah. Then, too, there were those whose stories were so abbreviated, I was amazed and pleased they were listed so I could get to know them: Serach bat Asher (granddaughter of Jacob), the Widow from Zarephath, and Rachav. Finally, there was a 23rd woman on the list, Vashti, the foil of Esther. The Rabbis certainly did not intend for her to be included as a Woman of Valor. However, as we look at the list today, Esther is no longer seen as completely without flaws or Vashti as completely without redeeming characteristics. Therefore, we must include Vashti who said "No!" to the king, and we amend the list to make it 23 women.

With this in mind, I imagine a group of Rabbis sitting in a circle on a rug in Yemen—debating about who is "in" and who is "out."

"What about Eve?" one proposes. "After all, she is the mother of all living."

"No, no," another retorts, "she lived too many generations before the Fathers (patriarchs) and Mothers (matriarchs), and besides, she did not obey her husband."

"But we must include Noah's wife, even though she did come many generations before Abraham and Sarah. The ark contained both male and female. As it says, "Noah was a righteous man; he was blameless in his age" (Gen. 6:9). So his wife was one of the first women of valor."

"You're right," another agrees. "Even though Noah's wife was not yet part of the covenant, she is just the kind of woman we are looking for—obedient, and so modest that she didn't even have a name. She can be first on our list, as it is written in the first line of the poem, *Eishet chayil mi yimtsa* (What a rare find is a capable woman).

The discussion continues until they settle on 23—one for each verse in the poem, with Vasthi and Esther sharing a verse. Even then, in later versions of this midrash, there would be different women included and excluded.[2] Now you, as the reader, can decide for yourself who belongs and who does not. Perhaps there are women you would add if you were creating this list. I believe the list is a stimulus to come up with other lists. Just as the Torah is a stimulus to come up with more wisdom and beauty in the form of midrash. Today, the meaning of "midrash" has expanded to take the form of music, dance, poetry, visual art, and story.

The list of women continued to haunt me. I had stumbled on a treasure trove. Learning this midrash would be like going on a special tour of the entire Hebrew Bible. This tour was for people with a passion about female biblical ancestors. It would be a way to get acquainted with some of the lesser-known women and to revisit some of the famous women such as Sarah, wife of Abraham, and Bath-Sheba, beauty queen and wife of King David.

What was even more exciting was that somewhere in this list of biblical women, I sensed there was a ritual for my daughter. Previously, I had seen several examples of rituals embedded in a text. I understand "text" to include a stimulus that is not necessarily written down: for example, an incident in someone's life, a painting, or a story from childhood.

For example, the women's Rosh Hodesh (New Moon) gathering, which is now quite widespread, took off from the seminal article written by Arlene Agus, "This Month Is for You."[3] Agus chronicled the rediscovery of the ancient festival of Rosh Hodesh by a women's study group she belonged to in New York in the 1970s called *Ezrat*

Nashim (a bit of an ironic name for a Jewish-feminist study group—literally, the women's section of an Orthodox synagogue).

A fairly new ritual object called *kos Miriam* (Miriam's cup), now found on seder tables among Jews of all denominations, came from a creative visualization that occurred during a Rosh Hodesh meeting in the 1980s in Boston. A whole series of ritual activities can be performed with Miriam's cup.[4]

When my husband and I were wrestling with infertility and had lost several pregnancies, I studied the story of Hannah daily. Eventually, we discerned a ritual for our losses in her prayer, which, in its silence and depth of feeling, is considered by rabbis to be a model for Jewish prayer. At that time, in the early 1980s, there were no Jewish rituals for infertility or pregnancy loss.

Each of these new rituals—Rosh Hodesh, Kos Miriam, and Hannah's Infertility Ritual—were part of a phenomenon called "invention of tradition."[5] All three are anchored to a Jewish written text: Rosh Hodesh as a special holiday for women has its roots in the Talmud (*Megillah* 22b and *Ta'anit* 1:6); Kos Miriam was inspired by the stories of the prophetess in Exodus and midrash; and Hannah's ritual is based on her story in 1 Samuel 1:1 and midrash.

As I considered the list of 23 women, I began to discern a ritual. What if we were to invite 23 women and girls to gather a few weeks before the actual bat mitzvah? What if we assigned one of the 23 Women of Valor to each guest and asked each to give Laura a blessing in the name of the biblical character—a blessing the character would have given the bat mitzvah girl if she could have been there that day? This bore some similarity to the *Zeved Bat* (Gift of a Daughter) celebration by which we had welcomed Laura into our family as a baby. At that ritual, everyone present was invited to say something to Laura—giving good wishes to a new baby is a Jewish tradition from Spain; the blessing could take the form of a poem, a song, good and wise words, a picture, or anything else the participants wanted to do.

Now we had to come up with our own list of 23 women to invite into our home for a "Make Your Own Midrash and Sundae" get-together. The day of the ritual, we placed in front of the fireplace a giant wicker throne chair—purchased back in the heyday of the *Addams Family* TV show. That was where Laura would sit to receive her blessings. The rest of us would gather around her in a circle of love and good wishes.

One by one, each person gave her blessing. Laura seemed to fill up with all the strong, positive feelings in the room the way a sapling takes in rain. It took about two hours for everyone to speak amidst plenty of tears, laughs, kisses, and hugs. Then we broke for ice cream with all the toppings a girl could want.

As one of my daughter's teachers—a Lubavitch woman who taught Hebrew and Judaic Studies—turned to leave, she told us, "That was the most beautiful bat mitzvah I ever attended!" And this was only the pre–bat mitzvah!

How the Book Came from the Ritual

After the "Ritual of the 23 Women" and Laura's bat mitzvah, I knew there was a book waiting to be written about this extraordinary list. What had been most powerful about the ritual was the way each woman and girl was able to enter into her ancestor's life and draw out a blessing for the bat mitzvah girl. I felt that these 23 Women of Valor needed a forum in which to speak and be heard.

I decided to study the stories from *Midrash ha-Gadol* in greater depth with a teacher. I approached a professor of midrash who was interested in my idea. He insisted that to study the midrash on the 23 women in the proper way would take a very long time. There were many sources in the text to research and link to the stories. There were different interpretations from the commentators to consider. To do justice to this text would take a serious commitment of time and energy. He did not have that kind of time, as he told me, but he thought my idea of bringing the women to life was worthwhile and that I should do it.

I appreciated his respect for the text, both the midrashic and the biblical one. I have learned in the course of writing this book that respect for the text requires being honest with it and with oneself. It means also respecting the long chain of tradition that has preceded current readings of the text. In writing *Praise Her Works*, all of the authors have learned to respect our ancestors, especially our female ones, who have a lot to say to us.

Jewish tradition is a well, from which it is possible to keep drawing water for sustenance and vitality. There is even a name for this: Miriam's well. Legend has it that on the second day of Creation, a well was created to keep the Jewish people alive in times of drought and scarcity, as well as in times of growth and plenty. There was too much material for me to study by myself in the midrash on "Eishet Chayil." Thankfully, there was a group of women who were willing to study it with me over the course of three years, to "become" the 23 Women of Valor in the best sense of the word. Then, later, there was a group of 15 women who agreed to "become" the ancestors and write down their own versions of the biblical stories.

Living in Torah

I hope this book teaches you how to step into Torah and leave behind the stance of "outside observer," which can hold you back from a more complete understanding of this timeless, sacred text. The Ethiopians in Israel taught me a great deal about living in the letters, words, and stories that had been the "Promised Land" of their ancestors when they were not living in Israel.

In 1991 in Israel, I was studying the Torah portion Noah with five Ethiopian women who had been living in Israel several years but never formally studied Torah. We read about the rainbow covenant between God and the people. They explained to me that in Ethiopia, a rainbow is a sign of blessing and wind is a sign of war. When I asked what thunder represented, one woman said, "When there is thunder, we all bow our heads and say, 'Moses is up on Sinai now.'" At that moment, I understood what it meant to be living in Torah.

The Hasidic Jews (a sect founded in the 18th century that strongly emphasizes ecstatic worship through dancing and singing) believe that coming closer to God is the most important goal of a Jew. They perceive all the biblical figures—accessible through study and contemplation—to be aspects of the divine, as well as aspects of the self. For example, learning the story of Sarah in depth, one is better able to identify with her and to know her. In turn, when one comes to a situation in which the strength of Sarah is called for, one knows that to summon her up will bring that particular kind of "Sarah" strength. Sometimes, Sarah may speak to the one who has called her. Sometimes, her presence is enough. Sometimes, she may ask a question for the summoner to answer.

I hope you will use *Praise Her Works* to get to know our female biblical ancestors, to see how each of these *nashei chayil* (women of valor) acted when faced with a serious challenge. Each woman has a unique power to transmit, from the steadfastness of the wife of Noah to the willingness of Rachav to lay her life on the line; from the faith Hatzlelponi had in the words of an angel to the daring Esther showed in revealing who she really was. We are the heirs to the ancestral strength chronicled in the Torah. We need only to study it deeply in order to receive our sacred legacy.

How This Book Is Organized

Each chapter follows a template, starting with the chapter title—which is a line from "Eishet Chayil" that the writers of *Midrash ha-Gadol* identified with a specific biblical woman—followed by the corresponding Hebrew excerpt from *Midrash ha-Gadol*. Something that the Rabbis who wrote *Midrash ha-Gadol* took for granted was that almost everyone who read the book knew the whole Bible by heart. That is why at times only half a verse from the Bible is quoted. The rabbis assumed that the reader knew the rest of the verse. Today, that level of biblical literacy cannot be presumed at all. Therefore, look up a citation when you don't understand it as written. This is an opportunity to learn more Bible.

Next, the Hebrew excerpt is translated. Then comes the story, which is a synopsis of the biblical account of this woman. After that, in a section called "Commentary," the contributor provides her personal perspective on the biblical woman's story. She explains how the biblical story connects to a line in "Eishet Chayil" designated by the Rabbis for that particular biblical woman. This section also seeks to understand the midrash from *Midrash ha-Gadol* in the light of her story. This, in turn, is followed by "So-and-So Speaks," in which each *eishet chayil* interacts with the reader, expressing thoughts she has not articulated over all these years, or she may clarify an action she took or a statement she made that she feels has been misinterpreted. After this, in a part called "A Message from the Woman of Valor," she distills down to a few brief paragraphs what she wants the reader to take away from this encounter. Finally, there is a section called "For Further Thought" to spur on more consideration of the meaning of this *eishet chayil's* story and words for the reader today.

Praise Her Works can be fertile reading material for groups as well as individuals. If you read it as a group and gather to discuss each chapter, you may want to "invite" different biblical women to join in the discussion. You may want to use props or even dress up. Some very unexpected conversations ensue when Serach and Miriam compare notes on prophecy or when Batya, Bath-Sheba, Esther, and Michal compare notes on life as royals. Sarah, Leah, Rachel, and Hatzlelponi can support each other around infertility. Vashti, Leah, and Michal may wish to form an "Unloved and Misunderstood Wives Club." Yocheved, Naomi, and Noah's wife may want to start a Memoir Group. Think of the get-together as Judy Chicago's "Dinner Party" meets "Women's Night in the Sukkah." The possibilities are endless.

I was fortunate to find a dynamic group of bold writers who were willing to go trekking with me into some of the more remote places in Torah. In order to do this, we had to open ourselves to discovering new and old ways to learn from our female ancestors.

I hope that as readers of *Praise Her Works* you will expand your ways of thinking about and experiencing your biblical ancestors. I hope that you will go trekking on your own and with others, constantly searching for ways of living in Torah. I hope that you will teach the next generation to do the same. May your mouth be open with wisdom. May a Torah of lovingkindness be upon your tongue.

Penina Adelman
13th of Shevat 5765
Newton, Massachusetts

❧ Chapter 1
Wife of Noah

PENINA ADELMAN

אֵשֶׁת־חַיִל מִי יִמְצָא וְרָחֹק מִפְּנִינִים מִכְרָהּ׃

"A woman of valor, who can find? Her worth is far beyond that of rubies" (Prov. 31:10).[1]

אשת חיל מי ימצא זו אשתו שלנח שהיתה מצדקת את בעלה כשאמר לו הקב"ה כי אתך ראיתי צדיק לפני. ורחוק מפנינים מכרה, שהיתה היא וכלותיה מעשיהן רחוקין ממעשה דור המבול.

A woman of valor, who can find? This is the wife of Noah, who caused her husband to be righteous, as God said, "... for you alone have I found righteous before Me in this generation" (Gen. 7:1). *Her worth is far beyond that of rubies.* Her deeds and those of her daughter-in-law were far beyond the deeds of the generation of the flood.
—*Midrash ha-Gadol*

Generations after Adam and Eve were cast out of the Garden of Eden, God sees that the people on earth are wicked. They think only of themselves; they stop at nothing to get what they desire; they are violent and destructive toward each other and the earth. God decides to destroy all that had been created.

God searches for the right person to carry out the plan. A man named Noah (comfort) is the choice. Noah is not an extremely righteous or virtuous person. However, he is the best compared to all the people around him. First, God instructs Noah exactly how to build an ark, where he and his family will live during the great destruction.

God says, "For my part, I am about to bring the Flood—waters upon the earth—to destroy all flesh under the sky in which there is breath of life and everything on earth shall perish. But I will establish My covenant with

you, and you shall enter the ark, with your sons, your wife, and your sons'
wives. And of all that lives, of all flesh, you shall take two of each into the
ark to keep alive with you; they shall be male and female"(Gen. 6:17–19).

Noah does just as God commands him. He builds an ark that
houses all the animals along with his family. The rain pours down for
40 days and 40 nights until even the mountains are covered. During
this time, God destroys every creature that creeps, walks, or flies.
Noah, his family, and the animals they are carrying on board are the
only beings alive. Time passes and the waters begin to recede.

Noah sends a dove out of the ark. It brings back an olive branch, sig-
nifying that dry land is nearby. When dry land is visible everywhere, God
commands Noah to bring all the animals and his family out of the ark.

"Then the Lord said to Himself: 'Never again will I doom the
earth because of man, since the devisings of man's mind are evil from
his youth; nor will I ever again destroy every living being, as I have
done.' ... God blessed Noah and his sons, and said to them, 'Be fertile
and increase, and fill the earth'" (Gen. 8:21, 9:1).

It was like a second Creation, a second chance—all but Noah
and his family have been destroyed.

Commentary

The poem "Eishet Chayil" (Woman of Valor), in its literal Hebrew
translation, starts out with a question: "Who can find a woman of
strength?" Not "Where is such a woman?" but "Who is the one capable
of finding her?" The question invites us to participate in the search, even
dares us. Right from the beginning, this poem tries to engage the reader,
who is too often a passive, silent being. This is the goal of Jewish study, to
urge the reader of the text to become involved in the learning process.

The legacy of Moses, who brought the Torah from Mount Sinai
to the Jewish people, is that we should take an active part in the trans-
mission of divine wisdom. Study is not worth much if it does not bring
about change in the student, if it does not matter a great deal in the
student's life.

The question "Who can find a woman of strength?" prefigures questions asked much later in *Pirkei Avot* (4:1), a tractate of the Talmud. For example,

> Ben Zoma said, Who is wise? He who learns from all men ... Who is mighty? He who subdues his passions ... Who is rich? He who rejoices in his portion ... Who is worthy of honor? He who respects his fellow men.

The questioner from *Pirkei Avot* shuns the obvious stock answers in favor of penetrating, even paradoxical, answers.

One answer to "Who can find a woman of strength?" is: only that person who possesses strength can find her. Who is the first woman that *Midrash ha-Gadol* points to as an example of this inner courage? Eishet Noach, wife of Noah. The "eishet" in both "Eishet Chayil" and Eishet Noach are not coincidental. As you study this midrash on the 22 women, you will find that this parallel is just the sort of hook the midrash is looking for to derive connections between the 22 lines of the poem and the 22 women of strength. (There are actually 23, not 22, women in this book, because we are counting Vashti as an *eishet chayil*, too, since she is included on the Rabbis' list, even though the Rabbis most probably did not intend for her to be a positive role model in the time during which they were writing.)

The wife of Noah is a woman of strength because "she made her husband righteous," according to the midrash. In a generation that is characterized by the commentators as particularly devoid of moral and just people, Noah and his wife stand out. At first glance, Noah's wife sounds like the typical "woman behind the man." After all, she gets no credit in the Torah for being the pillar that enables Noah to stand straight and accept God's challenge. She doesn't even have a name. However, perhaps that is precisely why the Rabbis of *Midrash ha-Gadol* bestow upon her the place of honor, which happens at the very beginning of their interpretation of the poem "Eishet Chayil."

The Wife of Noah Speaks

You found me. How many thousands of years it has taken, but you found me. I'm not asking why or how. That you did it is a miracle. I've learned you can't force things, just like we couldn't force God to stop the rain. I had hoped that one day someone would come and want to know more. Survivors need to tell their tales of survival, but there must be willing listeners. Sometimes the silence between words is all there is. Listening requires waiting. Not many have the time or the patience. You do, and so your energetic listening will draw my story out like water from a well where the pump needs a little priming.

Rain seeped into us day and night. I'm not a water creature, so it wore me down. Nor could I fly away like the free birds above us. Some of the birds circled us and we were afraid they knew our end was coming. They were ready for it.

The animals minded the water, too. They were trembling bundles of wet fur and feathers. And the smell. It hung there day and night like a sopping wet curtain oozing with urine, excrement, snot, vomit, sperm, and sweat. Not to mention the breath of so many creatures living together in a small space. Only the fish were at peace.

Our food was soaked through. Nobody felt like eating. I tried rolling up cakes of flour and rainwater. Tasteless crumbles.

How did we get through it? I asked the One Who Knows All Things for strength to live through the water. The One made it pour harder. At night in the deluge, Noah turned to me as we huddled together in our soggy straw bed. He cried and his tears were indistinguishable from the rain. "How can we survive another day of this?" he pleaded with me as if I could stop it. "People are not meant to live this way. It's against our nature not to have shelter, not to be dry and warm."

I caressed his head and held it close to my breasts as I remembered my mother doing for me when I was frightened. "I don't know," I told him, "but we will get through this. We will survive this flood."

Comforting him, I felt better. It was out. We were both terrified. You know, I was pleased when he cried since he did it so rarely. Noah could be hard. He could look at our sons crying when they were very small and tell them to stop. Because he couldn't stand to see them that way. I think their tears melted him and he was afraid of what was under the tough skin he had grown. He had to grow it because of the people who lived around us. They cared only for themselves, their homes, their children, their work, their fortunes. They had a god for each one of these. They didn't care for One God, and certainly not for other people. So Noah had grown this protective armor that he wore even with me. Why didn't I need to wear it? Where I came from, at the coming-of-age ceremony, a girl learns how to speak her true voice. That is her protection.

I could not imagine not making it through those terrible drowning days. I had said we would get through this, but what was I basing that on? A dream I kept having. Parts of it would haunt me during the long days when the horizon was invisible—softening the sky and sea into one gray vastness, as in the days before Creation.

> In the dream, I see a bow in a cloud. I had seen this once before when I was young, after my friend Ozia's coming-of-age ceremony. She and all her female relatives had been dancing all night as I and other women pounded on the drums. At one point, there was real thunder that seemed to be drumming back to us. Then rain started coming down, lightly at first like a band of butterflies, then a downpour. Just as quickly, the skies cleared and there was a bow in the cloud.
>
> In my dream, an invisible hand pulls back the bow and releases an arrow of many shimmering colors that fly across the sky: ruby, jasper, topaz, emerald, sapphire, and amethyst. Whenever I thought about this bow of many colors, my heart leapt up like a fish toward the sky. I had hope. I would envision those colors leaping across the sky in this seascape of no color and my heart would lift, too. As it says in King Solomon's poem, "Her worth is far beyond that of rubies," meaning I will not be sold for anything less than the entire sky, streaming with the colors of precious jewels, let alone the entire sky itself.

I once heard of a family that was starving because of a drought. Do you know what got them through this trial? They would dream of the most delicious foods they had ever tasted. They would describe them to each other, and in that way, they survived their hunger. They dreamt of a feast where there was none. I dreamt of a feast for the eyes where there was none.

Of course we did make it off the ark onto dry land in due time. We tried to pick up our lives, or I should say we began all over again. It was not easy to do. Noah and I barely left our new home after that. We were content to stay put. I never went into a large body of water again. I didn't even want to see one. I could not stand the taste of fish or anything from the sea. Watching the sky, especially when the light blossomed in the early morning or when it faded at the end of the day, always comforted me. And it comforted Noah. too.

By the way, I do appreciate your listening. And please call me by my name. It was never recorded in the Bible; it only appears later, in the Rabbinic writings. I am called Naamah, which means "pleasant."

A Message from Noah's Wife

There will come a time in your life when you must endure something terrible, something that does not seem to be in the natural order of things, such as a death, the end of a relationship, the loss of a job, illness, war, or natural disaster.

You could come out of it having achieved much inner growth. Crisis can teach you that you are not the creator of the story of your life, but you can be the one to fill in the gaps by making sense of the contradictions, the way midrash does for the biblical text. Crisis can teach you how not to keep washing up on the same shore over and over again like a creature in a shell, passively going where the water takes you—rather to pay attention to the patterns of your life and learn from them. You could also choose to ignore any lessons this crisis is trying to teach you, and come out of it battered and in deep despair. But that will lead to nothing fruitful.

The flood sobered me. It put me on notice that life is not going to wait for me to wake up. That I'd better recognize what I have to be grateful for. Noah. My children. Clear sky. Sunshine. My life. A new earth. No more do I take any of these things for granted.

For Further Thought

Consider the issue of women's silence, a phenomenon that is common in the Bible. What do you make of the silence of Noah's wife in Genesis? How is it different from, or the same as, Sarah's silence when Isaac is taken by Abraham to be sacrificed in Genesis 22? How is it different from, or the same as, Hannah's silence before she goes to Shiloh to pray for a child in 1 Samuel 1:1–9? The silences of biblical women are the reason why many Jewish women today feel compelled to use the medium of midrash to understand and fill those silences.

Tillie Olsen, a Jewish writer born in 1912 in Omaha, Nebraska, is the author of *Silences*, a fascinating treatise, both scholarly and personal, on why artists do not always have the luxury of expressing themselves. It is particularly pertinent to the "Wife of Noah" story and the stories of the other biblical and postbiblical women we do not know. She writes:

> The power and the need to create, over and beyond reproduction, is native in both women and men. Where the gifted among women (*and men*) have remained mute, or have never attained full capacity, it is because of circumstances, inner or outer, which oppose the needs of creation.
>
> Wholly surrendered and dedicated lives; time as needed for the work; totality of self. But women are traditionally trained to place others' needs first, to feel these needs as their own …; their sphere, their satisfaction to be in making it possible for others to use their abilities.[2]

A contemporary midrash with a different take on the meaning of silence is "The Unbinding of Sarah." It is part of a collection of contemporary midrashim by Norma Rosen called *Biblical Women Unbound* (Philadelphia: The Jewish Publication Society, 1996, 2001), pages 46–60.

Chapter 2
Sarah

PENINA ADELMAN

בָּטַח בָּהּ לֵב בַּעְלָהּ וְשָׁלָל לֹא יֶחְסָר:

"Her husband puts his confidence in her, and lacks no good thing"
(Prov. 31:11).

בטח בה לב בעלה, זו שרה שהיה לבו שלאברהם בטוח בה שאמר לה
אמרי לי אחי הוא. ושלל לא יחסר, שהיתה מכנסת את האורחין תחת כנפי
השכינה.

The heart of her husband trusts in her. This is Sarah, in whom the
heart of Abraham trusted, as he said to her, "... say ... He is my
brother" (Gen. 20:13). "And lacks no good thing," for she used to
invite in guests under the wings of the *Shekhinah.*
—*Midrash ha-Gadol*

Sarah's husband, Abraham, gets the call from God to leave his land
and his birthplace and his father's house for a land that God will
show him. He is 75 when God summons him, and Sarah is about that
old as well, which in biblical terms is quite young. God promises Abraham that once he reaches this land, he will become father of a vast
nation, he will be blessed, and his name will become great. Sarah and
Abraham leave with Abraham's nephew Lot and his family, in addition to all the people that were moved to join them in their divinely
inspired journey.

Sarah and Abraham travel to the Negev, where they learn there
is a famine, so they decide to go down to Egypt for food. Abraham is
aware that once they are in Egypt he and Sarah will be subject to the
laws of the desert. Since they will travel among strangers, they are
prone to being captured. In all likelihood, their captors will take the

beautiful Sarah and kill Abraham. Fearing this, Abraham instructs Sarah to tell whomever they meet on their way that they are brother and sister. Sarah does so and comes dangerously close to having sexual relations with the Pharaoh and with King Abimelekh, but for the grace of God. The Holy One intervenes and causes the kings to give Sarah back to Abraham.

Much later, after Sarah has borne Isaac, God intervenes again, this time saving Isaac from being sacrificed by his own father. However, it is too late for Sarah. Although we don't know exactly what happened, it seems that Sarah intuited that her son was in danger. Perhaps she bargained with God to take her life instead of her son's, and in this way he was spared the knife. Or perhaps she died of shock once she perceived that her husband had taken her only child to the altar to be offered up to God. We can only speculate because we never hear from Sarah again. According to the Bible, by the time Isaac returns from his near-sacrifice, Sarah has died.

What is known is that Abraham mourns for Sarah and weeps for her. He remembers how together they had journeyed into the unknown to make a better life for their descendants. He remembers how together they had always kept their tent open on all four sides to welcome strangers, feed them, give them drink and a place to rest. He remembers how together they had been able to face any hardship, any sorrow, and any opportunity.

Commentary

At first glance, Sarah, the second *eishet chayil* (woman of valor), does not seem to fill her own place. She seems a mere appendage of Abraham. He trusts in her and he will have no lack of gain, states the poem. The midrash confirms this by stating how Abraham's trust in her is well deserved because she does exactly as he asks. She tells those they encounter that he is her brother, again and again, in order to prevent his certain death. Besides, continues the midrash, she never fails to welcome strangers into their tent—a sign of Abraham's constant gain through her. Allowing the world to come into their tent means that Abraham has a chance of many, many encounters with beings human and divine. Providing hospitality to strangers means that something positive might happen, that their lives might improve in some way.

One could conclude that Sarah's entire reason for being revolves around her husband. This is a common complaint of some women reading "Eishet Chayil" today. It describes a woman who is a wife, mother, hard worker, teacher of children, and a provider for her family, but is she somebody in her own right?

This question draws me to the poem now. Sarah has a name and a voice. Her story bears reading more than once in order to answer the question: "Is Sarah an individual in her own right?" Sometimes I find myself judging another woman who has not chosen the same path as I have. "How can she live that way?" I ask myself. "Isn't she missing _____ (fill in the blank)? How can she make those choices?"

Of course, each woman has her own valid reasons for choosing her life's path. She could easily look at my life and decry some of my decisions. Is it possible to learn about Sarah's life and respect her choices, rather than judge them? If we read deeply enough it is possible to know Sarah in an unexpected way.

Sarah has trouble conceiving—a plight shared by Rebekah, Rachel, Hannah, Hatzlelponi, and the Shunammite woman. She proposes to Abraham that he couple with her servant, Hagar, so that she can bear Sarah an heir. This was not an uncommon practice at the time. The biblical text states, "And Abraham heeded Sarah's request" (Gen. 16:2). He takes what she says seriously and follows her wishes. This indicates a relationship of mutual respect.

What follows from Sarah's wishes is heartache and strife when Hagar bears a son, Ishmael. The relative positions of the two women become reversed for a time. Sarah is dependent on her servant for a child. Hagar knows she has something valuable that her mistress wants. Sarah and Hagar are rivals, battling for the favor of one man. Sarah is not meek and docile in this situation. She feels threatened in her very being, whereas when pretending to be Abraham's sister she went right along with the plan.

Sarah is a complex woman, not an appendage of her husband. True, she sets aside her own needs to do what Abraham asks of her as they make their way through strange lands. This is what is meant in "Eishet Chayil" when the poem says, "Her husband puts his confidence in her." However, at another juncture, Sarah changes the course of history by directing Abraham to have a child by Hagar. Perhaps it would be more accurate to say, "And they will have no lack of gain." Sarah's actions bear consequences she could not have foreseen, including bringing to fruition God's promise that she and Abraham each heard in their own way—the promise of enduringness, strength, and family.

Sarah Speaks

Welcome to my tent, open on all sides, as always. Come in, come in. I am especially pleased you have come because you seem to listen so hard. And that goes for all of us, *nashei hayil* [women of valor, strength]. We speak, knowing you take our words seriously, knowing you will make sure to pass our words on to others by writing them down this time.

Naamah [Noah's wife], you remind me of how hard it was to leave my land and my birthplace and my family to go into the unknown. You didn't know if there would be anywhere to go once God stopped ranting and raining. I knew the world would remain, but I couldn't imagine where I would be in it.

Do you know the hardest part? I was traveling with a man I barely knew—my new husband, Abraham. I didn't trust him yet. He didn't trust me either, I'm sure. How could we? We hadn't been through anything together yet.

Leaving home was the first time we were forced to depend upon each other. There were no parents, no friends or relatives to turn to.

Just the group of souls who came along with us because they believed our calling was true. We had both heard God telling us clearly to leave all we knew and loved, to go to a different place and start a better life. These people were looking to us for guidance. It would not have been fitting for us to ask them for help.

Of course God spoke to me, as well as to Abraham, though not in words the way he seems to have heard it. But it was speech, nonetheless. Let me explain. When I was a young girl, we celebrated the coming of our first blood. Mine came much later than all my friends' had. I kept asking my mother and my aunts and my girl cousins, "When will it come?"

They tried to reassure me. "B'sha'ah tovah, in its own good time. It'll come when you stop expecting it, when you are ready."

"But I'm ready now," I protested. "I don't want to wait anymore."

"Sarai, you must be patient," warned my mother, using the name she and my father had given me before God changed my name and Abraham's to reflect our coming closer to the Holy One. "Your blood will come."

She was right. But I just hated being out of step with my friends. One friend in particular, Anat, had her first blood long before the rest of us. She told me the Goddess had chosen her to be a Great Mother, promising she would bear many, many children, each one more perfect than the next. She made me swear not to tell anyone that one of her children was destined to become a god.

Anat became pregnant. She beamed as she told me she was holding the future of the world in her belly. Yes, I was jealous. I wanted to hold the future inside me, too. I wanted to know from inside what my mother meant, announcing as she did at every birth, "When a child is born, it has the potential to save the world."

Anat gave birth to a little boy. Immediately the priests of the temple claimed him for the Goddess. Anat scratched and bit when they came for her baby.

"He belongs to the Queen of Life and Death," they proclaimed, "not to you. You are a mere vessel. Go home and wait until you are called upon again to do the Goddess's bidding." They had to pry her away from her son.

I had dreadful dreams after that, ones in which I would keep getting pregnant, giving birth, and surrendering baby after baby to the Goddess. Needless to say, I was no longer so sure I wanted my first blood to come.

But whether I wanted it or not, sooner or later I would have to step out of my cramped, but so familiar, girl skin and get used to the ripe, expansive skin of a woman.

One day I was sitting on a windy hilltop while my goats nibbled the grass. I closed my eyes because that allowed me to know my surroundings better. When I opened them, the green grasses in front of me were bobbing and bending. They were saying something. I sat so still, I almost stopped breathing to listen better.

"Go, take yourself from this place where you have grown up," they advised. "Seek out a new place where your understanding will increase, where your wisdom will be heard, and where your compassion will help many others.

"You can no longer grow and thrive here. You recognize the futility of sacrificing children to make the unyielding land thrive again. Go to a place where your descendants will be as numerous as we are."

It was true. My mother and I talked often about the Goddess's unceasing hunger for innocent children. How the priests seemed to take gory pleasure in offering babies to her devouring Presence. My mother taught me how to pray, as she did, that no more children would be taken.

I had asked, "Who do you pray to? Surely not the Goddess!"

"I pray to a divine power that the Goddess is only part of, the way you and I and all of us here are also part of something greater than we are. That power is everywhere and does not exist only in the hands of the priests or the belly of the Goddess. But you mustn't talk about this or they will think you are not like the others. They might even—my stomach gnarls to think of it—offer you to Her!"

I understood that I must pay attention to the grasses. They were guiding me to something better if only I were brave enough. I could not imagine leaving by myself.

When I was joined with Abraham, I soon learned that he, too, had heard that it was necessary to leave our home. Of course, you know his story.

But you don't know the story of how we came to trust each other. Twice during our travels, he told me to say that I was his sister so that his life would be spared. Each time the king of that place nearly took me into his bed. I hated doing this. I felt that my own husband was offering me as a sacrifice. But each time, the Divine One intervened and I was spared. Then I began to wonder, is Abraham telling me to pretend to be his sister because he knows something that I don't? Should I trust him the way I trust the Divine One even though I'm not always sure I should?

Why does the world have to be such that no stranger can be trusted? I have been a stranger in a strange land and I know what that is like. Abraham and I had to pretend to be brother and sister traveling together, not husband and wife. As wife, I am my husband's property, which a king might fancy for himself. He might even have to kill my husband to get the desirable goods. As sister, I am ripe for plucking by any man who sees me, most of all the king.

Abraham and I were on a journey together. We came to trust each other because we needed to, in order to survive—to bring to life the revelations we each had had in our native land. That was most important. To teach others how the Divine One inhabits everything, how the Divine One speaks to us if we know to listen, how each of us knows this deeply from the moment the rhythm of life beats inside us.

Remember how we each learn the secrets of the whole Torah from the angel teaching us in the womb for nine months? Then as soon as we are born, we forget it all. Because of that, we spend the rest of our lives relearning what we have already learned. Abraham and I were blessed to be reminded, before we met, of our prenatal schooling. When our lives were joined together by our parents, we understood why.

A Message from Sarah

As I look back over my life now, I see things I would have done differently. Of course, at the time I was certain that I was right, but the years have given me the freedom not to be so sure. Don't wait for the end, as I have, to allow yourself to see what is really there, to act on what your heart is telling you. But then, only when my face is right up against the end do I see what I could not see for all these years. Perhaps you are not destined to wait this long, until it is too late to change anything.

This is what I would have changed.

I would not have cast Hagar out. I would have seen that our two sons needed each other, that they each had something to teach the other. I would have known that Hagar was part of our family even though I couldn't accept it at the time.

I would have argued with God about taking Isaac for a sacrifice. I would have demanded to be included in that decision as well. I would not have allowed Abraham to take our son up to the mountain. I would have lived to see Isaac grow up.

I would have known my daughter-in-law Rebekah. I would have enjoyed having her in a tent next to mine. I would have been proud to teach her all I knew about cooking, men, marriage, children, wilderness, and listening to God. I would have advised her against deceiving Isaac to get Jacob the birthright.

I would have advised Isaac not to play favorites with Esau, my first grandchild. I learned that the hard way through Isaac and Ishmael.

I would have found a way to pass on to future generations what it was really like in the desert with Abraham and me. In my chronicle, I would have included our conversations.

For Further Thought

What were your impressions of Sarah, the Matriarch, when you were a young girl? Compare them to your impressions now.

What are the strengths and weaknesses of Sarah's relationship with Abraham? What enabled their marriage to last?

Many contemporary midrashim have been written about Sarah. A short one called "Re-Visioning Sarah: A Midrash on Genesis 22" by Ellen Umansky appears in the landmark sourcebook that she edited with Dianne Ashton, *Four Centuries of Jewish Women's Spirituality* (Boston: Beacon Press, 1992), page 235.

A book-length midrash written by Savina J. Teubal (author of chapter 14 on Bath-Sheba in this collection) is called *Sarah the Priestess: The First Matriarch of Genesis* (Athens, OH: Swallow, 1984).

The Feminist Companion to the Bible, edited by Athalya Brenner (Sheffield, UK: Sheffield Academic Press, 1993, retitled in 1999 as *Genesis: The Feminist Companion to the Bible*), contains a provocative series of modern commentaries dealing with Sarah's role as a woman and wife in the biblical period. The author, Fokkelien van Dijk-Hemmes, compares and contrasts Abraham's exploitation of Sarah with sexual trafficking today. This article is called "Sarai's Exile: A Gender-Motivated Reading of Genesis 12:10–13:2," pages 222–234.

Chapter 3
Rebekah

PENINA ADELMAN

גְּמָלַתְהוּ טוֹב וְלֹא־רָע כֹּל יְמֵי חַיֶּיהָ:

"She is good to him, never bad, all the days of her life" (Prov. 31:12).

גמלתהו טוב ולא רע, זו רבקה. וכי מה גמול גמלה ליצחק, שבשעה ששלח
אברהם את עבדו ואמרו נקרא לנער ונשאלה את פיה, מנהגו שלעולם
אדם משיא את בתו לאחד אפלו השיאה לעבד מתביישת היא לומר
כלום, אבל רבקה כשאמרו לה התלכי עם האיש הזה ותאמר אלך. ד״א
שהיו מעשיה דומין למעשה שרה, דכתיב ויביאה יצחק האהלה שרה אמו.

She is good to him, never bad, this is Rebekah. And what kind of
good did she do for Isaac? At the time that Abraham sent his servant, and they said, "Let's call the young girl and make a request of
her" (Gen. 24:57); now it was customary in the world that when a
man would wed his daughter to someone, even if it were a servant
he was wedding her to, she would be embarrassed to say anything.
But when Rebekah was asked, "Will you go with this man?" …
she said, "I will" (24:58). Another thing: Rebekah's deeds were
like Sarah's, as it is written, "Isaac then brought her to the tent of
his mother Sarah …" (24:67).

—*Midrash ha-Gadol*

As soon as Sarah died, Abraham woke up to the fact that his son
Isaac needed a wife. He sent his trusted servant, Eliezer, to find
a suitable woman back in the land he had left years ago. When
Eliezer asked what he should do if this woman were not willing to
leave her land to marry, Abraham told him to return without her.
Above all else, Abraham did not want his son to return to the place
where he, Abraham, had grown up. He dared not send him back to
a land where people bowed down to statues and believed that these

gods of rain and thunder and grain and fertility could be won over with gifts.

So Eliezer set out for Aram-naharaim, birthplace of his master, to find a wife for Isaac. He brought 10 camels with him as a bride-price.

When he reached the city of Nahor, he stopped at a well where the women drew water. He said, "Lord, God of my master Abraham, grant me good fortune this day, and deal graciously with my master Abraham: Here I stand by the spring as the daughters of the townsmen come out to draw water; let the maiden to whom I say, 'Please, lower your jar that I may drink,' and who replies, 'Drink, and I will also water your camels'— let her be the one whom You have decreed for Your servant Isaac."

No sooner had Eliezer spoken these words in his heart than Rebekah came out with a vessel on her shoulder. She was the daughter of Bethuel, Abraham's nephew. Eliezer asked her for a drink and she replied, "Certainly, my lord and when you are done drinking, I shall draw water for your camels also."

These were the words Eliezer had been waiting for. God was certainly full of mercy to let him know so quickly that this was the girl meant for Isaac. Abraham's servant gave her two golden bracelets and one golden earring and asked if her family had room for him to spend the night. She said, "Yes, of course you can stay." When Eliezer found out that she was actually related to Abraham, he was even more certain Rebekah was the wife for his master's son.

Then, on behalf of Isaac, he asked for Rebekah's hand in marriage. Her family asked if she could stay with them a few more days before leaving. After all, they would probably not see her ever again. But Eliezer wanted to make haste. He requested that she come with him right away. Her mother and brother asked her if she wanted to go so soon and she said, "I will."

Eliezer brought Rebekah home to his master. Isaac took her into the tent that had belonged to his mother, Sarah, and he loved her. He felt comforted by her after the death of his mother.

Commentary

"*G'maltehu tov v'lo ra kol yamei hayeiha* (She is good to him, never bad, all the days of her life)." What is the good that the midrash sees in Rebekah? It is not that she gave Eliezer drink and his camels as well. It is not that she did good deeds for her husband all the time or that she was just looking for the next good deed to do. According to the midrash, the good she did for Isaac was saying, "I will go," without giving it another thought, when asked by her family if she really wanted to undertake such a journey.

Being decisive was the good she did for her husband. Remember, Isaac was a wounded soul. When he was young, his father had brought him to the sacrificial altar and would have offered him up to God if that had been required. It's easy to understand how Isaac may have had a hard time making decisions after knowing that he would have been dead, had God decided something different, up on Mount Moriah. Perhaps what he needed more than anything was to be with someone who cared about him and could make the hard decisions for him—or at least *with* him. Rebekah demonstrated she could do this when her family asked, "Will you go with Eliezer?" She was not shy about answering and she said, "Yes, I will," immediately.

Rebekah and Isaac share an interesting parallel in their stories. The Torah never states how old Isaac was when Abraham brought him up to the mountain to be sacrificed. Neither does it state Rebekah's age when Eliezer took her home to Isaac. In each case there is one midrash which puts both Rebekah and Isaac at less than ten years old; then there is another midrash which puts each at a much more mature age for these two events—Isaac at 37 and Rebekah somewhat younger.

What does this mean? Perhaps their actions were not linked to their ages. Perhaps each one was born with both the mentality of a child and that of an adult—the child being full of wonder and innocence and the adult being full of experience and wisdom. Even when they were children, they did not act like children. Isaac saw his life and death flash before his eyes. Most children do not have such knowledge. Rebekah saw ahead to her destiny as a mother in Israel and knew she would have to leave her family, tribe, and place of birth. She said yes and did not look back.

The other aspect of the good that Rebekah did for Isaac is alluded to in *Midrash ha-Gadol*: She was good in the same way Sarah was good. There is a midrash claiming that as long as Sarah was alive, the *Shekhinah* hovered, cloudlike, above her tent; the dough she made with her own hands was always rising; and her candles stayed lit from one Shabbat to the next. When Sarah died, all these things passed away with her. Only when Rebekah came to inhabit her mother-in-law's tent did the cloud, the dough, and the light return.

In the same way, there is a holy thread of knowledge that began with the first woman, Lilith[1] (according to midrash, she was Adam's first wife before Eve, born from the earth just as he was) or Eve, and has continued through the wife of Noah, the Matriarchs, and all the other righteous women who have lived until this day. These women extend the thread to you. Where will you take it? To whom will you pass it on?

Rebekah Speaks

You say you want me to tell you my first memory. I'll tell you that one and then a more recent memory.

My ema [mother] had a ring that looked like a red, red flower. I used to play with it as I sat on her lap. I would twist it and rub it, even smell it. I could see a little face in it. Whose face?

"Lu, lu, lu," Ema crooned, "May you be a mother in Israel. Lu, lu, lu. May myriads of children come from you. Lu, lu, lu. May your deeds be fragrant as the perfume of many flowers rising up to heaven. Lu, lu, lu."

I looked up into her eyes and saw that same little face. I smiled. The face smiled back at me. I laughed. The face laughed too.

Then one day when I am old enough, Ema sends me to the well by myself for the first time. The warm dust rises in clouds as I walk.

I am three or four summers old. I am alone on the road and so I start singing. While I'm singing I hear it: a voice singing with mine. Our voices are like two different colors, two shades of the sky blending to make a new color. The other voice stops. I strain to hear it. Where did it go? I keep walking, longing to hear the voice sing again. The place where our two voices had merged is waiting.

I come upon the well, hardly feeling I had walked at all. As I let the pail down into the deep, I wait to hear it touch water. Silence. The pail whizzes back up to me without my even pulling it. I look in to make sure the water is inside.

I see a face shimmering in the water—the same face I had seen in Ema's ring and in her eyes. The singing begins again. Who is singing so beautifully? Who is staring back at me?

I remember the stories Ema used to tell about the Creator making human beings in the image of the Divine. Male and female united and individual. It sounds so simple, but it means I have male and female in me, too. In the water, they swim together. On earth, they separate. As I separate from my mother. As she sent me away from her to bring water. I am a human being. It is *my* face in the water and it is God's face.

Eliezer, trusted old servant of Abraham, is leading me to my new home. I am excited and nervous, the way I guess a bride is supposed to be when she is about to meet her lifemate. Will I be a help to him as Eve was to Adam? I don't take orders well.

Usually I figure things out for myself first and then I decide what to do. But as soon as dusty, wrinkled Eliezer approached me for water, I could feel the hand of God in it. I knew exactly what to do. I let down my vessel so he could drink and drink and drink. I thought of the camels, also—poor faithful beasts, standing so patiently in the heat. I let down my pail for each one of them to drink its fill.

Eliezer noticed my willingness. He asked if I were ready to take the long journey to marry the son of his master. He was leaving shortly, and so I had to come with him immediately or not at all.

I said, "Yes, I will go," even though my mother and brother begged me to stay and not make such a hasty decision.

"After all," said Ema, "you have just begun to bloom. I want to see the flower you will become."

"God calls me," I told her, and we fell into each other's arms, weeping.

For days we ride on the camels. I have lots of time to think and dream in the shimmering heat.

I see my new husband as an infant at birth. Sarah and Abraham act like newlyweds, exuberant and hopeful even as they approach the end of life. They drink the fruit of the vine together from one cup, then dip their fingers in, to place a few drops on their son's lips.

I see Isaac scampering alongside his father in early morning, climbing Moriah, the fateful mountain. He looks to Abraham for a clue as to what they are going up to do. Abraham looks at him with sad determination, "For what I am about to do, may God and Sarah forgive me."

In that instant, Sarah draws her last breath, and Isaac feels a pang in his heart as if he had been stabbed. Abraham lets go the knife and notices the ram caught in the bushes.

I shall never know my mother-in-law in the usual way, but I shall know her as she rests peacefully in the souls of her son and her husband.

Suddenly I hear a shout from Eliezer, "We're home. There is your husband, Isaac!"

My husband stands with his back to the setting sun. He is deep inside with God. Wrapped in the waning light, he seems to be growing out of the very earth we are riding upon. I have an urge to fly to him for my feet will not take me fast enough. I leap off my camel and land abruptly on the hard ground. Maybe I cannot fly but I can run.

A Message from Rebekah

Learn how to listen, to yourself as well as others, to the world around you as well as God.

Trust the voice and voices inside yourself. Only by being completely honest can you achieve this.

When faced with a fork in the road, I usually ask myself: Do you really have to go that way? What about the other way? Where could that way bring you, or why might you need to continue along the road you are on? Is there another road, a better road, a clearer way?

Ask yourself, in the deepest place you can: Why should I go this way? Listen for the answer. It might not come right away, but it will come. You will know in your whole being if it is right or not.

Another way I sometimes handle a difficult decision is to ask Mother Sarah, my mother-in-law, in whose tent I now dwell. I ask her what she would do in my situation. She never fails me, even though she does surprise me at times with her answer.

For Further Thought

What other reasons can you come up with that might explain why Rebekah so readily agreed to go with Eliezer and to marry Isaac?

Rebekah is considered a prophetess by the Rabbis, as were all the other Matriarchs. What do you think was the vision she had for herself, for her sons, for her people?

Rebekah speaks, as well, in another contemporary Bible commentary—one with a bold name—*The Five Books of Miriam*, by Ellen Frankel (New York: G.P. Putnam's Sons, 1996). This book is modeled on the Talmud, in which the Rabbis converse with each other, except here all the voices are female. See chapter 6, *Toldot*: "Family Politics," pages 39–48.

Jewish women in 18th-century Central and Eastern Europe composed prayers to the Matriarchs. Here is an excerpt from a prayer called a *tkhine* that addresses all the Matriarchs on the Day of Judgment, Yom Kippur:

> And I also ask our mother Rebekah to plead for our fathers
> and mothers, that they may not, heaven forbid, be separated from
> us ... When Eliezer, the servant [of Abraham], took you away
> from your father and mother to your husband, Isaac, you also

wept copiously. Therefore, you know how bad it is without a
father and without a mother. ...

This translation of "Tkhine of the Matriarchs for the Shofar"
is from *Voices of the Matriarchs* by Chava Weissler (Boston: Beacon
Press, 1998), pages 177–178.

Chapter 4
Leah

PENINA ADELMAN

דָּרְשָׁה צֶמֶר וּפִשְׁתִּים וַתַּעַשׂ בְּחֵפֶץ כַּפֶּיהָ:

"She looks for wool and flax, and sets her hand to them with a will"
(Prov. 31:13).

דרשה צמר ופשתים, זו לאה שראתה ברוח הקדש שעתיד לצאת ממנה בן
שהוא מתיר דבר אסור בישראל. ואיזה, זה לוי. בישראל כתיב לא תלבש
שעטנז ובאהרן כתיב ועשו את האפד שהב תכלת וארגמן ותולעת שני
ושש. והיתה מתחמדת לינשא ליעקב ושדלה באחותה ויכלה.

She looks for wool and flax, this is Leah who saw through the holy
spirit that in the future would come from her a son who would allow a thing which is forbidden in Israel. And who is it? It's Levi. In
Israel it is written, "Do not wear *shatnez* [a mixture of materials
such as wool and flax]" (Deut. 22:11). And it is written about
Aaron, "Make the ephod [priestly garment of woolen cloth] of gold,
blue, purple, scarlet and linen. And she (Leah) really desired to
marry Jacob and so she coaxed Rachel [to help her marry him] and
she succeeded" (Exod. 28:8).

—*Midrash ha-Gadol*

Leah is the older daughter of Laban, brother of Rebekah. Laban
manages to manipulate the situation so that Leah will be married
before her younger sister, Rachel, even though no suitor is asking for
her hand.

Jacob encounters Rachel on his way to Haran to look for a wife.
He falls in love with her. She is beautiful in bearing and appearance.
The only bit of Leah's appearance that is mentioned in the Torah is her
eyes. Leah has *eynayim rakot* (gentle, tender eyes). It is hard to know
what her eyes look like. The word *rakh* can also be translated as "weak"
or "soft." But her eyes are all we know of what Leah looked like.

The story about Leah is famous—of how Laban switches her for Rachel at the last minute and forces Jacob, his future son-in-law, to marry both sisters. If arranged marriages are difficult for our modern sensibilities to accept, then this one is doubly difficult to understand. Leah is the daughter her father feels pressured to marry off, and on the train of Rachel's wedding gown no less. Rachel is most likely quite resentful of her sister for taking her rightful place as the bride of Jacob, who she finally weds seven years later. Jacob probably feels that his father-in-law has duped him. Laban gets not seven but fourteen years of labor out of him in exchange for the two daughters. Besides, Jacob cannot be with his true love, Rachel, until he pays for her by marrying Leah. Being a co-wife is difficult enough, as we know from the stories of Sarah and Hagar, Peninnah and Hannah. Being a co-wife with one's sister is certain to be even more difficult.

However, despite all these troubles, Leah, Rachel, and Jacob manage to live together in a more or less peaceful way. How they achieve this is not known to us from the Torah. We can only imagine.

Leah starts having children right away because God wants to compensate her for not being loved by her husband. What follows is a chronicle of Leah's relationship with Jacob as expressed by the names she gave her children.

She calls her first child Reuben (*Reuven* in Hebrew, derived from "The Lord has seen my affliction"); it also means: "Now my husband will love me" (both Gen. 29:32).

She calls her second child Simeon (*Shim'on* in Hebrew, derived from "has heard"). "This is because the Lord heard I was unloved and has given me this one also" (Gen. 29:33).

She calls her third child Levi (derived from the Hebrew for "accompany"). "This time my husband will become attached to me because I have borne him three sons" (Gen. 29:34).

She calls her fourth child Judah (*Yehudah* in Hebrew, derived from "God will be praised"). "This time I will praise the Lord" (Gen. 29:35).

Leah does not bear any more children for a while. It seems that after her third son, she no longer spends so much of her energy hoping that her husband will come to love her. She begins to value her children for more than being the way to Jacob's heart. She simply gives thanks to God for granting her another child, Judah.

At the time of her marriage, Leah's father had given her a handmaiden named Zilpah. When Leah ceases to give birth, she sends Zilpah to Jacob. Because Zilpah is a servant, the children she bears are considered to be Leah's children.

Leah calls the first child Zilpah bears Gad. In naming him, she says "What luck!" (Gen. 30:11) for that is the meaning of *gad*.

Zilpah bears another son whom Leah calls Asher (derived from the Hebrew for "success" or "good fortune"). She says, "What fortune!" meaning, "Women will deem me fortunate" (Gen. 30:13).

Then Leah's son Reuben brings some mandrakes to his mother. Mandrakes are plants that grow in the woods with roots in the shape of a human form. They were thought to have aphrodisiac powers. When Rachel hears that Leah has some of these potent plants, she begs her sister to give her some. Remember, Rachel has not yet borne a single child. But Leah refuses to grant her sister's request, saying, "Was it not enough for you to take away my husband, that you would also take my son's mandrakes?" (Gen. 30:15).

Rachel concedes the point. How each sister is wracked with guilt toward the other. Rachel knows that Jacob loves her more. Leah knows that God must look more favorably upon her than upon her sister to keep giving her more sons.

Leah sleeps with Jacob under the influence of the mandrakes, and "God listened to Leah, and she conceived and bore Jacob a fifth son" (Gen. 30:17). Leah names him Issachar (Yisskhar in Hebrew, derived from "God will reward"). She says, "God has given me my reward for having given my maid to my husband" (Gen. 30:18).

Leah has one more son after this whom she calls Zebulun (derived from the Hebrew for *zeved* meaning "gift" and *yizbeleni* meaning "he will dwell with" or "exalt me"). She says, "God has given me a choice gift; this time my husband will exalt me, for I have borne him six sons" (Gen. 30:20).

Finally, Leah has a daughter whom she names Dinah. She says nothing about Dinah's name, in sharp contrast to her unique explanations for each son's name.

Commentary

Leah's only female offspring, Dinah, represents the culmination of her childbearing years. Dinah comes from the Hebrew root *dalet-yud-nun*, meaning "to judge." Dinah's story of leaving the fold to see the neighboring territory and getting raped might be a judgment. But who is the judgment for? Why such a violent condemnation (Gen. 34).

God seems to have felt compassion for Leah's sense of isolation and rejection by Jacob. What, then, can be the meaning of her only daughter's tragic fate? Did Leah have to learn the hard way that suffering does not only produce bounty? Did Leah come to realize that results are never under our control, even if they spring from the best intentions?

The *nashei chayil* listed in the midrash "Eishet Chayil" represent women who, although stepping out of normal, expected behavior in various ways, did not leave convention behind altogether. However, many of the biblical women connected to these *nashei chayil* by birth, friendship, marriage, or circumstance did not adhere to expected norms. These women are not listed in *Midrash ha-Gadol* by the Rabbis.

In Leah's case, her daughter's story begins with the words, "Dinah, the daughter of Leah, whom she had borne unto Jacob, went out to see the daughters of the land" (Gen. 34:1). In sharp contrast to Leah—who did exactly what her father told her, in order to become married—Dinah did what was explicitly forbidden to biblical women: She went out. We know it was forbidden because of the way families, and especially fathers, protected their daughters from the outside world until they came of marriageable age. Think about the midrash's comment on Rebekah, who immediately agrees to leave her family home and go with a stranger to the home of her husband-to-be. The midrash says it was not the custom in those days for a girl to express herself directly when asked by her father if she wanted to marry a particular man. Rebekah was certainly not a customary girl and spoke up for herself.

Sarah also left her family to go with a man who professed knowledge of one God and one God only. Abraham was taking a new path, an unorthodox path, and when he invited Sarah to accompany him, she did not hesitate.

Imagine that Dinah had in mind two women—her grandmother and great-grandmother—when she "went out to see the daughters of the land." Alternatively, perhaps Rebekah and Sarah were not even in her mind at the time. Perhaps she had inherited enough of their spunk that she felt an urge to explore and to socialize with the unfamiliar girls living around her, and she did not stop herself.

Dinah was unlucky, unlike her female ancestors. She went out and was raped. She went out and provoked her brothers to avenge her defilement. She went out, and because of her honor being lost, all the men of a city were murdered, and their wives and children were taken prisoner.

The downfall of Dinah affirmed Leah's conservative stance. Was Dinah rebelling against her mother's obedient, "incidental" marriage? Was Dinah trying to take her life into her own hands—an action that brought on such a devastating and unforeseen result? A certain degree of active behavior is all right, but not too much, or one's life will be ruined.

What happened to Dinah after this? We never hear from her in the Torah again. Did she ever marry or have children? Did she find happiness? Did she make peace with what she had done? Or did she carry the burden of her mistake with her for the rest of her life? We learn so much about Leah by knowing the story of her daughter, Dinah.

Leah Speaks

Dinah, I mourned for you till the day I died. Yes, that's right. And still, even now, you are never far from my thoughts. Not a day goes by that I don't see your face in front of me, accusing: Where were you, Ema [Mother]? When I needed you most, why didn't you come?

What can I say to you now? That the men blamed me for letting you go out in the first place? That they kept saying to me, "What kind of mother lets her daughter leave her side and go out by herself? To a place where strange men from other tribes would like nothing better than to get their filthy hands on her. To a place where dangerous wild beasts roam."

What can I say? That I was afraid, even as a girl, to leave the safety of home and so perhaps I let you go because I didn't want you to be like me. I wanted you to go when and where you wanted, even though I was well aware of the risks.

I believed God had blessed you and me. When you were born, I was so grateful to have one daughter among all my sons. Someone to go to the *shuk* [market] with, someone to cook with and teach all my recipes to, someone as fair to look upon as your Aunt Rachel. Someone to talk to about women's things, about the pride and burden of being a descendant of Rebekah and Sarah, about how to know a good man when you see one, how to marry for property if you're lucky—and for love if you're able to throw caution to the wind the way Rachel did.

But you were not blessed, my sweet Dinah. You were cursed with the worst thing that can befall a young girl, to be violated by a strange lover of whom your father and brothers did not approve and then to have him killed by them.

How horrible, Dinah, how hopeless your life was after that.

Yet, in spite of it all, you have lived out your days in dignity, staying close to me in the tent, shunning your father and brothers. But you have never shunned me.

I beg your forgiveness, Dinah, my daughter. In my estimation you are an *eishet chayil*. I pray for the day when you will tell your story in your own words.

A Message from Leah

If there is anything I have learned in my life, it is that you must speak the words you have inside before they become too ripe. Or else you fill up with all this sticky-sweet language that eventually rots and makes you sick.

I wish I had been honest with Jacob and talked to him about our being manipulated to marry. In all those years, we never spoke about it and it festered. Is that why he wouldn't listen to me when I begged him to resolve Dinah's defilement himself and not let our sons, Simeon and Levi, take matters into their own hands?

Because Jacob never trusted me after I became his wife, I came to accept that our marriage was only an arrangement made by my father. I got used to holding back my words from him, words that could have been a bridge. The crisis with Dinah came and we had no way of coming over to each other's side.

Don't wait to speak, as I did, until your words rot and turn back into the earth.

For Further Thought

Imagine you are Leah. Dinah returns from her venture out of the tent to see the daughters of the land. She tells you the story of what happened. What do you say to her? What wisdom can you give her?

Think about the mother of sisters Leah and Rachel. She is not mentioned in the biblical text. How do you think she related to her daughters? How was her relationship with them different from Laban's relationship with them?

Two contemporary authors, Rhoda Kaplan Pierce and Sandie Bernstein, have written a novel whose main character is a woman named Leah Applebaum. As she faces events in Israel before the intifada of 2002, she embodies the character of Leah the Matriarch. The book is called *Leah's Blessing* (Wayland, MA: Kehillah Press, 2002).

For a fascinating summary of the Rabbinic view of marriage, focusing in part on the marriages of Leah and Jacob and Rachel and Jacob, see "Fruitful Vines and Silent Partners: Women as Wives in Rabbinic Literature" in *Midrashic Women: Formations of the Feminine in Rabbinic Literature,* by midrashic scholar Judith R. Baskin (Hanover, NH: Brandeis University Press, 2002), pages 88–118.

Ellen Umansky, scholar on Jewish women, has written an essay on friendship between women in Jewish literature, in which the relationship between Rachel and Leah serves as one model influencing the fate of Dinah. See "Seeking Women's Friendship" in *Lifecycles: Jewish Women on Biblical Themes in Contemporary Life,* edited by Rabbi Debra Orenstein and Rabbi Jane Rachel Litman (Woodstock, VT: Jewish Lights Publishing, 1997), pages 62–67.

A beautiful poem by the contemporary Hebrew poet Rivka Miriam gives an inkling of what it was like to be Leah when Jacob thought she was Rachel. It is called "A Song to Jacob Who Removed the Stone from the Mouth of the Well" and is found in *Four Centuries of Jewish Women's Spirituality: A Sourcebook,* edited by Ellen Umansky and Dianne Ashton (Boston: Beacon Press, 1992), pages 195, 227.

Chapter 5
Rachel

IRIT KOREN

הָיְתָה כָּאֳנִיּוֹת סוֹחֵר מִמֶּרְחָק תָּבִיא לַחְמָהּ:

"She is like traders' ships, bringing her food from afar" (Prov. 31:14).

היתה כאניות סוחר, זו רחל שאמרה ליעקב הבה לי בנים ואם מתה
אנכי. אמר לה יעקב התחת אלהים אנכי. ואין תחת אלא לשון ביוש, כענין
שנאמר חתו ובשו. אמר לו הקב׳׳ה לא דייך שלא בקשת רחמים על הצדקת
הזו אלא אף שביישתה, חייך שאני זוכרה ונותן לה בן ואינו נקרא על שמך.
הדא היא ויזכר אלהים את רחל ולא אמר את יעקב.

She is like a merchant fleet, this is Rachel, who said to Jacob: "Give me
children, or I shall die!" (Gen. 30:1). Jacob responded, "Can I take
the place of God … ?" (Gen. 30:2). This is nothing but a language
of shame, as it is said, "they were afraid and ashamed" (Isa. 37:27).
The Holy One, Blessed be He, said to him, "Isn't it enough that you
didn't pray for mercy for that righteous woman, but you embarrass
her, too? By your life, I shall remember her and give her a child, but
he will not have your name." Thus it is written: "Now God remembered Rachel" (Gen. 30:22) and Jacob is not mentioned.
—*Midrash ha-Gadol*

When Rebekah and Isaac send Jacob to Haran, to find his first
wife—among the daughters of Rebekah's brother, Laban—
Jacob obeys. His brother, Esau, had rejected his parents' wishes by
taking a wife from his Uncle Ishmael's children.

Jacob meets his cousin Rachel, younger daughter of his Uncle Laban
who is pleased that Jacob has come. He has an older daughter, Leah,
who is described as having eyes that are unappealing in some way, and
Rachel is described as having great beauty. Jacob falls in love with Rachel
and agrees to work seven years for Laban as a bride-price for Rachel.

Laban tricks him, though, and under cover of darkness, he puts Leah in Rachel's place in the marriage tent. Jacob wakes up the next day, discovers the deception and cries: "What is this you have done to me? I was in your service for Rachel! Why did you deceive me?" (Gen. 30:25). Laban's answer is: "It is not the practice in our place to marry off the younger before the older" (30:26). Laban agrees to give Rachel to Jacob on the condition that he will work seven more years for her. Jacob, yearning for Rachel, agrees to this condition.

However, Rachel and Jacob's life together is still not simple. Leah gives birth to son after son, but Rachel is unable to conceive. Finally in desperation Rachel cries to Jacob for help: "Give me children, or I shall die." Jacob is incensed by Rachel and says, "Can I take the place of God, who has denied you fruit of the womb?" (Gen. 30:1,2). *Midrash ha-Gadol* responds to this bitter exchange between husband and wife and takes the side of Rachel. She then gives birth to Joseph, the favored son who is rejected by all his older brothers and who saves his family when he rises to power in Egypt many years later.

Commentary

The midrash views Rachel as a trading ship. Indeed, Rachel shows throughout her life a talent for trading. First she trades being a bride for the continued love of her sister. The sieges describe how she provides Leah with certain signs known only to her and Jacob so he will remain convinced that he is spending his first night of married life with Rachel. Years later, when both sisters are married to Jacob, Rachel sells Leah another night with Jacob in return for the mandrake plant that Leah's son Reuben has given her. She trades love for the possibility of fertility. When that doesn't work, she offers a harsh trade to Jacob: He must give her sons or lose her forever.

The second part of the midrash focuses on the interaction between Rachel and Jacob that results from the trade she is proposing. The midrash severely judges Jacob's answer to Rachel because he showed no empathy toward his wife in her grief and distress. Compare the tender way

Elkanah answers Hannah when she stops eating and sleeping for lack of a child. He says, "Am I not more devoted to you than ten sons?" (1 Sam. 1:8). Jacob callously rebukes her. According to the midrash, Rachel is a righteous woman; thus she conceives a son. Jacob's punishment, according to the midrash, is that "… God remembered Rachel" (Gen. 30:22). She is remembered by God, not Jacob. Rachel finally bears a boy and she is the one who names him Joseph. Jacob is not even mentioned as part of the process.

Rachel and Leah represent a co-wife dynamic similar to the ones between Sarah and Hagar, and Hannah and Peninnah. "Any two pairs of women … are always defined as two rivals who are interlinked by family ties and interlock in social combat, as if no alternative pattern of social behavior is conceivable for them in such a situation."[1] Rachel's and Leah's jealousy toward each other ends up destroying them both, not only on a personal level, but on a national one as well. Their children internalize the jealousy of their mothers. This paradigm contrasts with other patterns found in the Bible that emphasize women's cooperation with each other for gaining the most from the patriarchal society in which they live. The relationship between Ruth and Naomi is an example.[2]

Once Rachel gives birth to her first son, Joseph, she returns to her womb competition with Leah, trying to keep up with her in producing sons. Yet Leah is always a few steps ahead. Because of Leah's success in this arena, Rachel perceives herself as worthless, a tragic figure. Even though she has Jacob's love, even though he talks only to her, and even though, when he prepares to meet his brother, Esau, he protects her more than all the others—Rachel is not content. She still envies her sister's ever-blooming womb. In her agony, Rachel cries out to Jacob—demanding he give her boys and threatening that she will die if he does not. Ironically, it will be the birth of her next son, Benjamin, that brings about her death.

There is an extraordinary midrash that claims that Rachel's craving for more children was her downfall. The *Akedat Yitzchak*, a 15th-century biblical commentary, contains this observation:

We learn from the two names that were given to Eve of the two purposes that women have in the world. The first name was Isha (Woman), thus it says: "Then the man said, 'This one at last is bone of my bones and flesh of my flesh. This one shall be called Isha (Woman), for from Ish (Man) was she taken" (Gen. 2:23). Thus the first purpose is driven by the name Isha. Like a man, a woman can develop her intellect and virtue, just as our Matriarchs, righteous women, and prophetesses did.

The second purpose of a woman is to become a vessel for fertility and raising children. This we learn from her second name, Eve, thus it says: "The man named his wife Eve because she was the mother of all the living" (3:20). Therefore, a woman who can't bring children into the world is unable to fulfill her small [and secondary] purpose in the world, but is not exempt from her bigger purpose; that is, being righteous and doing good deeds like a man who is infertile. Jacob became upset with Rachel because she looked only at her small purpose—her fertility—and saw no meaning in living without fulfilling that purpose.[3]

How extraordinary it is for Rabbi Yitzchak Arama to refer to the fertility aspect as the "small purpose" of the woman. Rachel, who focuses on her lack of fertility, feeling it defines her, ends up losing all. She dies while giving birth, losing her husband's love and missing out on her sons' growing up. The irony of Rachel's death is that Jacob, who works seven years for her—years that seem to him "but a few days because of his love for her" (Gen. 29:20)—and then works an additional seven years, is the one who indirectly brings her demise. Jacob swears that the one who stole Laban's idols will die, not knowing that his beloved wife is the thief. Rachel dies in childbirth and is buried alone on the road to Bethlehem.

Perhaps because of Rachel's early, tortured death, she remains in the collective memory of Israel as the great and merciful mother. She is the one who cries and begs before God when the people of Israel, her sons, are expelled from their land. She is the one God comforts. She is the one to whom God makes a promise that her children will return from the land of the enemy, on account of her merit (Jer. 31:15).

Rachel Speaks

Silence. Only I am awake in the tent.

Around me the women are dozing: Leah and our handmaidens, Bilhah and Zilpah. The men are in the tent next to us. Now, silence.

Two contractions and the baby has not yet emerged. For two days now my cries fill the emptiness of the tent. They can be heard from one end of the world to the other. My strength has waned and so has the strength of my loved ones. I told Jacob to go rest. It has already been two days since he began fasting for my sake. And my sister, my love and my rival, is completely worn out from taking care of me. She lies exhausted at my feet, dreaming.

Now, it is quiet. From the roof of the tent, the moon shines down on me, almost full, but still not quite full—like me. The hyenas are laughing from afar and a hot wind can be heard whispering, like a se-cret melody, a dirge. I already know that my death is coming. I just have to give birth and bring forth another little boy and afterward, I can sleep, sleep. My body is dying, I have no more strength, as if my spirit and my blood have been sucked out of me and I am an empty sack. At this moment, as the pain stops, calm falls over me. My spirit is free even if my body is not. In a little while, I'll leave this behind. And through my dull senses, I am able to see episodes of my life, this one turning to that one, the times all mixed up. There are still so many words that need to be said and in a little while it will be too late. Now, before the pain returns. Now, if only you can all hear me.

My dear sister, Leah, how often we fought and how jealous we were of each other. You lusted after a love that was not for you, and I lusted after sons I could not have. It was to prove that I have a purpose, that I am not empty, that I, too, can be a mother. My sister, the two of us have been barren, you from love and I from children. I still don't know today which kind of barrenness is more difficult. Believe me when I say to you that I love you with all my heart. Believe me when I say to you that my heart shrank when we walked together and they made fun of you, of your delicate eyes. Believe me, that is not how I wanted it to be, the two of us fighting over the love of one man and his seed. How it distressed me when I saw the hurt in your eyes as you looked at Jacob and me, when you saw the love I received from him without even trying. As for me, I could not help but be jealous of your womb, ever fertile with children. Leah, there have been many nights when I prayed that my husband who is yours also would learn to divide his love between us. But he never did. Jacob is a man of one love and even now, I see that he loves Joseph more than all his sons, and I know that this is not a good thing, not at all. Jealousy is mighty as *She'ol* (the underworld). It is hard to face the fact that love is given to one and not to the other. Believe me, I wanted the two of us to be loved and to love each other and to give birth to sons and daughters. But fate did not want it this way …

Will you forgive me, my sister, for the harsh words and insults I said in the thick of anger and weakness? Doesn't your blood course through my veins? How can I hate you? The thought that in a little while our paths will separate brings tears to my eyes. So, be certain that there is a reward for all you have done, that kings are going to come from you, my very own sister, great kings.

Now, suddenly an image jumps out at me: the well where Jacob and I first met. Jacob, you wept when you saw me. Oh, Jacob, my heart, my heart is with you, for now you will be left with many sons, but without your beloved wife. Your love for me was difficult, not only the fact that you were with my sister and I brought this upon myself, but also that you did not sense my desires. I wanted a child and you thought that your love for me would be enough. I forgive you, for I know that you were helpless and that this pain was what caused you to berate me when I turned to you in my bitterness. Jacob, will you instruct your children with wisdom? Will you teach them that hatred and love are forces that one must learn to control with restraint and patience? Will you learn at last how to divide your love equally? Will you remember fondly your beloved wife who died at the crossroads and did not merit seeing her children grow up? Children or perhaps there will be only one child ...

Joseph, my precious son with such a beautiful body and such a beautiful face. How will you grow up without a mother's love? How can I abandon this world and leave you an orphan? How can I not live to see the man you will become one day? Can you believe that my soul will continue to protect you? Will you be able to remember your mother's love? Will you grow up to be always good and merciful? Will you learn to forgive the wrongs that will be done to you?

The light is shining now and the pain is starting to return. Contractions and crying and whispers in the tent. Here is my sister and here are Bilhah and Zilpah and in a short time Jacob will come running. It is all a fog and the words aren't coming to me and all I hear are sobs and murmurs hovering above my head. Here I am, giving birth. Crying, pain, contractions. "A son," they are shouting, "A son!" They place him at my breast. "Ben-oni, son of my suffering," I whisper. My boy, my love. But my throat is dry and the words are not coming and there is still so much I wanted to say. Now I am separated from them and I am at peace, I am leaving you, but my soul will continue to protect you, if only you will believe it. If only you will believe.

A Message from Rachel

Please, try not to fail where I did. See your larger purpose in life. Consider what you, and you alone, can bring to the world. I got all caught up in seeing myself only as a vessel for fertility. My sister was the perfect vessel, bringing child after child into the world for Jacob while all I brought him was emptiness.

Jealousy blinded me; it nearly destroyed my relationship with Leah. Why do we women do this to each other: mothers to daughters, sisters to sisters, friends to friends? Sometimes I wonder: What do we want so badly that we fear we won't get enough of it? Why is another woman seen as the ideal, the threat, the obstacle?

For Further Thought

Consider the difficulty Rachel had in conceiving. How did she feel about her infertility? What did she think was the solution? Compare this to the difficulties and solutions experienced by other *nashei chayil* (women of valor); for example, Sarah, Hannah, the Shunammite Woman, and Hatzlelponi.

Rachel is considered throughout Jewish history to be a model of compassion. Rachel's Tomb outside Bethlehem is a place where people go when they need healing, especially women who are experiencing infertility. In a midrash from *Lamentations Rabbah*, Rachel challenges God, saying that just as she was able to overcome her jealousy of Leah, who married Jacob before she did, God should be able to overcome being jealous of foreign idols, for which reason the Holy Temples were destroyed. This midrash can be found in a collection called *The Defiant Muse: Hebrew Feminist Poems from Antiquity to the Present* (New York: The Feminist Press, 1999), Poem 24 on page 63. What do you make of Rachel's challenge?

For a creative analysis of the classical midrashim that focus on the relationship between Rachel and Leah, see the chapter called "'A Separate People': Rabbinic Delineations of the Worlds of Women" by Judith Baskin, scholar on Jewish women, in *Midrashic Women: Formations of the Feminine in Rabbinic Literature* (Hanover, NH: Brandeis University Press, 2002), pages 145–150.

Chapter 6
Batya

SUSAN BERRIN

וַתָּקָם ׀ בְּעוֹד לַיְלָה וַתִּתֵּן טֶרֶף לְבֵיתָהּ וְחֹק לְנַעֲרֹתֶיהָ:

"She rises while it is still night, and supplies provisions for her household, the daily fare of her maids" (Prov. 31:15).

ותקם בעוד לילה, זו בתיה בת פרעה שראתה ברוח הקדש שעתיד מושיען שלישיראל להתגדל על ידיה והיתה משכמת ומערבת היא ונערותיה להטייל על היאור וכיון שבא משה לידה נתן לה הקב"ה מה שביקשה ושמחה הרבה, דכתיב ותפתח ותראהו את הילד.

She rises while it is still night, this is Batya, daughter of Pharaoh, who foresaw by the Holy Spirit that in the future the savior of Israel would be raised by her. In the evenings and mornings she and her handmaids used to stroll by the Nile. When Moses came her way, God had given her what she had requested. She rejoiced a great deal, as it is written, "When she opened [the basket], she saw that it was a child, a boy crying" (Exod. 2:6).

—*Midrash ha-Gadol*

When the Children of Israel are living in slavery—growing in numbers and seeming to become a thunderous power—Pharaoh proclaims an edict to kill all of the Hebrew baby boys. The daughter of Pharaoh goes to the river. Some midrashim say she is seeking relief from the pain of leprosy. Other midrashim say she is seeking absolution from the impurity of idol worship in her father's palace. The young woman sees the floating ark amidst the reeds of the river and asks one of her maidens to fetch the basket. When the princess opens it, she finds a weeping baby boy. She realizes that it must be one of the Hebrew babies, and although she initially thinks to leave the baby to its fate, she has a change of heart as the baby wails and cries.

The princess takes the baby home to the palace, where they live among the Egyptian royalty. Her father rules the land with a ferocious will and temper.

Commentary

Upon hearing Pharaoh's edict to have all baby Israelite boys killed, two Hebrew slaves, Yocheved and Amram, choose not to risk a pregnancy that might result in the birth of a death-warranted son. But after some time, their daughter, Miriam, prophesies that her parents will give birth to a prophet, and she urges them to resume conjugal relations.

A son is soon born, and after three months of hiding, Yocheved takes the baby to the Nile River and deposits him in a small floating ark she has made. She leaves, but Miriam remains to watch from the bulrushes as Pharaoh's daughter, Batya, also known as Thermutis, retrieves the floating basket. So Miriam appears and offers to bring a Hebrew woman as a wet nurse. The princess approves of this plan. Miriam and her mother take the baby back home. Sometime later Miriam brings the baby to the palace.

Throughout the uncertain moments in the river, water surrounds and protects Moses as he is reborn as Batya's son. *Mayim chayim* (living waters) become his second womb and the Nile River his second birth canal.

Batya goes to the Nile to heal. According to midrash, she is leprous, a condition later shared by Moses' sister Miriam (*Exodus Rabbah* 1:23). Batya's handmaidens bring her the baby's basket. With an outstretched arm,[1] she touches the basket and is healed. The basket not only holds baby Moses; beside him is the feminine spirit of God, the *Shekhinah* (literally, the indwelling presence of God, the spirit of God that resides in all of Creation). It is this divine light that bathes the baby's body with extraordinary beauty and shields his soul as he is placed in the Nile. The light, however, withdraws from him during his years in the palace, only to return when he ascends Mount Sinai.

The light then stays with him, and it is this light that allows him "to survey the whole of Palestine in the twinkling of an eye" (*Zohar* 2:11b).

The river, serving as a second birthplace to Moses, is also Batya's healing place and her place of renewed birth. She is birthed as a mother through the Nile's living waters. Living waters are her *mikveh* (place of ritual immersion).

With his rebirth, the baby boy is renamed "Moshe" by the princess—"*ki meshitihu*," she said, meaning "for I drew him out of the water" (Exod. 2:10). Batya mothers Moshe as her own child, nurturing him with all of her unassuming love, wrapping him in comfort with the long, sinewy arms that reached toward his basket in the water.

Even though Moshe is not a Hebrew name, it is the name that remains with him throughout his life. Some say it is because of Batya's deep and abiding love for Moses—the love of a mother for a child—that God, too, calls Moses by this name. We refer to him as Mosheh Rabbenu, Moses our teacher.

With her immersion, the princess is also renamed. She sheds the old Egyptian name Thermutis and becomes Batya, literally, "daughter of God."

Moses brings Batya close to God, and it is said that her change of name reflects that closeness. "When he [Moshe] came into the world he brought nearer to God those who were far away from Him, namely Batya, the daughter of Pharaoh" (*Deuteronomy Rabbah* 7:5). Because she treated Moses as a son, God treats her as a daughter. There is deep reciprocity in the relationship of Moses and Batya. She saves him from the edict of death, giving him life in a palace. Later, he saves her (*Exodus Rabbah* 8:3) from God's decree that all Egyptian firstborn shall die (she is a firstborn of Pharaoh).

In the Torah text, we find three women, barely mentioned, who play pivotal, redemptive roles in the opening chapters of Exodus: Shiphrah, Puah, and Batya.[2] Batya is not even named, and the midwives Shiphrah and Puah receive only cursory attention. Through midrash, we learn about these women and how they significantly alter the history of the Jewish people. They defy the injustices around them, imaginatively and resourcefully giving, in effect, rebirth to the Israelite babies. Each of them, in their relative textual anonymity, is "Other." Batya is "Other" in three ways: she is a woman, a non-Israelite, and a leper. Her transformation as Moses' adoptive mother suggests a movement from inwardness, that is, hiddenness, to an unfolding of her redemptive self—her outstretched arm to redeem the baby and her own renaming as God's daughter. When we read this story as a parable of human nature and the human condition, we find Batya to be a woman of significant insight with stunning imaginative power.

Midrash recounts that she leaves Egypt with the Children of Israel and, along with them, is liberated. Water remains her agent of transformation, her *mikveh*. From the Nile, where she is given a new name, to the Sea of Reeds, where she removes her royal garments, water purifies her spirit and bathes her soul.

Batya Speaks

Welcome to my chamber in Paradise.[3]

Here I sit in the first of Paradise's six chambers. For my virtue as the one who saved Moshe, I was allowed to enter Paradise alive. In the chamber next to me sits Serach bat Asher. In the third chamber is Yocheved. Deborah the Prophet sits in the fourth; and our Matriarchs Sarah, Rebekah, Rachel, and Leah sit in chambers next to her.

In my life I lived in a palace where evil and goodness sat side by side. As a young princess the palace was my home, its gardens and surroundings the place where my soul grew. I traveled to the river to bathe and to cleanse myself of my father's temper. Into the water I immerged as Thermutis; out I came as Batya—daughter of God, adoptive mother of Moses. God changed my name when I redeemed the baby prophet from death's door. In silence I cared for and nurtured the boy, raising him as a prince.

The *Shekhinah*, hovering beside Moses as his miniature ark floated in the Nile, was the spirit that tickled the sleeping boy into wails and bellowing tears that caught my attention at the river's edge. The *Shekhinah* watched over him as he grew to manhood. Although this divine light was withdrawn during the palace years— that is, he knew not that the spirit hovered near him—I knew the *Shekhinah's* gaze was following the boy when he spoke of miracles, when he challenged my father's curses, when he stood face-to-face with God.

But I did not know that the *Shekhinah* also watched me as I watered Moses' soul with love. She watched my love for the boy grow; she spoke with the angels. The *Shekhinah* stood at the gate to the Garden of Eden to welcome me. Wings grew from the tips of my painted fingers. Arms outstretched, fingertips pointing upward. Not even death drew life's breath from my lungs, although they filled with water. And from deep in the river of life I soared toward the heavens.

Now, with the *Shekhinah*, I welcome you to Paradise.

A Message from Batya

Outstretch your arms and gather within your reach the abundance that lies beyond your dreams. Goodness is found in such unlikely places. And each of us bestows common blessings, unaware of our actions.

Outstretch your arms and gather new friends. Bring into your ample bosom friends from near and far. Draw them close so that your breath and their breath mingle. Open your home. Let the aromas of your kitchen waft into the desert, beckoning friends and strangers to feast at your table.

Outstretch your arms and gather new adventures. Experiment with the rivers. Wade into the waters up to your ankles. Fear not; and wade just a bit more deeply. Soon your calves and knees and thighs and waist are submerged. Continue until you float. Soon, you are moving with a new current and heading to a fork in the stream.

Outstretch your arms and gather new moments of time. Sometimes an hour is but 60 minutes. But other times an hour is gloriously slow—filled with passion and delicately nuanced in rhythms of dance. Make each of your hours full and riveting. Each 60 minutes might be a treasure of time.

Your outstretched arms fold memories into daily life. Behind your eyes are pictures of the generations that bear your name. Tucked into the pictures are stories and threads of song, laughter, and tears that flow as a river—the one whose waters you wade into for adventure.

They might be the waters of the River Nile, where I, Batya, the daughter of God, redeemed Baby Moses. My baby who grew into a man who became a prophet, a teacher, and a leader of our people. He brought us from slavery into freedom.

These are the waters of my life. These are the tears that burn behind sad eyes. These are the tears that flow with joy at a wedding.

For Further Thought

What is the interplay between divinity, belief, and love in the story of Batya? Consider how these shifted proportionately for each of the people in her story.

What does Batya's story teach us about compassion and outreach toward an individual or an entire people? Consider what causes transformation to take place. How did Miriam, Batya, and Moses influence each other? What are the reasons to wish for transformation—of yourself, your close relationships, the place where you live, or another nation?

For more commentary on Batya, see Louis Ginzberg's *Legends of the Jews* (Philadelphia: The Jewish Publication Society, 1938 and 2003), page 271.

For an intriguing view of life in Pharaoh's palace, read Julius Lester's *Pharaoh's Daughter, A Novel of Ancient Egypt* (New York: Harcourt, Inc., 2000). Although this book is for younger readers, it gives a firsthand account of the life of Batya as imagined by an accomplished author who likes to challenge traditional ways of looking at the Bible.

An appealing new look at biblical women takes place in a collection of tales and commentary by Vanessa Ochs: *Sarah Laughed: Modern Lessons from the Wisdom and Stories of Biblical Women* (New York: McGraw–Hill Ryerson, 2004).

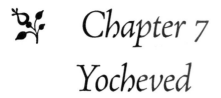

Chapter 7
Yocheved

PENINA ADELMAN

זָמְמָה שָׂדֶה וַתִּקָּחֵהוּ מִפְּרִי כַפֶּיהָ נָטְעָה כָּרֶם:

"She sets her mind on an estate and acquires it, she plants a vine-yard by her own labors" (Prov. 31:16).

זממה שדה ותקחהו, זו יוכבד שעל ידיה נקראו ישראל כרמו שלהקב'ה, שנאמר כי כרם ה' צבאות בית ישראל. ולמה נקרא שמה יוכבד, שהיו פניה דומין לזיו הכבוד.

She sets her mind on an estate, this is Yocheved, because of whom Israel was called vineyard of the Holy One, Blessed be He; as it is said, "For the vineyard of the Lord of Hosts is the House of Israel" (Isa. 5:7). And why was she called Yocheved? Because her face was like Ziv HaKavod (Majestic Splendor).

—*Midrash ha-Gadol*

Yocheved's story begins before the Jews went to Egypt. She is born on the way to Egypt to the tribe of Levi. She comes into the world in freedom, moving with her family to Egypt because of the terrible famine in Canaan.

Because the Jews are such a hearty and prosperous people, they become a threat to Pharaoh. He enslaves them in order to oppress and eventually destroy them.

Yocheved spends the first part of her life as a free person. By the time she marries Amram, also from the tribe of Levi, she is a slave. Her children, Aaron and Miriam, are born into slavery.

When she gives birth to Moses, the conditions under which the Jews live are worsening. Pharaoh decrees that all the baby boys should be killed as soon as they are born. Yocheved cannot bring herself to do this. She hides Moses for three months. When he becomes too big to hide, Yocheved fashions a little ark for him. She places him in the reeds on the banks of the nearby Nile River and then leaves.

Moses' big sister, Miriam, goes down to the river and hides in the tall reeds to keep an eye on him. Pharaoh's daughter, in the midst of her bath, discovers the baby and takes pity on him. She realizes that he is an Israelite child. Miriam, who has been watching all this time, steps forward.

She asks the princess, "Would you like me to bring one of the Hebrew women to nurse the baby for you?"

"Yes, please go at once," replies the princess.

Miriam goes to fetch Yocheved. Pharaoh's daughter asks if Yocheved would nurse the baby for wages. Yocheved assents gladly and keeps her son with her until he is weaned.

Commentary

Yocheved is not mentioned by name until long after she first appears as "a Levite woman" (Exod. 2:1). Four chapters later, in 6:20, it says, "Amram took to wife his father's sister Yocheved, and she bore him Aaron and Moses ..." Why does the story take so long to name her?

We have seen in the Bible that many women are unnamed: the wife of Noah, the Shunammite woman, the widow from Zarephath, the wife of Obadiah. In Yocheved's case, she is eventually named. However, by not being named at the beginning of the story, she becomes part of the mystery surrounding the Hebrew midwives. They are mentioned before Yocheved even enters the plot (Exod. 1:15).

There were two women who resisted Pharaoh at great danger to themselves. Known as Shiphrah and Puah, they refused to kill any of the male babies they helped birth. If not for their courageous and defiant acts, there might be no Jewish people today. In midrash, the midwife named Shiphrah is identified as Yocheved (*Sotah* 11b). Puah is identified as Miriam, and sometimes as Elisheba, wife of Aaron. But no one knows who the midwives really were because their names were not given in the Torah. Did Yocheved and Miriam remain unidenti-fied to protect their secret work as midwives?

Anonymity does not end there. In the first part of the story, Miriam is not mentioned by name either. She is called "his sister" (Exod. 2:4). Even Pharaoh's daughter has no name at first. She is called simply bat par'oh (Pharaoh's daughter). Nor is Moses' father, Amram, mentioned by name. So, in the story of the birth of the hero Moses, all the figures around the boy are unnamed until much later in the story. Only Moses has a name, which Pharaoh's daughter gives him when Yocheved brings him back after he is weaned. Wouldn't it be interesting to know what his birth family called him for those three months?

Being unnamed recalls Creation. Only after everything had been created did God bring all the animals "to the man to see what he would call them"(Gen. 2:19).

Exodus begins with a description of the slave conditions of the Israelites in general and then shines the spotlight on one family. It happens to be the family in which Moses, the leader of the Jewish people, was born. Nobody has a name at first until Pharaoh's daugh-ter bestows one on her adopted son, Moses. She, like Adam, the first person on earth, has the power of naming. Without her, as we learned in chapter 6, there might have been no Jewish people. Without the creation of a first human being on earth, there would have been no "rest of humanity."

The midwives are the ones who bring the Jews to life by guiding them out of the womb. They are partners in God's creation. Whether in her role as the mother who brought Moses into the world or a mid-wife who ensured the lives of thousands of Jewish babies, Yocheved is a Giver of Life, and in that way, she recalls Eve, "the mother of all the living" (Gen. 3:20).

There is a mysterious line in the story of the midwives that has puzzled interpreters for centuries: "… He [God] established households for them [the midwives]" (Exod. 1:21). This may bear on Yocheved's line in "Eishet Chayil" that reads, "She sets her mind on an estate and acquires it; she plants a vineyard by her own labors."

A house symbolizes family extending from the past into the future. When God rewarded the midwives with "households," God was ensuring them of their future. The work the midwives did, bringing Israelite baby boys into the world against Pharaoh's will, also ensured the future of the people "Israel."

The midrash on "Eishet Chayil" states that the beginning of the line "She sets her mind on an estate and acquires it; she plants a vineyard by her own labors" denotes Yocheved, "because of whom Israel is called the vineyard of God. As it is said, 'For the vineyard of the Lord of Hosts is the House of Israel'" (Isa. 5:7).

Considering a field and buying it are active deeds. So were the acts of resistance Yocheved and Miriam performed every day as midwives—that is, bringing baby boys into life, not death. She and her daughter were obeying the divine leader, not the earthly one.

In the second part of the line, "… by her own labors" (literally, the fruit of her hands) means Moses, Aaron, and Miriam, as well as the countless children she brought into the world. Yocheved is linked to this particular line of "Eishet Chayil" because she is credited with no less than cultivating the sacred grapes in the vineyard that is the House of Israel.

Grapes are the fruit of her hands because grapes are used to make the wine used in the sacred rituals of the Jewish people. Yocheved's children, both her flesh-and-blood children and the children of her sacred work as a midwife, are the "seeds" with which she plants a vineyard. Year after year and generation after generation grow the grapes containing the essence of the Children of Israel.

Yocheved stands on the threshold between two worlds: freedom in Canaan and slavery in Egypt. She looks backward and forward at once. She carries within her the seeds of freedom that the Children of Israel brought from Canaan. She also bears the dreadful responsibility of birthing children into slavery. Because her husband, Amram, was not willing to claim this responsibility, he divorced Yocheved so they would not have any more children to add to Pharaoh's slave army.

Miriam's prophetic powers revealed that Yocheved would bear a future leader of Israel. According to a midrash, Miriam convinced Amram to take back Yocheved by saying, "Pharaoh has decreed that only the baby boys should not be allowed to live. Now that you have divorced Ema (Mother), you are decreeing there will be no baby girls alive either! How can you?"

Miriam's words convinced her father to take back Yocheved and marry her again.

Yocheved Speaks

There I was, washing his clothes in the Nile, the sun cooking me as the day burned on. Miriam came to see what I was doing. She usually awoke before dawn like me. That's when we talked and told each other our dreams. We would try to figure them out together.

I'd had a dream of foreboding several nights in a row.

A strange man knocked on our door. I answered it because Amram was not there. I suppose he was at the construction site.

"What do you want?" I demanded, thinking he was probably one of the taskmasters giving us the usual bad news about the diminished food supply or increased workload. Although, how the workload could be increased any further was beyond me. We were already up to 18 hours straight.

With a snarl, he announced, "We will no longer be needing your services."

"But, but ..." I tried to get the words out but my tongue was a heavy stone I couldn't move. I was thinking frantically: Who will help all the babies be born?

"That's right, we'll no longer be needing you," he repeated, his voice supremely self-confident. He turned his back on me and vanished.

I asked Miriam what she made of my dream.

Without hesitating, she said, "Ema, your destiny is to bring into being the leader who is going to show us how to emerge from our slave bodies into our new free bodies. A snake already knows how to shed its old skin, but this redeemer will need to teach us."

"But," I answered, "Abba has already said he will not be the conveyor of new souls in this world as long as they will be born into Pharaoh's prison."

"Abba is wrong!" she retorted. "I see it as clearly as the clearest water. You are meant to give birth to the leader of our people!"

She was right. I, too, had the gift of deep seeing from God, as did our Mothers: Sarah, Rebekah, Rachel, and Leah before me. But it was difficult for me to put what I saw into words. Miriam had no problem speaking her visions whatsoever. I envied her at times. But it was not my way. Neither had it been my mother's way.

Now you'll understand why what happened next stunned me so that my entire being was trembling.

I was getting ready for bed. Checking on Miriam and Aaron when they were fast asleep was one of my only pleasures. As I was getting ready to lie down next to Amram, he said in an unfamiliar tone, "I must talk to you."

I sat next to him on the pallet and waited for him to speak. I placed my hand on his. He slid it out from under mine. Dread, cold and clammy, started spreading from my gut and filled my heart, throat, and shoulders.

He did not look at me. He did not say my name as he told me, "I am leaving you. I can't bear to bring one more child into this." He held up both hands, revealing the utter emptiness of "this." "Don't ask me to stay. I am no longer a man. I'm a slave without a soul. I'm a dried husk, not a husband or a father. I see every baby you bring into the world becoming another brick in Pharaoh's enormous edifices of death. I can't bear it any longer. I must go."

I broke at that point. What he said was true. Our lives meant nothing. If he were an empty husk, I was a hollow womb of no use to anyone.

Looking into my soul's depths, I saw future generations of women whose men would be driven to despair by what they had to endure as Jewish men. I saw generations of Jewish men and women driven to despair by the cruelty of their oppressors. I also saw some who managed to hope.

I remembered our wedding when Amram and I stood together before our families and God. I could feel the vibrant currents of our ancestors coursing through us, intersecting with each other, cross-fertilizing, winding our destinies together. How could we split apart?

A Message from Yocheved

Of course, you know how it all turned out. How my brave little Miriam stood up to her father and shamed him into realizing that he had become crueler than Pharaoh. I never pleaded with him to come back. I knew he would. Moses had to be born. I would nurse him so he'd have enough from me to thrive like a tough little vine in Pharaoh's house for the rest of his growing-up years.

I was patient with Amram as I was patient with God. I knew God did not ultimately control Pharaoh's heart. I knew God was watching us, waiting for us to rise up so we could learn Torah at Mount Sinai.

But that is another story. I was blessed to be married twice to the same man, and yet, my first and second marriages were completely different. Remarried, Amram and I were leagues apart from that young bride and groom who so innocently faced the beginning of their lives together.

With all my knowing what was supposed to happen, that my Moses would lead us out of Egypt, I was never absolutely sure. What if my inner sight was not showing me the truth? What if this "seeing" was not a gift from God but a curse from Satan? I only knew for certain I had been right when I was blessed to be standing there at the mountain while my youngest child and God spoke to each other. And I was blessed to be alive when we entered the Promised Land once more.

I had trusted what I knew to be true. The children I brought into this world were the grapes in God's vineyard.

This is my message to you: Trust what you know to be true; listen to what your heart tells you; act on it.

For Further Thought

How do you think it felt for Yocheved to be the mother of three such strong and talented children: Miriam, Aaron, and Moses, especially as they were growing up?

When we look at all our responsibilities, many of us feel trapped—a bit enslaved—by some aspect of our lives. How can dreaming of change help us move toward regaining a measure of the simplicity and freedom we knew in childhood? If you were talking to Yocheved about your dreams, how might her attitudes and her experiences, going from freedom into slavery, be useful to you?

Yocheved is rather difficult to locate in Jewish literature, in contrast to her well-known children: Miriam, Aaron, and Moses. However, in *The Five Books of Miriam: A Woman's Commentary on the Torah* (New York: G.P. Putnam's Sons, 1996), page 303, author Ellen Frankel cites a poignant Rabbinic midrash on Yocheved's grief at the death of Moses.

Aviva Gottlieb Zornberg, a Bible scholar who combines a knowledge of the traditional commentaries with a comprehensive background in English literature, has written about the midwives in her book, *The Particulars of Rapture: Reflections on Exodus* (New York: Doubleday, 2001), page 22.

Chapter 8
Miriam

MARSHA PRAVDER MIRKIN

חָגְרָה בְעוֹז מָתְנֶיהָ וַתְּאַמֵּץ זְרֹעוֹתֶיהָ:

"She girds herself with strength, and performs her tasks with vigor" (Prov. 31:17).

חגרה בעוז מתניה, זו מרים שאמרה לאביה כשגירש את אמה קשים
גזירותיך משלפרעה. הוא גזר על הזכרים ואתה גזרתה על הזכרים ועל
הנקיבות, הוא רשע ספק גזירותיו מתקיימין ספק אין מתקיימין ואתה
צדיק ותגזר אומר ויקם לך. ולא עוד אלא שראיתי שעתיד לצאת ממך מי
שמושיע את ישראל. מיד החזיר אשתו וכיון שילדה משה והשליכתו ליאר
טפחה לה אמה על פניה ואמרה לה היכן נבואתיך, מיד ותתצב אחותו
מרחק, שעמדה בנבואתה.

She girds herself with strength, this is Miriam who said to her father when he divorced her mother, "Your decrees are harder than Pharaoh's. He decreed against the boys and you have decreed against the boys and the girls. He is evil and so there is a doubt about whether his decrees will come to be or not. 'You will decree and it will be fulfilled' (Job 22:28). Not only that, but I have seen that in the future there will come from you one who saves Israel." Immediately he remarried his wife, and since she gave birth to Moses and had to throw him into the Nile, her mother slapped her [Miriam] across the face and said to her, "Now where is your prophecy?" Immediately "... his sister stationed herself at a distance" (Exod. 2:4). She stood by her prophecy.

—*Midrash ha-Gadol*

Pharaoh is worried that the Hebrews are multiplying so quickly they could become a potent enemy. He decides to enslave them and later decrees the death of all Hebrew baby boys. To protect Moses, his mother, Yocheved, places him in a small ark by the reeds of the Nile. We meet the young Miriam, introduced not by name but rather as Moses' sister, when she hides in the reeds to watch the baby. Soon Pharaoh's daughter, Batya, finds the basket with the crying baby and takes pity on him. At that moment, Miriam appears. She asks Batya whether she would like a Hebrew nurse for the baby, and the princess agrees. Miriam brings Yocheved to nurse her son, and later the princess adopts Moses.

Years pass. Moses grows up as an Egyptian prince, runs away to Midian, and marries the daughter of a Midianite priest. One day as he shepherds his flock, he notices a bush that burns but is not consumed. Moses stops to hear the voice of God commanding him to return to Egypt and free the Hebrews from slavery. An insecure and ambivalent Moses agrees. After the hardships and tragedy of 10 plagues, Pharaoh finally agrees to free the Israelites.

But not for long. Soon the Egyptians pursue them, and the Hebrews are trapped in front of the Sea of Reeds. Scared and pessimistic about their future, the Hebrews are again saved by the Eternal, who splits the sea when Moses lifts his rod. The Israelites cross on dry land, the sea closes, and the Egyptians pursuing them drown.

At that moment, we meet Moses' sister for the second time. Now she is named Miriam and she is called a prophetess. What does she do after being designated a prophetess? She picks up her timbrel, and all the women follow her as she dances.

Time passes. Moses receives the Ten Commandments at Mount Sinai. The Israelites continue their journey toward the Promised Land, more frightened and discontent as the years pass, until Moses himself has a crisis of confidence. At this point, we meet Miriam again. She and Aaron, Moses' older brother, are talking together because of the Cushite woman. Who is this mysterious woman? We don't know for sure because there is no further explanation in the Torah.[1]

Miriam and Aaron then begin to complain, "Has the Lord spoken only through Moses? Has He not spoken through us as well?" (Num. 12:2). Hearing this, God is angry and calls all three siblings to the Tent of Meeting. Speaking to Miriam and Aaron face-to-face, God chastises them for not recognizing the uniqueness of the relationship between

God and Moses. When God leaves, Miriam is white with *tzara'at,* a kind of painful skin condition. We don't know if Miriam is suffering. We don't know how she feels because she doesn't speak. In her stead, Aaron begs Moses to intervene with God on Miriam's behalf, and in a beautiful short prayer, Moses begs, "O God, please heal her" (12:13). God responds to Moses' prayer, but insists that Miriam stay out of the camp for seven days. Nobody journeys until Miriam returns.

The last time we meet Miriam is when we hear that she died in a place called Kadesh. She never reaches the Promised Land. But she brings song and dance with her on the journey through the wilderness, and she bids us to do the same.

Commentary

Miriam has always been an inspiration to me. She is identified as the woman of valor who "girds her loins" (literal translation) with strength. The strength that I see rising from her is spiritual, emotional, and psychological. It allows her to challenge the powers of her time and to celebrate in the midst of uncertainty. Unlike other biblical women, she is never introduced as a wife or as a mother. Miriam is a sister and a prophet. Her commitment to her brother and to God enables her to demonstrate the far reaches of her strength.

Midrash ha-Gadol tells us that when Miriam was a very young child, her parents were thought to divorce because her father did not want to give Pharaoh any opportunity to murder a son that the couple might produce (*Sotah* 12a). Miriam confronted her father, admonishing him for being worse than Pharaoh, since Pharaoh decreed the death of the boys while her father prevented the birth of girls as well. Listening to their daughter, who was so strong in her faith, her parents reunited and Moses was born.

Miriam, no matter how entrenched in her faith, did not seem to accept the idea of leaving the situation up to God. Instead, she developed a partnership with God, believing that "God helps those who help themselves," as the old adage goes. She hid near the water, available to take a proactive role if necessary in saving her brother's life. From her hiding place, she witnessed the princess coming down to the Nile, the river that was the grave of so many Hebrew baby boys. She witnessed the princess looking at the baby with pity in her eyes. And before the princess had a chance to change her mind, Miriam was there, a powerless slave looking at a powerful regent, offering her a way to live by her conscience. Miriam suggested to the princess that Moses be nursed by a Hebrew slave. The princess not only allowed Miriam's mother to nurse the baby, but paid her for doing so. Miriam's relational strength permitted her to see the possibility for righteousness even in the daughter of an evil monarch, and then speak up in a voice of faith and love.

Miriam's emotional and spiritual strength shone when the Hebrews crossed the Sea of Reeds. They watched their only road back being flooded by water; they watched the Egyptians drowning. They looked ahead and saw limitless wilderness, interminable land without water or food. They looked behind and saw the deep, uncrossable sea. They witnessed a God who both saved them and scared them. This God could both kill firstborn sons and liberate slaves from their suffering. This God could open the sea for them and permit them to cross safely. What awe they must have felt, what fright. What do we do when we encounter life-altering events with potential for both great happiness and great tragedy? Miriam knew. She danced.

That is why she is called a prophetess. Her job is to tell us what God wants from us. She did just that with song and dance rather than with words. Imagine what it would be like for us at such moments, if we had Miriam's spiritual and emotional strength. Someone is going through tests for cancer. One site is clear. Can she celebrate that moment of finding one site clear? Or will she be consumed with fear that she may not be as lucky when the next results are in? Miriam danced.

But Miriam also suffered from the constraints of being a caretaker who felt responsible as a big sister. Miriam had a hard time when Moses paid little attention to his wife, Zipporah. Miriam expected Moses to treat women lovingly. After all, she, her mother, and the princess had collectively raised him with those values. So Miriam confided her concerns in Aaron.

At the same time, Miriam also must have been concerned about Moses' psychological state. After leading these scared, complaining people through the wilderness for so many years, Moses felt defeated. He cried to God, "I cannot carry all this people by myself …. If You would deal thus with me, kill me rather, I beg You …" (Num. 11:15). How could Miriam, the sister who watched from her hiding spot in the reeds, sit by and watch her little brother suffer? She may have wanted to use her relationship with God to take on more responsibilities and assist her little brother.

God had other ideas. Sometimes we need to witness the doubts and fears of those we love without stepping in to take the burden from them. It is so easy to call a teacher as soon as our children find something at school is upsetting—and so much harder to hear them out and be supportive of their attempts to deal with the situation. Miriam tried to protect Moses and got in the way of his growth.

God became angry. When God left, Miriam was white. We are never told that God turned her white. Perhaps the knowledge that she had strayed from what God wanted and what was best for Moses led to a psychophysiological reaction.[2] We also know that she didn't say a word. Sometimes, it takes strength to allow others to make discoveries without our intervention. During that silence, Aaron showed Moses that he had faith in Moses' leadership ability—he asked Moses to intervene with God on Miriam's behalf. And, for the first time, the little brother took direct action to assist his big sister. Moses prayed to God to heal Miriam. God agreed but ordered Miriam to travel outside of the camp for seven days. During that time, the once fragmented community did not travel on, but instead waited for the woman who led them in dance and song.

The last time we hear about Miriam is when she died in Kadesh, a name that means "holiness". Her holiness came from her spiritual and psychological fortitude. She girded her loins with strength: the strength to choose gratitude over fear, to speak truth to power, to love and act on that love, and to learn about her own faults and be able to change. This is the meaning behind the new tradition of placing Miriam's cup on our seder table. We fill it with water, reminding us of the well that followed her through the desert.[3] Then we dip our hands in the water, taking in the sustenance that she provided so that we too feel girded with the strength to celebrate life.

Miriam Speaks

The night air gets cold in the wilderness. Here. Take the shawl and wrap it around you. Please, sit with me as I tell my stories and hear yours. For that is what we do: We women tell stories that connect us to the past and offer us a pathway toward our future. Then we'll pick up our timbrels and fill the crisp night air with sound, joyous sound, for we must choose between joy and despair. And, with our timbrels, we choose joy.

I am not the first of our women to sit in the wilderness under these glowing, uncountable stars. Our first foremother, Sarah, entered this wilderness, leaving behind all that she knew, to join her husband Abraham on a journey of faith. Hagar, Abraham's second wife, ran to this wilderness twice. God saw her and heard her here, and promised her a future.

Our foremother Rebekah's footprints are also in this sand. She knew that the land of her birth held no spiritual promise or sustenance. At a young age she left all that she knew to travel to a new land, to marry a stranger who was our forefather Isaac.

Our foremothers Leah, Rachel, Zilpah, and Bilhah also walked these sands. With their husband, Jacob, as their guide, they too found a home in the Promised Land. And now we sit under the same stars, guided by the same God, not knowing what the future will bring but knowing that this moment is complete and whole.

You say I am strong and have courage, that I can enter the wilderness with song and dance. Yes, I can. But the courage doesn't come only from me. It comes from all the women whose feet made prints in this sand, from all of those who gave up everything, only to find that what once sufficed as everything was not sufficient at all. Ah … each day we get closer to the Promised Land. But each day I also am more enchanted with the journey.

You ask how I felt when we crossed the sea. That's not so simple. The moment I stepped in, all my experiences of past, present, and future whirled around me and became one. I returned to my childhood. Arguing with my father, telling him that he should not prevent the birth of the baby who might lead us from slavery. I stood by as my mother made the ark for my baby brother and left him in the reeds.

I knew my mother loved the baby and loved God, but I believed she was making a big mistake. Whoever this God was, it hadn't shown its Eternal Self to us in hundreds of years. Babies were being murdered by the day. This God was not being very energetic. Still, deeper than my anger and even deeper than my fear was my unshakable belief that this God was there. But it wasn't my mother's belief. I felt that I was God's partner and prophet, and that my job was to try to carry out God's will on earth.

And so I hid by the river, a young lioness, crouching, ready to jump, keeping myself still. And then she came—the princess dressed in her golden clothing, younger than I had imagined, determined, walking quickly, two handmaids following her, concern on their faces. She stopped short and looked toward the water. Her animated eyes dimmed. She fell to her knees. She didn't stir. She looked at the remains of all the babies killed by her father's orders, drowned in this river of life and death. As she knelt there, my brother's cries burst forth and became louder. She turned in the direction of the cries, and saw him. She ordered her handmaids to reach for him and bring him to her. Tears began brimming in her eyes. Then I knew that God had sent me to hide at the reeds and that God would be with me as I made my presence known.

I can't explain what made me speak up to the princess. I can only say that I had the same feeling when my father and mother divorced, and a force in me, greater than me, pushed me to confront my father. I understood that it came from God, and that I, God's servant, had to act. My acting came from a deep, passionate love. For God? For my parents? For my brother? I don't know. Now it surfaced again with the princess. How did I know? Because of the tears in her eyes, because of her gaze into the water. We women have the potential to make and support life. Nobody should be able to destroy that potential. "Princess?" I asked, my stomach tight, my mind resolute, "May I get a Hebrew midwife to nurse the baby?"

That day changed my life and the life of the princess. I was no longer simply Moses' sister, and she was no longer simply Pharaoh's daughter. We were God's daughters, an army of resisters, with our weapons of love and faith, determined not to let the babies die. God renamed Pharaoh's daughter Batya, daughter of God. And, of course, I'm Miriam, the rebel. Together, we rebelled in the name of God. The mothers were told to put the babies in arks by the water; the Egyptian women scoured the weeds and plucked the little boys out of the water. The Hebrew mothers fed them; the Egyptian women raised them in safety. All right under Pharaoh's nose. That's the strength of women of faith.

We all left Egypt together, a mixed multitude: the Hebrews, the resisters, the babies now toddlers and children and adults, who were brought up across ethnic divides but within God's boundary.

No, I did not birth my own children. I feel that I have so many children, so many scared, awkward, at times lost children. I use my strength to strengthen them.

So that's what I was thinking as we crossed the sea. When my feet touched dry land, I felt such profound gratitude, uncertainty, relief, and fear. Then I had to choose. With all those feelings grappling for dominance, which would triumph? I chose gratitude. I knew that we could die in the wilderness, but at that moment, we were alive and safe. *Dayenu.* I knew that there was no water or food in sight but at that moment, we weren't hungry or thirsty. *Dayenu.* And then the water closed over the charioteers and their horses, and any path back to Egypt was cut off forever. So what now?

We dance. Not because the enemies have died. They too are the children of God. Not because the future is easy. No, because we are here now, surrounded by loved ones, witnessing the greatest miracle of our lives against all the odds. We dance.

A Message from Miriam

I have seven days now outside our camp. Seven days to create a better understanding of myself and what I might have done differently. The air is fresh and hot. The sand glistens and stretches eternally. I scoop some up and let the grains slip through my fingers. Each one of us who was or ever will be is one of these grains.

Most people think that I was frightened when I turned white. I was. But I felt much, much more than fear. Aaron had begged Moses to help me! Nobody had ever done that for me before. But Aaron immediately tried to rescue me. And then my little brother, my Moses, responded as soon as Aaron spoke. I heard him, the one who stuttered, eloquently pleading with God to heal me.

I brimmed with gratitude and sadness. I realized that I never expected anyone to take care of me before. I advised my parents from the time I was a small girl. I helped save my baby brother. I led the women in dance. The well of water followed me. I was a prophetess with no children to care for me in my old age. I took care of everyone, but who took care of me? Until that moment, I assumed God would do it. But when I heard my brother's plea, I knew that God is manifest in each human being, and that all these years, I had never counted on people to help me.

Please, dear friends, find God in all the people who surround you. Take in their love even as you give your own. Be cared for along with doing the caretaking. What enormous relief I felt when Moses' voice cried out to God. For the first time, I felt truly cared for. My connection with God grew stronger from the gratitude I felt toward my brothers.

Alone, away from our camp, I feel uncertain. Who am I if not the nurturer? The prophetess? The caretaker? Who is Miriam? Then I dance, and from this I know that the greatest gift I can give myself and my people is to dance in the face of uncertainty. Life can be a dance of gratitude, if we choose to make it one. And that is the life I would choose again.

For Further Thought

Think back to a time when you were feeling fearful because of some uncertainty in your life. For a moment, place yourself in that time. Imagine yourself in a particular location. Imagine what you are thinking, feeling, seeing, hearing. Now imagine that Miriam enters the place where you are experiencing this uncertainty. How would she enter the space? How would she look? What would her nonverbal messages be? What would she say to you? How might you respond? Continue to allow the interaction to unfold until you are able to experience some helpful change in your perception of your experience, thoughts, or feeling. Imagine how you would carry this new information with you as Miriam leaves the space and you reenter your current time and space.

Speaking truth to power is one important strategy in social change. Think of a change you would like to make in society. How would Miriam approach this challenge? How would she speak truth to power today?

Tikvah Frymer-Kensky's chapter, "Saviors of the Exodus," in *Reading the Women of the Bible* (New York: Schocken Books, 2002), analyzes how women in their everyday roles acted with courage and ethical uprightness to subvert Pharaoh's orders to kill Hebrew baby boys.

Marsha Pravder Mirkin's recent book, *The Women who Danced by the Sea* (New York: Monkfish Press, 2004), explores biblical stories from a psychological perspective. It connects the issues we deal with in our contemporary lives with those faced by our foremothers. Chapters on Miriam explore how we can find blessing and gratitude in the

moment, even when uncertainty looms in front of us, as well as Miriam's—
and our own—roles in the birth of an ethical community.

Rebecca Schwartz, editor of *All the Women Followed Her* (Mountain View, CA: Rikudai Miriam Press, 2001), has brought together a number of talented writers, Jewish scholars, and poets who present their understanding of Miriam from many different perspectives.

Chapter 9
Hannah

PENINA ADELMAN

טָעֲמָה כִּי־טֹוב סַחְרָהּ לֹא־יִכְבֶּה בַלַּיְלָה נֵרָהּ:

"She tastes that her merchandise is good; her lamp never goes out at night" (Prov. 31:18).

טעמה כי טוב סחרה, זו חנה שטעמה טעם תפלה, שנאמר ואשפך את נפשי. לא יכבה בלילה נרה, ונר אלהים טרם יכבה ושמואל שוכב בהיכל ה׳.

She sees that her business thrives, this is Hannah, who tasted the taste of prayer, as it is said, "... I have been pouring out my heart to the Lord" (1 Sam. 1:15). *Her lamp never goes out at night*. "The lamp of God had not yet gone out, and Samuel was sleeping in the temple of the Lord ..." (1 Sam. 3:3).

—*Midrash ha-Gadol*

There is a man named Elkanah who has two wives, Hannah and Peninnah. Hannah is his favorite. But there is one thing she does not have that Peninnah has: children. Peninnah has many children. Hannah has not been able to bear even one child.

Every year when they go to pray and offer sacrifices in Shiloh, Elkanah always gives each wife a portion. He gives Hannah even more than her share, because he loves her and God has closed up her womb. Peninnah taunts Hannah mercilessly because of this. Each year Hannah has to go through this taunting by her co-wife. She cries and stops eating. Elkanah tries to assure her that he does not love her any less because she cannot bear children. "Am I not more devoted to you than ten sons?" (1 Sam. 1:8) he challenges.

This year, when Elkanah, his wives, and children all go to the shrine at Shiloh to pray, Hannah takes even more time to pray than usual. She is bitter in her soul and desperate to have a child. She weeps as she prays. She also makes a vow, "O Lord of Hosts, if You will look upon the suffering of Your maidservant and will remember me and not forget Your maidservant, and if You will grant Your maidservant a male child, I will dedicate him to the Lord for all the days of his life; and no razor shall ever touch his head" (1 Sam. 1:11). She keeps speaking to God deeply, from her heart. Her lips are moving and no sound is coming out.

The priest at Shiloh, Eli, sees Hannah immersed in prayer. He mistakes her for a drunk and says, "How long will you make a drunken spectacle of yourself? Sober up!" Hannah answers him, "Oh, no, my lord! I am a very unhappy woman. I have drunk no wine or other strong drink, but I have been pouring out my heart to the Lord" (1 Sam. 1:14–15).

Eli realizes his mistake and tells her, "… go in peace, … and may the God of Israel grant you what you have asked of Him" (1 Sam. 1:17).

Hannah thanks him and goes on her way. She is lighthearted and the thought of eating is appealing. When she arrives home, she and her husband have intimate relations right away. This time, she does conceive, giving birth to a baby boy whom she calls Samuel, which means "God has heard." True to her word, she keeps her son only until he is weaned. Then she brings him back to Shiloh where Samuel ministers to God in front of Eli.

In those days, God did not speak directly to people very often. But one day when Samuel is in the temple, he hears someone calling him. He rushes over to Eli to see what he wants, but Eli had not called him. This happens again. Eli then understands that God is calling Samuel. He tells the boy that the next time he hears the voice calling him, he should say, "Speak, for Your servant is listening" (1 Sam. 3:10).

God lets Samuel know that the house of Eli will be destroyed because he and his sons have sinned by acting dishonestly in the temple. When this comes true, all of Israel knows that Samuel is indeed a prophet who listens to God.

Commentary

Hannah's tale is one of victory. She is fighting for her fertility with all her heart, all her soul, and all her might. Her co-wife and rival, Peninnah, tries to wear her down with cruel words and taunts. Hannah can only cry and stop eating in response. She seems to be losing the battle. Even when her husband, Elkanah, tries to fortify her, his rhetorical question, "Am I not more devoted to you than ten sons?" (1 Sam. 1:8) brings cold comfort.

What are the weapons Hannah brings to bear? They are prayer and deep faith. How Hannah forges these out of her despair and depression is the crux of the story here, demonstrating why she is an *eishet chayil.*

At this point in the Hebrew text, several roots are used doubly—a biblical Hebrew convention for emphasis. These are the words used in this way: "*U-Vacho, tivcheh/* She wept bitterly." (1 Sam. 1:10); "*Vatidor neder/* And Hannah vowed a vow" (1:11); "*HaShem, im ra'oh tir'eh ba'ani amatekha/* God, if You will look and see the affliction of your handmaid …" (1:11).[1]

The doubling of roots is a Hebrew device that makes the extent of Hannah's suffering clear to reader and listener. Her suffering has no audible words as the story says, "Now Hannah was praying in her heart; only her lips moved, but her voice could not be heard. So Eli thought she was drunk" (1 Sam. 1:13). The words of the narrative echo within each line, in sharp contrast to the silence Eli mistakenly perceives.

In fact, Hannah is not silent. She is carrying on an inner dialogue with God, which could look like prayer or it could look suspiciously like drunken, psychotic behavior. *Hannah ta-amah ta'am t'fillah* (literally, "Hannah tasted the taste of prayer"). This indicates how

Hannah was experiencing her prayer. According to the Rabbis who came up with this comparison, prayer is like food which comes from outside and enters the body through the mouth. Usually, words come from the inside of a person and out through their mouth, the inverse movement. Food nourishes a person as prayer can do. Prayer can also be savored like tasty food.

Because of the way Hannah prays—silently, savoring the words in her mouth, concentrating deeply—she is considered to be the model of Jewish prayer. Hannah herself says, in response to Eli's misjudgment of her, "I have not been drinking wine out her soul or strong drink; only I have been pouring out my soul before God." Pouring out her soul is another reversed food metaphor. Eli has accused her of putting drink into her mouth. Hannah replies that her soul is the "drink" that she has been pouring out before God in hopes of a divine response. She understands her prayer as God's drink, as her offering. Much later in Jewish history, with the destruction of the Temple and the end of sacrificial rites, that is exactly how prayer is depicted, as an offering to God in place of an animal sacrifice.

Samuel is also an offering that Hannah and Elkanah present to God. Samuel is called "her light" in *Midrash ha-Gadol*. He is the part of her that never ceases doing God's work. Whether Samuel is in the temple watching over God's place or Hannah is at home conversing with God in prayer, both of them are human instruments of the divine. Hannah's special quality as an *eishet chayil* is that she knows how to gain access to the mysterious part of herself that is connected to the life source. Her son Samuel gained access to that profound part of himself by living inside her for nine months. Children emerge from the womb, the *rechem*, the seat of compassion,[2] the deep place inside a woman that can be one of her conduits to God.

In addition, Hannah refers to herself in her prayer in 1 Samuel as *amatekha* (your handmaid) three times. Is she making sure God has no doubt about who wants a child? Perhaps she worries that up until now God has mistaken her for someone else, possibly assuming, God forbid! that she already has children. Let there be no mistake about it: Hannah is asking for a child from God. She is so certain God can fulfill this request that she commits this child to God, even before he is born. She figures it is only proper that a child who comes from God belongs to God. This is one way in which Hannah distinguishes herself from her bullying co-wife, who has kept all her children.

Hannah Speaks

Words have left me. Their little, black, insect selves have scampered into nooks and crannies where I cannot follow them. I need to tell you something, but can't. I haven't found the words.

No, I have not always felt like this. I was a girl in the morning of my life. A squash flower opening to drink light from the sun. A new promise shining in the golden ring on the bride's finger.

But words can die on the vine, breathing with life one minute and the next minute gasping for air. Just because I haven't found the words for what I want to say doesn't mean they aren't moths fluttering around and around inside my head. Spinning and spinning, I am wild with meaning.

He calls me a drunkard and I go right into the familiar habit of swallowing my words. Right down my throat into the pipe that's too narrow. Once they squeeze their way out of there, they get stuck in my belly. I feel bloated, pregnant with my own words.

God, please help me. I don't know how to say what I need to say. I'm full with words that need to be born. Give me the strength, the faith of Yocheved and Miriam who steered baby after baby out into the wide-open world.

A baby is innocent as the first breath of day. How does a baby know what it needs to do? The same way a blade of grass knows how to drink the rain. The child spends nine months in the womb learning Torah and only then is it ready to come out into the daylight. How do words know when it's time to be born?

The words I swallowed when he called me "drunkard" burned on their way down, scorching and seething like big pills of anger. But I choose not to bear those words. I will only bring into this world words that will bear fruit. That means I mustn't talk too much, that I must keep silence like a precious pregnancy. Let the words grow inside me as they will.

"B'reshit bara Elohim et hashamayim v'et ha'aretz (When God began to create heaven and earth)—v'ha'aretz hayeta tohu v'vohu (the earth being unformed and void)—v'khoshekh al p'nei tehom (with darkness over the surface of the deep), v'ruach Elohim m'rakhefet al p'nei hamayim (and a wind from God sweeping over the water) ..." (Gen. 1:1,2).

God speaks. Light is born. A word contains a world.

God, I am trying to tell you something. Please listen to me. There are millions vying for your attention, I know, but I'll only take a minute.

You have put everything here on this earth for a reason: trees, insects, stones, water, mountains, animals, children of Adam and Eve. All have a reason to be.

If I can't bear a child, I have no reason. Why did you put me here, God? Is it for Peninnah, my co-wife, to taunt me? Is it for Elkanah to feel sorry for me? Is it my punishment? Is it to make me wonder if this all there is? Did I bud and bloom to bear no fruit?

Then what fruit is that? Why can't I know it? I don't understand what you are getting at.

You say children are not the only fruit. What other fruit can there be? What else do I have to give?

When I close my eyes and look inside, there is only this yearning that feels like the brown dust rising up after a horse has galloped through my innards. My youth is escaping on that horse. Why are You letting this happen?

But if it isn't You, then who is it? Who is responsible for my life's blood being sucked away, for my future being pulled out from under me?

I see. I need to find other avenues for my fertility. To be open to other ways of growing living beings inside me, other ways of giving birth, other ways of suckling and feeding, other ways of teaching Torah.

And still, will I be a woman even if I never give birth to my own child? Yes, yes, I know ... What is "my own" child anyway? It passes through my womb on the way to the world, but in no sense is it mine.

God, I'll make a bargain with you. Let me bear a son and I will give him up to you as soon as he is weaned. Never will a razor touch his head, neither will he drink strong drink. He will be Your servant.

Just let me have the experience I was born for. Let me grow a child in my womb. Let me have a garden and cultivate a flower for You.

Please, God.

A Message from Hannah

I was patient for too long. I waited. I believed in my heart everything would turn out alright. When in my short life had I ever known anything to go so wrong? I endured the words of my co-wife, even though they chomped on my unwitting flesh and drew blood.

I tried to find comfort in Elkanah. He didn't care if I was childless. Why should it bother me?

But it did.

Don't let something so big bother you for as long as I let it.

Tell yourself how much it hurts. Tell God.

Tell it and tell it until you must do something about it.

Telling it, you are giving birth to words that must come out so they can live in the world and not only fester in your soul.

So others can hear them and hold them and help you raise them and answer them and let them grow on their own.

As they must.

For Further Thought

What might be different ways for handling Hannah's co-wife, Peninnah, and her taunts? Discuss their relative merits.

There is a midrash in which a man asks Elijah, the prophet, "My master, why is the joy of having children withheld from some householders in Israel?" [Elijah] replies, "Because, my son, the Holy One who loves them with an utter love and rejoices in them, purifies them [through suffering] and brings them to entreat Him urgently for mercy." What do you think of this reasoning? This midrash can be found in Judith Baskin's *Midrashic Women: Formations of the Feminine in Rabbinic Literature* (Hanover, NH: Brandeis University Press, 2002), pages 134–135.

The Song of Hannah (1 Sam. 2:1–10) is the subject of a chapter in Susan Ackerman's book *Warrior, Dancer, Seductress, Queen: Women in Judges and Biblical Israel* (New York: Doubleday, 1998), pages 257–264. In it, Ackerman describes a cult of drinking, singing, and dancing in which Hannah's song must have figured prominently.

In the essay, "The Womb and the Word: A Fertility Ritual for Hannah," Hannah became the anchor for Penina Adelman's own dive into the deep ocean of grief for a child she could not have. See *Four Centuries of Jewish Women's Spirituality*, edited by Ellen Umansky and Dianne Ashton (Boston: Beacon Press, 1992), pages 247–257.

Chapter 10
Yael

ANDREA COHEN-KIENER

יָדֶיהָ שִׁלְּחָה בַכִּישׁוֹר וְכַפֶּיהָ תָּמְכוּ פָלֶךְ:

"She sets her hand to the distaff; her fingers work the spindle" (Prov. 31:19).

ידיה שלחה בכישור, זו יעל שבא סיסרא לידה שנאמר וסיסרא נס
ברגליו. ותפתח את נוד החלב ותשקהו. לידע אם דעתו נכונה עליו אם
לאו. שתה ונשתכר תבעה לדבר עבירה, מיד ותתקע היתד ברקתו. וכתיב
ידה ליתד תשלחנה וימינה להלמות עמלים. לפי כך נתברכה באהלי תורה
בבתי כנסיות ובבתי מדרשות, שנאמר תברך מנשים יעל.

She sets her hand to the distaff, this is Yael[1] and how Sisera came to be in her hands. As it says, "Sisera fled on foot to the tent of Yael ... She opened a skin of milk and gave him some to drink" (Judg. 4:17–19), to see if his mind was right or not. In his drunken stupor, he wanted her. "... she drove the pin through his temple" (4:21). Deborah later sings of this act in a poem, saying: "Her left hand reached for the tent pin, Her right for the workmen's hammer." (5:26). Thus she is blessed amongst the tents of Torah, in synagogues and study halls. As it is written: "Most blessed of women be Yael, wife of Heber the Kenite, most blessed of women in tents" (5:24).

—*Midrash ha-Gadol*

Yael lived in the period of the judges, roughly 1600–1200 b.c.e., from the time Joshua crossed over from the desert into the Promised Land until the establishment of the Israelite monarchy. The Israelite tribes settled in among the other various tribes of the region. Leadership patterns emerged that were somewhat regional. Many tribal or regional leaders were fairly amoral military types and were useful to the needs of the moment. Conflicts erupted and alliances shifted frequently.

The prophet and judge Deborah emerges. She is more of a civil judge than a military leader, but she becomes involved in a military matter. She summons Barak son of Abinoam and instructs him about a specific military strategy against Sisera, an army commander. Barak only agrees to go with Deborah at his side. Deborah seems to chide him, saying that the credit for the battle will fall to the hand of a woman.

Indeed, the battle goes well for the Israelites, but Sisera, the chief general of the allied nations against Barak, escapes on foot to the tent of Heber the Kenite. Yael comes out to greet him and invites him in. She soothes him and feeds him. He rests.

"He said to her: Stand at the entrance of the tent. If anyone comes and asks you if there is anybody here, say 'No.' Then Yael wife of Heber took a tent pin and grasped the mallet. When he was fast asleep from exhaustion, she approached him stealthily and drove the pin through his temple till it went down to the ground. Thus he died" (Judg. 4:20).

Deborah tells the story of these deeds in chapter 4 and then sings a poem about it in chapter 5. Yael is blessed and praised for her acts. She is placed squarely in the lineage of the other mothers of Israel. To call her one of the "women of tents" places her in the line of the Matriarchs of Israel.

Commentary

Yael and Deborah represent two faces of womanhood: public and private. As a female prophet and judge, Deborah is social, public, and anomalous. She judges, calls, and leads. She is assertive, albeit at the word of God. The rabbis found her annoying. Reading into small textual cues, in good midrashic style, they said she lost her prophetic power at one point due to her arrogance. Deborah's leadership becomes a sign and a byword for a generation of men who will not step up and do things right. She had to summon Barak, but his weak leadership made Deborah's intervention necessary. The rabbinic mind reads this story to tell us that women take on these public roles when men have failed in some way. God puts the ultimate credit not in Barak's hands or in Deborah's, but in Yael's.

Yael gets a lot done, hardly ever leaving her tent. But she does go out and even calls to the fleeing Sisera. She invites him in, feeds him, and covers him. Then she kills him, using both hands. She uses a tool that belongs both to a woman in a tent and to a workman. Her aggressiveness and self-assertion is praised in the midrash. Yael strikes a potent balance between power and feminine wiles.

For this reason, our midrash states that Yael is blessed among tenting woman and has a place at the other future homes of the *Shekhinah* (indwelling presence of God). The houses of learning and prayer are tents for the Divine Presence. Her assertiveness protects the tents of Israel. She has a share in the future dwelling places of the Divine Presence.

It is precisely the balance between staying in and going out that yields Yael's blessedness.

Yael Speaks

Hey, girls, I am probably what you would think of as a southern girl. We Kenites lived off to the west and south a little bit. But we go way back with the Israelites. The father-in-law of our teacher Moses was Reuel, a Kenite.

Our clan has been around a long time, and we basically had alliances with everyone in the region. It just always felt like it was not our fight, and we tried to be straight with everybody. Heber, my husband's name, even means *haver*, "friend"! "Alliance," too. He was known that way. My story intersected with the Hebrews' in a way that I do not understand. The struggle between the Hebrews and the local clans literally followed me into my tent in a night I will never forget. I believe the Lord of Israel was using me in some way. This story is nothing but my own and it feels bigger than that too.

The Israelites and the nations battled it out at Wadi Kishon, which was near me. Heber was out with the flocks and a strange storm came up real fast. The weather was so dark that day. I didn't know which way things were going. I sat alone as a lookout at the tent opening and finally saw one man, running and running and running. I just knew that it was Sisera and he was the sole survivor of his troops.

I called to him. I didn't know yet what I was going to do. For the sake of all our alliances, I knew I had to offer him shelter. He would have stormed right in anyway. But in the meantime, I had just invited an embattled, grief-stricken man into my tent.

I did everything I could to calm him, while I tried to remain calm myself. I walked in an expansive, relaxed way. I sat him down. He raged and ranted and came out of his frenzy once in a while to leer at me. I fed him, saying, "You must be tired, my lord. Let me get the good bowls, my liege. What can I get you?" Eventually he would fall asleep. The question was whether he would rape me before he slept.

He asked for water and I gave him milk, nice thick curds. "No water for you, my lord. Have our richest food." I tried to mother him, to be asexual. I covered him. I still did not know what I was going to do but when he slept, I got ready. I sat down as close to him as I dared, with the tent peg in the one hand and the mallet in the other. He slept fitfully and would rouse himself with lurid thoughts of me from time to time.

I sat ready. "Come 'ere," he muttered, pulling me toward him. I let myself be drawn to a squatting position over him and simply stuck him through the temple in one move. He gasped and arched a little and then just fell flat. He died that day and I did not.

A Message from Yael

I learned to stay focused when faced with one who was a friend of my people even as I felt him to be my enemy. Moment by moment, alone with that man in the tent, I did not know what I was going to do. So I rooted myself right there in the moment and asked myself what was really important.

I had to stay alive. I had to find a way to get rid of him. If he defiled me, my life would be over. Heber could not take me back into his bed. I could not show my face anywhere. Any tenting woman would say that I had a right to kill a man who tried to take me in my own tent. It was the only thing to do. I wished I did not have to do it. And yet, I would do it again.

I hope that if you encounter moments like this, you will be able to do what needs to be done. I hope you will listen to God, Source of Strength and Wisdom, and to yourself. If you had told me before all this that I would have to use my mallet and a tent peg to finish a story, I would not have believed you. I could not have imagined using the instruments of tent-building to save myself, or to harm someone. I acted as one woman, alone, outside of the battle scene and the political alliance. I can't know or understand if the God of Israel used me to settle another score, but I do know that I saved my own life that day.

For Further Thought

Think of Yael as a warrior in the mode of Deborah the Judge (Judg. 4:4–16) and Judith (Book of Judith in the Apocrypha). Imagine how these women would have prepared themselves psychologically and spiritually for what they had to do. Then, consider these questions:

What is righteous anger and what is the right way to express it? And what, then, is unrighteous anger? And what is the wrong way of expressing it?

Is killing ever justified?

How do you hold and balance your power? Consider power as an aspect of your relationships: with children, with parents, with teachers, with the government, with animals, with nature, with men, and with women.

In the Apocrypha—the book of writings that was not considered to be part of the biblical canon—read the Book of Judith to see what Judith did when faced with a life-and-death situation in her community.

For a discussion of the many parallels between Yael and Judith, see Sidnie Ann White's article, "In the Steps of Yael and Deborah: Judith as Heroine," in *"No One Spoke Ill of Her": Essays on Judith*, edited by James C. VanderKam (Atlanta: Scholars Press, 1992), pages 5–16.

Also, see the story of Tamar in Genesis 38. It is an account of a different kind of biblical "warrior," one who stood her ground even when threatened with being burned to death. She resolved to have a child, and she had to maintain a warrior stance in order to do so.

Chapter 11
Widow from Tzarephath

LEAH SHAKDIEL

כַּפָּהּ פָּרְשָׂה לֶעָנִי ...

"She spreads out her hand to the poor ..." (Prov. 31:20).[1]

כפה פרשה לעני, זו צרפית שאמר לה אליהו תני לי מעט מים. ומה שכר
נטלה על כך, כד הקמח לא תכלה וצפחת השמן לא תחסר.

She spreads out her hand to the poor, this is the Tzarephit, the woman from Tzarephath, to whom Elijah said, "Please bring me a little water " (1 Kings 17:10). And what was the reward that she took for this? "The flour jar shall not be finished and the oil cruse shall not be lacking" (1 Kings 17:14).

—*Midrash ha-Gadol*

Before we meet the prophet Elijah for the first time, we receive the background to his mission. He is up against the mighty King Ahab, ruler of the northern Israelite kingdom. Ahab, together with his wife, Jezebel, daughter of the king of Sidon, has outdone all his predecessors with his sins, especially idolatry. Elijah appears when circumstances are so extreme that only drastic measures may help. He announces that rain and dew, keys to life, will be withheld until further notice. And indeed, God sends him to hide in a riverbed until he sees the river dry out completely.

Now God sends him to Tzarephath by Sidon, to be fed there by a widow. He does find a widow collecting wood at the town's gate and asks her for water. When he asks her for bread, too, she reveals that she has almost no flour or oil left for herself and her son. She fears they will starve to death. Elijah promises her that if she feeds him first from the little she has, she will lack no flour nor oil until the drought is over. This comes true, and, miraculously, she has an abundance of food.

Then the widow's son falls so seriously ill that he is left breathless. She blames Elijah for intruding into her life and killing the boy for some sin of hers. Because there is no previous mention of any sin, she tries to understand her son's illness as God's punishment for some sin unknown to her. Elijah picks up the son from her lap, takes him up to the attic where he is staying, puts him on his bed, and calls out to God: "Are you even visiting evil upon the widow in whose house I live, to kill her son?" "O Lord my God, please return this child's soul unto him!" (1 Kings 17:20,21). He lies down over the child three times until God answers his prayers and revives the boy. Elijah then takes the child down to his mother.

Only then does the woman say, "Now I know that you are a man of God and that the word of the Lord is truly in your mouth" (1 Kings 17:24).

Commentary

The Tzarephit's place in Elijah's life cycle is framed as foreshadowing the "grand narrative" of the people of Israel. Only dramatic, unprecedented miracles will make them adopt again the God they abandoned.

The biblical story is woven around Elijah, but *Midrash ha-Gadol* provides the opportunity to reread it with the woman as the protagonist. This biblical narrative nourished later Christian myths referring to Jesus, and even Jewish readers have since been unable to avoid the analogy. Focusing on the role of the child's mother in this drama, the image that comes to mind is the *Pietà*—Mary holding the dead Jesus in her arms. Infinite grief and pity overtakes the woman at the moment of her bereavement when she is in utmost despair. She holds her dead son in her arms while she is experiencing the immanent presence of God and His utmost compassion.[2]

The Book of Kings includes two parallel stories of this kind. One involves Elijah and the widow from Tzarephath. The other involves Elisha, Elijah's heir, and the Shunammite woman (see chapter 20). Both women are counted in the list of women in the *Midrash ha-Gadol*, but the Tzarephit gets only half a verse, whereas the Shunammite woman figures more prominently. Also intriguing is the fact that the Shunammite narrative is included in the haftarah readings, as are extensive parts of the Elijah cycle, whereas the story of the Tzarephit is not. One particular attribute makes her story different from the other *Pietàs*: She is a widow.

In ancient societies where agriculture combined with patriarchy as the foundations of civilization, the widow epitomized not only poverty, but also helplessness and total dependence. She had to rely on the generosity of the field owners and on the wisdom of lawmakers, who turned the giving of alms into specific obligations, just like other taxes that were imposed on produce. As a woman she could not own land. Her very survival depended on a male who would "spread his wing over her" (Ruth 3:9),[3] be it father, brother, husband, or son.

A motherless son in antiquity posed no problem to society as long as he had his father to take care of him. In the Torah, only a fatherless son is designated as a *yatom* (orphan), as was the Tzarephit's son. Together with the *ger* (landless stranger), the widow and the orphan became the subject of emphatic Torah laws, such as the following: "All widows and orphans you shall not torture" (Exod. 22:21).[4] No wonder the term *yatom* in the Torah is later replaced by *ben almanah* (widow's son). *Almanah* and *yatom* are a pair. Since *yatom* is always fatherless, it follows that a *yatom* can have a mother who is an *almanah*, a dyad of mother and son in utter poverty. An *almanah* may be completely alone; she may seek another man; or she may have a son. The widow becomes the metonym for utmost tragedy in biblical stories as well as in midrashim. Within the prophetic tradition that describes the relationship of God and the people of Israel as that of man and woman, the widow (with or without her sons) becomes the metaphor for Israel's suffering, her helpless victimhood, and her sense of abandonment in the period of destruction and exile

The widow from Tzarephath, then, is an even stronger *Pietà* image than that of the Shunammite woman. However, the sages in our midrash turn the tables here. They attach her to the half-verse, "her hands are stretched out to the poor!" (Prov. 31:20)[5] Moreover, they place her above Elijah the prophet, who is reduced to "the stranger in your gates" (Exod. 20:10) that she feeds. Thus, in *Midrash ha-Gadol* she goes from being depicted as a dependent mother to a provider for those who are even in greater need than she. This brings her closer to the ideal of *hesed* (lovingkindness), exemplified by Ruth. Charity saves lives, not only the lives of those who receive it, but notably the lives of those who dispense it. The sages transform the Tzarephit from the one saved by outside help to the one saved through helping others.

Elijah and the Tzarephit live in the same house and share the food provided first by her and then by him. Eventually they even share a son—born to her biologically and then reborn with Elijah's breath. Does this detailed, suggestive intimacy veil a formal relationship? Indeed, some talmudic sources make her vent a false accusation—that he had made a sexual advance, and now she is punished for the sin he had forced on her. According to these texts, Elijah prays for her and asks God to forgive her for lying in her sorrow and frustration.[6]

The Tzarephit is an assertive, proud, wise woman of deep faith, who is, at the same time, acutely aware of the various abuses of patriarchy to which she is subjected. She is simply too wise to rationalize them away and pretend that all is well in God's world. Though bitter and angry, she is also an optimist who does not give up on the potential of the world to be improved. Neither does she dismiss her own power to participate in *tikun olam* (repairing the world). She participates not because she is ordained to do so, but because she insists on going beyond that which is formally ordained.[7]

Widow from Tzarephath Speaks

I have no name, as if I do not matter. He knew the name of the town he happened upon, that's all. Tzarephath, near the city of Sidon, up north by the sea. So I should consider myself lucky for being named more than just "The Woman." Why should we put up with this anonymity, as if we were nothing but a milestone along the males' travels through space? They engineer our lives at their will, and they also control the narrative afterwards, his story, the man's, and His Story, God's Bible.

He must have known I was a widow by my special clothes, when he saw me doing the man's work of collecting wood by the town's gate. A newcomer, all right, so it was easier for him to ask for water and bread from me. Still, why did he have to embarrass me this way, to make me tell him the reason I had no bread for him was that my son and I were practically starving to death. But I am smart too, and with one look I knew he was a man of the God of Israel, that he was probably on some mission, and was only testing me to see if I was the one he had been sent for. So I slipped into my reply the code words of the oath, "By Your Living God." Maybe that was my mission, to spread my hand out to the poor man, the stranger at the gate.

It worked: He prophesied immediately that if I fed him first, then ate, myself, and only then fed my son, there would be an abundance of flour and oil until the day when God sends rain to end this drought. Are men all the same, always putting themselves first? Even if he is a priest and gets his portion of all the dough?

Yes, he could work miracles and we had more than enough to eat. But did he have to force himself on me in this way, to take rooms in the attic of my house without properly taking me for a wife? I have my reputation to protect, after all. If it were not for my son, I would have kicked him away. But none of this was the boy's fault, of course. It looked like this man of God's holy mission was to keep me and my son alive through the drought. I blessed God and his messenger every day after we had food.

Still, I am only a woman, only an instrument in this plan. I am to live through the men of my life, especially my son. I am lucky this is not a daughter, for I would have had to make him marry her to have food, even though he is so many years older than she would be. I am even luckier than the childless widows who are too old to have any hope. Every day I spread out my hand to all the poor of this town. Manless women first, though when they talk about me, they say I am compassionate to "the poor" in general.

But then my boy became ill. I could not watch him die. I climbed the stairs to the attic, furious. What was he doing in my house anyway? I should have paid attention to the rumors. They said that this man of God could curse too, not only bless. They said he was the very cause of the drought and the famine. They said he had punished all of us in the land for the sins of the king and the queen. That he was the one who had visited death on all the sons of Hi'el from Beit-El, because Hi'el broke an ancient oath. Why be surprised that he was now digging up some sin of mine so he could kill my son?

He said nothing and followed me downstairs. I froze when I saw that my boy looked like a dead corpse, so thin and yellowish. He picked him up in his arms and carried him to his own bed in the attic. I was watching coldly, beyond despair, as he murmured beseeching prayers, then leaned on the boy and blew his own breath into him. I looked on, the way his father had looked on while he came out of my body in great agony. Women give life like animals. When death is at work, why can't we mothers ever revive our sons? Why are we called upon to mourn for them or cry for a male helper to save us by saving them?

I do not know how long I stood there at the door, staring at this strange scene. My son was reborn on that bed, and the man of God fathered him this second time. Everything changed forever at that moment.

I could not bring myself to use the man's name aloud after that, because it was God's name twice, *Eli-yahu* (My God is Yah). So I gave him another name, Amitai (Truthful). Long after he had left my house and become famous for purging the land of idolatry, he went up to heaven in a chariot of fire. People never tired of hearing about these events. I had to assure them this was the truth, that there were miracles, but also that Elijah was unrelenting and unforgiving in his certainty, that he knew what the one and only God wanted.

My son, Yonah (Jonah), son of Amitai, the man of God, was changed too. Years later, he went on pilgrimage to Jerusalem, which very few from the kingdom of Israel ever dared to do. I hear he became a prophet, like his second father. I hear he had his own complications with God. I wish I could have been as resigned to his departure from me as Hannah was when she gave her Samuel to God. Maybe she was a happier person. After all, she had a name and a loving husband. I had two men but they both left me. And I have no name.

A Message from the Widow from Tzarephath

A letter to my son, Yonah, the prophet, son of Amitai:[8]

My heart goes out to you with compassion and love. I want to hold you in my arms again, to hug you closely, to comfort you with my song and tears. I hear you were running away from God, in a ship. I hear there was a bad storm and they threw you out to sea to calm God's wrath. I hear a fish swallowed you and then threw you up on the shore. I hear God insisted that you go to Nineveh. I hear they repented and that you had a hard time accepting that. I hear that God taught you another lesson, the hard way, with the tree over your head that dried out in the sun.

How many times must a man almost die, before he can learn how to love people? Yonah, my only son, I named you after the bird that brought hope in her beak to Noah in the ark after the flood. I want you to learn from me, your nameless mother, how to hope and hang onto life, through famine and other disasters, and strange signs that you don't begin to understand, sent by God. Keep your hand spread out to the poor at all times, whether they be people of God or sinful dwellers of Nineveh. Yes, find yourself a good woman and bring her home to me. And give her a name if she does not have one. You will never regret this.

For Further Thought

Can you think of a time when you encountered a stranger and this encounter turned out to be crucial, even transformative, in your life? What were your thoughts when you met the stranger? Were you receptive or not?

Compare the widow from Tzarephath's story to that of the Shunammite woman and to the wife of Obadiah. All three of them had encounters with Elijah or Elisha, the prophets. What were the encounters like? What were the different attitudes of each woman toward the stranger?

In the Apocrypha, the Book of Judith tells the story of the widow Judith, who saved her town through cleverness and courage.

Compare the story of the widow from Tzarephath to the stories of Naomi and Ruth (chapters 12 and 21, respectively), two widows of different generations.

Little has been written thus far on the Tzarephit, so we must go to another widow, Naomi, to understand her better. Two essays in *Reading Ruth*, edited by Judith A. Kates and Gail Twersky Reimer (New York: Ballantine Books, 1994), address the status of the Jewish widow in the person of Naomi. One is "The Journey Toward Life," pages 125–130, by Patricia Karlin-Neumann, and the other is Lois Dubin's "Fullness and Emptiness, Fertility and Loss: Meditations on Naomi's Tale in the Book of Ruth," pages 131–144.

On women's marginality in canonical narratives, see Carol Gilligan, "Woman's Place in Man's Life Cycle," *In a Different Voice*, (Cambridge, MA: Harvard University Press, 1993), pages 5–24.

🌿 Chapter 12
Naomi

RUTH SOHN

... וְיָדֶיהָ שִׁלְחָה לָאֶבְיוֹן:

"... her hands are stretched out to the needy" (Prov. 31:20).

וידיה שלחה לאביון, זו נעמי שהכניסה את רות תחת כנפי השכינה,
דכתיב ותרא כי מתאמצת היא ללכת אתה ותחדל לדבר אליה.

Her hands are stretched out to the needy, this is Naomi, who brought
Ruth beneath the wings of *Shekhinah* (indwelling presence of God),
as it is written, "When [Naomi] saw how determined she was to go
with her, she ceased to argue with her" (Ruth 1:18).
— *Midrash ha-Gadol*

Naomi's story begins in Bethlehem in the time of the Judges, shortly before the monarchy is established. Her husband, Elimelech, is,
according to later lore, one of the great men of his generation. When
Judea is struck by famine, Elimelech decides to leave with Naomi and
their two sons, Mahlon and Chilion. They settle in Moab, the country
east of the Dead Sea. There Elimelech dies and leaves Naomi a widow
with two sons. Perhaps they should have returned to Bethlehem, but
the boys marry Moabite women, Orpah and Ruth, and stay on in Moab
for about 10 years.

When Mahlon and Chilion suddenly die, Naomi is left mourning these new losses along with the loss of her husband, for whom she
has never stopped grieving. Naomi hears that there is a great harvest
back in Israel, and she returns home with one of her daughters-in-law,
Ruth. There, by chance, Ruth gleans in the fields of Boaz, a member
of Elimelech's family. When Boaz discovers Ruth is gleaning in his

fields, he greets her warmly and urges her to continue working through the harvest, for he has already heard of and been impressed by her devotion to Naomi. Boaz sends Ruth home at the end of the day with an unusually large amount of barley. When Naomi learns that it was Boaz who treated Ruth so generously, we hear for the first time a note of hope in Naomi's voice as she recalls that he is a redeeming kinsman, a member of Elimelech's family. This implies that he could marry Ruth and continue the family line.

At the end of the harvest, Naomi advises her daughter-in-law to approach Boaz and let him know that she would be interested in marriage. Boaz responds favorably and makes the necessary arrangements to marry Ruth. Ruth later gives birth to a son, and the women of the town sing out God's praises and celebrate Ruth's love for Naomi. Naomi helps nurture and raise the new baby, whom we are told will one day be the grandfather of David.

Commentary

We first meet Naomi as a woman all but swallowed up in grief at the loss of her two sons. The loss of a child, even a grown child, is one of the greatest tragedies a human being can experience. Anyone who has suffered loss will be able to identify with Naomi's deep grief. The loss of both sons, terrible in itself, has reawakened the pain at the loss of her husband, Elimelech, 10 years earlier. As our tradition teaches, "The death of a man is felt by no one as much as his wife, and for a woman, by no one as much as her husband" (*Sanhedrin* 22a).

Naomi first shares her pain and hopelessness when she begs her two daughters-in-law not to follow her but to return to their own families where they have the chance to begin anew. Naomi's grief is compounded by the recognition that she cannot bear more children, and even if she could, she still could not help her daughters-in-law marry and bear children of their own.

"Turn back, my daughters, for I am too old to be married. Even if I thought there was hope for me, even if I were married tonight and I also bore sons, should you wait for them to grow up? ... My lot is far more bitter than yours, for the hand of the Lord has struck out against me" (Ruth 1:12,13).

When Naomi and Ruth arrive in Bethlehem, Naomi again gives voice to her grief, this time even more powerfully as she renames herself. "Do not call me Naomi," she replies. "Call me Mara, for Shaddai has made my lot very bitter. I went away full, and the Lord has brought me back empty" (Ruth 1:20). Naomi's sense of herself stands in striking contrast to her external reality. Having left Bethlehem during a great famine, she has returned at the start of the barley harvest; but, grieving for her sons and her husband, she herself is now empty. She makes no mention of Ruth, who is by her side. Consumed by her grief, Naomi is blind to the love of her daughter-in-law who has left her own family and bound her life and soul to her mother-in-law. The bountiful new harvest points to the possibility of sustenance and new life. However, Naomi's words lead us to wonder, will Naomi ever again enjoy these blessings?

This brings us to the question that most interests me about Naomi: What allows Naomi to move out of the pain and despair that she gives voice to so eloquently? Where will Naomi find the strength that will transform her into an *eishet chayil*? Loss and pain are woven into the fabric of all of our lives. We are hungry for the lessons Naomi can offer from her journey.

The women in Naomi's life—first Ruth and then the women of the town of Bethlehem—play a significant part in Naomi's journey. They provide the rope for her to hold onto in her darkest moments. They are a loving presence by her side, at times not fully appreciated, but much needed all the same. It is perhaps this loving presence of friends that provides Naomi with the confidence to explore and to discover deep within herself the power to transform her pain. In reaching out to help Ruth find her way to Boaz, Naomi pulls herself further out of despair. This is the turning point for Naomi and, in some sense, for her people. Finally, when Ruth bears a child, Naomi's life is restored.

The women of Bethlehem sing out to Naomi in the Book of Ruth as a Greek chorus. Their collective voice at key points in Naomi's story points to the women's important role in her life. And, like a Greek chorus, they alert us to the fact that Naomi's story—of love turned to grief and loss and back again to renewed hope and life—is more than the story of an individual and her family. It is the story of our people. We, like Naomi, have traveled the roads of exile and return, famine and harvest, despair and hope, again and again. The child Ruth bears brings new life to herself and Naomi. One day this child will become the grandfather of King David, holding the seeds of Israel's future redemption. From pain and loss we can again discover new life and hope.

"V'yadeiha shilcha l'evyon" (Her hands are stretched out to the needy). This verse connects to Naomi in several ways. As the midrash notes, Naomi reached out to Ruth by allowing her to travel with her back to Bethlehem when Ruth so lovingly expressed the desire to stay with her, "For wherever you go I will go ... your people shall be my people ..." (Ruth 1:16). However, at the time, Naomi was so overwhelmed by her own grief that her reaching out to Ruth was minimal: She simply allowed Ruth to come with her.

Ironically, the verse can better be understood as relating to Naomi as the poor person. Brought low by grief, Naomi needed to allow others to reach out to her and help her begin to heal. When Naomi was better able to deal with her own pain, she was moved by Ruth's plight and acted decisively on her behalf. Now Naomi could reach out to Ruth again, this time more fully. She took her daughter-in-law under her wing and guided her toward a marriage with Boaz and a new life. Naomi's life is the story of people reaching out to each other in loving compassion, weaving together a living fabric that lifts up the fallen and provides hope and sustenance for everyone.

Naomi Speaks

How wonderful to be part of such a gathering of women! Long ago I learned the power of listening, and the gift it is to be listened to.

This is the story I am about to share with you, how the loving and attentive listening of women brought me out of pain so great it was pulling me down into She'ol (literally, the grave or depths of despair). But I am getting ahead of myself. How affirming it has been to hear the stories of those of you who have already spoken and to see parts of my life in new ways. I hope my story does the same for all of you, even if you have not suffered such losses as the death of the love of your life or, God forbid, a child.

At first the pain of losing my two sons was so great it was too much for me. Why had God forsaken me? Why had my prayers dissolved into ash on my tongue? I was afraid of my own pain and anger.

I raged against God and cried out against Elimelech for abandoning me; and yes, I was angry even with my poor sons for dying. But mostly I was angry with myself for having failed as a mother, for having failed my sons when they needed me most, even if I had no control over the fever that had raged in them and finally taken away their breath.

Gradually I sank deeper and deeper into the dark. Everything came to be cloaked in shadows. I felt so alone. Ruth never left my side, God bless her; but I see now that even as we traveled on to Bethlehem, back to my home, I was growing more and more isolated in my grief.

Then in Bethlehem, after their initial shock—I saw it in their faces and heard it in their whispers—"Is this Naomi?"—my dear old friends, their hearts and eyes softer with age, embraced me. Over those first days and weeks, over cups of hot tea, they listened. They allowed me to tell them the story again and again. They cried with me. They did not judge me. They held me with love and patience. For the moment the pain would be bearable. But later, in the dark of night, the pain would sweep over me again and suck me into its powerful current, and threaten to pull me still deeper into the dark, downward spiral of grief. I gradually came to know that the morning light would always come again, and I could trust that the dark of the night was only temporary.

Then one night as I sat alone—Ruth was already sleeping—I again started thinking over all that had happened. When I came to my sons' death, the pain swept over me anew, a dizzying wave of grief and loss. But this was different. I did not fight it. I did not say "why me?" I did not struggle. This time, almost curious, I opened up to the pain itself. I allowed the pain to wash over me and fill me up. One moment later, my heart racing, I found myself gasping for breath. For a terrifying moment, I thought the pain would choke the breath out of me. But I stayed with it. I sat with the pain without pushing it away. Then something wonderful happened. It was as if a pool opened up inside me. The pool was my own pain, but now it did not frighten me. Rather, it calmed me and my heart opened up to it.

Then the pool itself opened and deepened, and suddenly I realized there were other people drinking from it. I saw women and men whom I knew in an instant came from distant places and spoke languages I had never heard. Yet there we were, drinking from the same pool of tears, the same pool of pain. We shared a quiet intimacy. The searing pain of a child snatched from life. The aching loss of a partner or parent we weren't ready to lose. The devastation of war. Raging fires, famine and floods. Lingering illness. Sudden death. My heart went out to each and every one of them, strangers, yet kin. In that moment, the pool of pain that was in my heart deepened and bloomed into a pool of *hesed* and *rachamim*, lovingkindness and compassion. Compassion for myself. Compassion for the pain of the world. In that moment, I knew if I could stay open to the pain and not close my heart in fear, new life could be born for me and for those around me.

From that night on, I felt different. Even as I was still grieving for my husband and my sons, I heard what people said differently. I cared again about what others felt. I was connected deeply to everyone and everything. I was alive.

The next morning, as I was cooking the afternoon meal, I found myself thinking about Ruth. She was so loving and devoted, she asked for nothing. Even though it had been her idea to come along— I had tried to talk her out of it—she must have sometimes been lonely for what she had left behind. But she never once complained or spoke of missing home. She would rub my back and my feet when they were sore without my asking, and would sing for us the songs of her youth. She seemed content. But this morning I was shaken out of my lethargy. What would happen to Ruth when I was gone? She was young and still had her whole life ahead of her. She should be taking care of a husband and children, and here she was taking care of me. I needed to help her find a husband. What about Boaz? He was family. She was drawn to him, I could tell. But she was shy, and he was only recently a widower. Someone needed to get things started here. Perhaps. There were possibilities.

When Ruth came in later for dinner, I shared with her a plan. At first she was a bit uncertain, but I assured her Boaz would respond well to her taking some quiet initiative. He was a good man and would know what to do, I told her. So that very night I sent Ruth out to the threshing floor where Boaz would be, and the next morning, Boaz went to the Elders at the Gate, and, well, you know the story.

After Ruth married Boaz, I was really alone for the first time, and to my surprise, I found I enjoyed it. After the baby was born, they asked me to move into their house and to help Ruth with the baby. How could I refuse? My life is full in a way I never dreamed it could be again.

One thing you may have wondered about. Why was it the women of Bethlehem who named my grandson? It is true; this was very unusual. You would have expected Boaz or Ruth to name the child. But there was an important reason, a beautiful reason.

You see, it was these women, my old friends, who saved my life in those darkest of days. They took me back into their hearts and lives after all those years, and they drew out of me some of my bitterness and anger. They listened and they held me. They helped me heal. When Ruth was big with child, I asked her and Boaz about the naming, and they loved the idea. So the women were granted this great honor. And what was the name they chose? Obed. One who serves

God. I hope we can succeed in teaching this child the fullness and the blessing of such a name. May God be gracious to Obed. And may Obed discover the blessing of an open heart: in our reaching out to each other, we can most fully serve God.

A Message from Naomi

Grief is the price we pay for the gift of love. The longer I live, the more I see that loss and grief and pain and, yes, suffering, are experienced by everyone over the course of life. Some experience it earlier than others, some more than others—more than their share, we might say. But everyone who escapes an early death themselves must at some point face the searing pain of loss, the ache of sadness and loneliness, the longing for what is no more and what might have been. And while we would never invite suffering our way, when it comes, it has much to teach us.

There are parts of this journey you will have to take alone, but not right away. Allow others to take care of you and help you heal. Let them in.

Do not be afraid of your grief. Do not close your heart to protect yourself. This will only bring you greater pain and suffering. It will make of your heart a bitter stone, pulling you down into a swirling current of anger and fear that will threaten to choke the life out of you. Allow your grief to open your heart to the pain of your loss. The irony is that in opening to the pain, you will also be able to feel more deeply again the love that is, in the end, what really sustains us.

Pour out your heart before God as Hannah did. Pour out your grief, your anger, your fears and longings. Allow yourself to be carried and held. And if you are wondering if God is really there, turn to God *as if God is there* and see what happens.

Allow yourself to see others' suffering from your own open heart and reach out. With a hand on a shoulder, with food and drink, with patient listening, and with words of comfort. Allow yourself to trust again in the power of love to touch, to heal, and to make whole. This is why God gave us life.

For Further Thought

What strikes you as the most important things that helped Naomi make the transition from pain and despair to renewed hope? Do any of these resonate with your own experiences?

Does Naomi's account offer any approaches to dealing with painful experiences that you have not tried in the past but that you might want to try or suggest to others?

Reading Ruth: Contemporary Women Reclaim a Sacred Story, edited by Judith A. Kates and Gail Twersky Reimer (New York: Ballantine Books, 1994), is a rich collection of essays, poems, commentaries, and stories by contemporary Jewish women on the Book of Ruth. Authors include Marge Piercy, Cynthia Ozick, and Francine Klagsbrun. Many of the pieces contain fresh perspectives and insights on Naomi.

See *Countertraditions in the Bible: A Feminist Approach* (Cambridge, MA: Harvard University Press, 1992), pages 98–117. The author—feminist biblical scholar Ilana Pardes—notes literary links between stories. She compares the love between Ruth and Naomi with the competition between Rachel and Leah, saying that the latter is more typical of the biblical motif of conflict found between brothers.

❧ Chapter 13
Rachav

STEPHANIE NEWMAN SAMUELS

לֹא־תִירָא לְבֵיתָהּ מִשָּׁלֶג כִּי כָל־בֵּיתָהּ לָבֻשׁ שָׁנִים:

"She is not worried for her household because of snow, for her whole household is dressed in crimson" (Prov. 31:21).

לא תירא לביתה משלג, זו רחב שהחביאה את המרגלים. ומי היו ר' יוסי אומר זה כלב ופינחס. ויש אומרין פרץ וזרח היו כשבקשה מהן אות אמר לה זרח את תקות חוט השני הזה תקשרי בחלון, זה שנבדקתי בו במעי אמי, דכתיב ותקשר על ידו שני. לפי כך זכתה ויצאו ממנה עשרה כהנים. ואלו הן חלקיה ירמיה שריה מחסיה ברוך נריה חנמאל שלום בוזי יחזקאל. ויש אומרין אף חולדה הנביאה, דכתיב אשת שלום בן תקוה בן חרחס ולהלן הוא אומר את תקות חוט השני.

She is not worried for her household because of snow, for her whole household is dressed in crimson, this is Rachav,[1] who took in the spies. Who were they? Rabbi Yosi says Caleb and Pinchas. Others say Perez and Zerah. When she requested a sign from them, Zerah said to her, "... you tie this length of crimson cord to the window ..." (Josh. 2:18), this is the scarlet thread which was tied to my hand in the womb to prove my birthright, as it is written, "... the midwife tied a crimson thread on that hand ..." (Gen. 38:28). Therefore Rachav merited having 10 priests as descendants: Hilkiah, Jeremiah, Seraiah, Mehasiah, Baruch, Neriah, Hanamel, Shalom, Buzi, Yehezkel. Others say also Huldah the prophetess, as it is said: "the wife of Shallum son of Tikvah son of Harchas" (2 Kings 22:14), and regarding Rachav it is written: *tikvat chut ha-shani*—"the scarlet thread."

—*Midrash ha-Gadol*

The Children of Israel are poised to enter the Promised Land under the guidance of their new leader, Joshua. He dispatches two men called *meraglim* (spies) to see the land, specifically the city of Jericho. The two spies, unnamed in the text (Josh. 2), stay at the house of Rachav, *ishah zonah*, (prostitute). When the king of Jericho finds out that the spies have gone to Rachav's house, he sends a message to her to deliver them to him. Rachav, however, has hidden the men on her roof under stalks of flax. She sends a message back to the king telling him that the men had indeed been to her house, but that she does not know where they are presently. The king's men continue to pursue the spies.

Rachav then goes up to her roof to speak to the spies. She tells them three things: First, "I know that the Lord has given the country to you." Second, "dread of you has fallen upon us, and all the inhabitants of the land are quaking before you. For we have heard how the Lord dried up the waters of the Sea of Reeds for you when you left Egypt ...." Finally, she requests from the men, "Now, since I have shown loyalty to you, swear to me by the Lord that you in turn will show loyalty to my family. Provide me with a reliable sign that you will spare the lives of my father and mother, my brothers and sisters, and all who belong to them, and save us from death" [when the Children of Israel enter the Land] (Josh. 2:12–13). The spies agree to her request as long as she does not tell anyone of their agreement.

Rachav lowers the men from her window by a rope, since her home is in the wall of the city. She tells them to hide in the hills for three days until their pursuers turn back, and then they should return to their encampment. They give her a scarlet thread to put in her window, and tell her that as long as no one leaves her house, they will be spared; however, if anyone leaves the house, or if she discloses this agreement to anyone, then the deal is off. The spies then hide in the hills for three days as Rachav has instructed them, and then they return to Joshua. They relay what happened and quote Rachav:

"The Lord has delivered the whole land into our power; in fact, all the inhabitants of the land are quaking before us" (Josh. 2:24). This assures their God-given victory over the Land.

Commentary

Why is Rachav counted among the *neshei chayil* (women of valor) of the midrash? She is, after all, a prostitute (or an innkeeper, according to some commentators) and seems to use her position to extract a promise from the spies to save her own family. Even more than this, she "knows the ropes" of the land. The king knows who she is and relies upon her for information vital to his kingdom. She is also aware of her importance to the governance of the land. There is even a talmudic dictum that states that there was no prince or governor who had not slept with Rachav, the harlot (*Zevachim* 116b). What makes her special enough to be counted amongst other *nashim tzidkaniyot* (righteous women)?

Upon closer examination of her words, one begins to see a more complex picture of Rachav. When she speaks to the spies, she informs them that fear of the Children of Israel has come upon her people. Yet her words reveal a personal belief in the God of Children of Israel: "I know that the Lord has given the country to you, ..." (Josh. 2:9). She has come to realize, over the 40 years that have passed since the Children of Israel crossed the Sea of Reeds,[2] that God is with them: "When we heard about it, we lost heart ... for the Lord your God is the only God in heaven above and on earth below" (Josh. 2:11). We recognize this statement of faith from our liturgy, first found in Deuteronomy 4:39 and later in the words of Rachav the harlot. She risks her life to help the Children of Israel conquer the Promised Land and betrays her own people to join the faith of this nation. Finally, in her request for an oath and a sign, she says: " ... swear to me by the Lord ..." (Josh. 2:12), again emphasizing her belief in the Almighty God of the Children of Israel. Indeed, a midrash describes Rachav's faith in God as second only to that of Moses (*Yalkut Shimeoni Joshua* 10).

Furthermore, in her request to be kept alive, she does not even mention herself: "... that you will spare the lives of my father and mother, my brothers and sisters, and all who belong to them, and save us from death" (Josh. 2:13). Because of the selflessness of her deed and her request, and because she keeps to the words of the oath, Rachav and her family are saved. Prior to the conquest of Jericho, Joshua gives special instructions regarding Rachav: "… only Rachav the harlot is to be spared, and all who are with her in the house, because she hid the messengers we sent" (Josh. 6:17). During the actual conquest of the inhabitants of the city, Joshua commands the two spies to bring Rachav and her family out of the city. After the conquest, when the city was burnt, we are told "Only Rachav the harlot and her father's family were spared by Joshua, along with all that belonged to her, …" (Josh. 6:25). A midrash on this verse posits that Joshua married Rachav, thus legitimizing her family's status within the Children of Israel and ensuring that "… she dwelt among the Israelites—as is still the case. For she had hidden the messengers that Joshua sent to spy out Jericho" (*Radak on Joshua* 6:25).

Now let's return to the *Midrash ha-Gadol*. The midrash weaves its story about Rachav around the scarlet thread that Rachav uses as a sign to the Children of Israel to save her household. Where else do we see this scarlet thread in the Bible? The midrash connects Rachav with Zerah, one of the twin sons of Tamar and Judah. We recall that Tamar (Gen. 38) disguised herself as a harlot in order to produce an heir from the family of Judah, since he had not married her to his one remaining son. When Judah realizes what she has done, he says, "She is more in the right than I, …" (Gen. 38:26). Tamar gives birth to two sons, Zerah and Perez. In their struggle to enter the world from her womb, Zerah reached out his hand first, and the midwife tied a scarlet thread around it. But then he withdrew his fist, and his twin pushed his way out first, thus earning his name Perez (one who has burst forth). Thus we see the link between Rachav and Tamar through the red thread of Zerah.

What is the symbolism of the red thread in these stories? Looking back at the verse in Proverbs, we see the image of snow and scarlet. The prophet Isaiah exhorts: "Be your sins like crimson, They can turn snow-white; Be they red as dyed wool, They can become like fleece" (Isa. 1:18). We call upon this imagery in our liturgy for the High Holy Days, as we pray for the atonement of our sins. We recall the service of the High Priest, who prayed on behalf of the people. If he were successful in procuring forgiveness for their sins, the red thread outside the Holy of Holies would turn white, bringing joy to all who witnessed the transformation. By securing a red thread to her window, Rachav was paralleling the actions of the High Priest, atoning for all of her past misdeeds. In choosing to join the Children of Israel, she hoped that her own life and the life of her family would be more pure. It would be like starting a new life with a clean slate. She took a risk to start a new life in a new nation. Her risk proved worthwhile—her descendants are both priests and prophets.

Rachav Speaks

I have been blessed. After all I have been through, after all I have seen and done, I have been blessed. With a husband who is none other than the leader of my new people. With a community of believers and moral exemplars who have welcomed me and my family as heroes and as equals. With my children happily married in their own families. With the assurance that my descendants will be priests and prophets. My dreams have come true.

I'll never forget how it started. I was 10 when I heard the rumor of the great miracle at the Sea of Reeds. I remember wondering how such a thing could be. They said there was a slave people saved by an invisible God and led by an Egyptian prince turned rebel. They said these slaves escaped from the Pharaoh and walked unharmed through the Sea of Reeds while their erstwhile captors perished in its waters! Absurd, yet the rumors kept reaching us from different sources: eyewitness accounts, bits of overheard conversations, actual contact with the nomadic tribes, children of the slaves. At first no one believed any of it, but the stories kept coming about this strange people who were now traversing the desert. Where were they going, what were they going to do next, how powerful were they, exactly?

I, of course, was in a position to hear all of the rumors firsthand and in great detail. How did I end up a prostitute? I would like to be able to say I made the decision, but in fact, at the time, I felt I had no choice. I needed the money to stay alive—my parents were ill and could not work; my brothers and sisters were struggling; and I needed to find a way to survive. So I did what I had to do, and I did it well. I had a way with words—it was like a magical power—and I used it to my advantage. Men would tell me everything. Soon I had earned a reputation as a confidante and a dealer in information. It was a very risky business, but I managed to keep it going for about 40 years.

It was close to the end of this time when the rumors stopped being rumors and turned into truth. It was when we heard how the Children of Israel defeated Sihon and Og, the two most powerful kings of the region, the longtime leaders of the Amorite people. This could not have been made up. It could not be a mere rumor. Therefore, to many of us this meant that the previous stories had to be true as well. Panic ensued. People tried to run away, but our king stopped them, closing the gates of the city and instituting enforced curfew. Suspected traitors or collaborators were tortured or burned. The new laws hurt my business, but it didn't matter. I had already made my decision. Somehow I was going to leave. The lure of a new life beckoned. I needed to leave my house in the wall and my past behind. I would join with the new faith, the believers in the One God.

And then the opportunity I had sought came knocking on my door. The two spies from the Israelites were ferocious men, yet steadfast in their mission and loyal to their leader. I saved their lives, risking my own and my family's lives. Thank God for the red thread. I still have it, as a reminder of all that has transpired, of all I left behind, and of all that is yet to come for my family and me.

A Message from Rachav

Here are lessons to take with you.

First of all, learn the sanctity of this nation, the Children of Israel. We have the potential to change the world through the power of our ethical and religious beliefs. We must immerse ourselves in the study of these beliefs and act on them in order to become a beacon amongst the nations, to make the world a better, more peaceful place.

Second, don't ever lose faith in the power of the individual. Through my perseverance, I was able to save my family and myself. I made a decision to leave my former nation, to seek a better life for us all. We don't always know if our decisions are good ones until we have already acted on them.

Finally, it is never too late to atone for past misdeeds. We need to examine our deeds and believe in our potential to change ourselves, as well as the world around us.

For Further Thought

Compare Rachav to other biblical women such as Tamar (Gen. 38) and Ruth. How do these comparisons shed light on Rachav's plight?

Consider the red thread. What else could it symbolize?

Why are we told the story of Rachav at all? Does her story tell us more about Joshua, or does it have value in its own right?

Encyclopedia of Biblical Personalities: Anthologized from the Talmud, Midrash and Rabbinic Writings (New York: Mesorah Publications, Ltd., 1994), by Yishai Chasidah, is an invaluable resource for finding references to a particular biblical figure in the traditional sources.

Judith Baskin has written about Rachav in her thought-provoking work, *Midrashic Women: Formations of the Feminine in Rabbinic Literature* (Hanover, NH: University Press of New England, 2002).

Chapter 14
Bath-Sheba

SAVINA J. TEUBAL

מַרְבַדִּים עָשְׂתָה־לָּהּ שֵׁשׁ וְאַרְגָּמָן לְבוּשָׁהּ:

"She makes covers for herself; her clothing is linen and purple"
(Prov. 31:22).

מרבדים עשתה לה, זו בת שבע שראת ברוח הקדש שעתיד לצאת ממנה
בן שהוא אומר שלשת אלפים משל דכתיב ויחכם מכל האדם.

She makes covers for herself, this is Bath-Sheba, who foresaw by the
Holy Spirit that in the future she would bear a son who would say
3,000 parables, as it is written, "He [Solomon] was the wisest of all
men: ..." (1 Kings 5:11).

—*Midrash ha-Gadol*

The biblical story of Bath-Sheba is told in two parts, in two books:
the first in 2 Samuel: 11,12, and the second in 1 Kings: 1,2.
Bath-Sheba's personality is so different in each of the books that
she does not sound like the same person. In the Book of Samuel,
Bath-Sheba is a woman acted upon, with no voice of her own,
whereas in the Book of Kings, Bath-Sheba is depicted as determined, confrontational, and perhaps even conniving.

The account in Samuel tells us more about David than it does
about Bath-Sheba; it is the low point in his career. In fact, in his deal-
ings with Bath-Sheba, David is depicted as the basest of characters,
amoral and ruthless. On the other hand, Bath-Sheba's role seems de-
signed to draw our attention to her and away from David.

The biblical scene opens with the statement: "At the turn of year, the
season when kings go out [to battle], David sent Joab with his officers and

all Israel with him, and they devastated Ammon and besieged Rabbah; David remained in Jerusalem" (2 Sam. 11:1).

One evening, while walking on the roof of his palace, David sees a very beautiful woman, bathing. The narrative explains that she is bathing because it is the time of her purification: she is observing the ritual of *mikveh* after her menstruation (Lev. 15:18–32). This implies that she was not pregnant by her husband, Uriah. David inquires about her and is told she is the daughter of Eliam and the wife of Uriah the Hittite. So David sends agents to fetch her and he lies with her. After she returns home, she finds she is pregnant and sends someone to inform David.

David has Bath-Sheba's husband, Uriah the Hittite, brought from the battlefield. For days David does everything possible to cause him to go to his wife; he even gets him drunk. But, to David's frustration, Uriah insists on maintaining sexual abstinence in order to observe the ritual purity of the battle camp in the presence of the Ark. He sleeps instead with the servants.

Unable to cajole Uriah into believing he has impregnated his wife, David writes a letter to Joab—which he sends with Uriah—telling the captain to place his officer where he will surely be struck down and die. Joab sends word back to the king that he has accomplished the mission.

When Bath-Sheba hears that her husband has been killed, she mourns for him. After the mourning period is over, David sends for her again. She becomes his wife and bears a son.

Nathan the prophet goes to David and accuses him, on God's behalf, of sinning; "You have put Uriah the Hittite to the sword; you took his wife and made her your own wife and had him killed by the sword of the Ammonites. Therefore the sword shall never depart from your House ..." (2 Sam. 12:9,10). David confesses his sin, but Nathan claims, "The Lord has remitted your sin; you shall not die. However, ... the child about to be born to you shall die" (2 Sam. 12:13,14).

Bath-Sheba's first child dies and she is struck with grief. David comforts her and lies with her again. She bears another son, whom she names Solomon.

Bath-Sheba's story resumes in Kings at a much later date, when David is sick and dying. Adonijah, one of David's sons, supported by Joab and Abiathar, the Israelite priest, is proclaimed king by them on the outskirts of Jerusalem. Nathan hears of it and informs Bath-Sheba. She hastens to the king's private chambers and says to him, "My lord, you yourself swore to your maidservant by the Lord your God: 'Your son Solomon shall succeed me as king, and he shall sit upon my throne.' Yet now Adonijah has become king, and you, my lord the king, know nothing about it" (1 Kings 1:17,18). David immediately has Solomon crowned. When Adonijah is brought before Solomon, the new king spares his life on condition that the would-be usurper ceases to rebel.

After David's death, Adonijah goes to Bath-Sheba with a request. He wants the queen to ask Solomon to give him Abishag the Shunammite, the beautiful young woman who had been taken to David's bed to keep him warm in his old age. Bath-Sheba goes to the king to speak to him about Adonijah. King Solomon rises to greet her and bows down to her. He sits on his throne and she sits on his right. Bath-Sheba relays Adonijah's message to her son the king. Solomon has Adonijah killed for sedition.

Commentary

The verse that the rabbis chose to represent Bath-Sheba in "Eishet Chayil" is revealing. It begins "She makes covers for herself"— implying that she had been uncovered. Biblical references to Bath-Sheba are sparse, but her introduction into David's story—being spied on by King David as she took her bath—is the image that has been the most popularized in literature, art, and film. This is unfortunate, in the first place, because, as I shall argue, the bathing event is unlikely. In the second place, the depiction of Bath-Sheba's public nakedness (in Samuel) disparages and belittles the initial image of a woman who is later (in Kings) described as resourceful and respected. This is expressed by the Rabbis in the second part of the proverb: "Her clothing is linen and purple," presumably referring to Bath-Sheba's transition from nakedness to royalty. I find the Samuel version of Bath-Sheba's role improbable, so I would like to examine this account in depth to make my case.

The first sentence in the Samuel story does not seem very consequential until we ask ourselves why David sent his subordinates on so important a mission and did not go to war himself, as he should have done. The texts do not depict him as either too ill or too old. Why does the author give no explanation for David's absence on the battlefield … or does he? Is the reason concealed in the story that follows?

At least two plausible explanations can be inferred from the narrative that comes after the initial statement. It is possible that the king had lusted after Bath-Sheba and had taken advantage of his royal position by abusing his power and violating the wife of one of his elite warriors while the man was away at war. It is also possible to conjecture that, for political reasons, David felt the need to marry a woman from Jerusalem, his newly acquired kingdom. Before David had conquered it, Jerusalem had belonged to a people known as Jebusites, possibly a branch of the Hittites. David had many wives at the time, all from Israel and Judah. He may have felt a need for a bond with the Jebusite people of Jerusalem, so he stayed behind in order to find a local woman to marry. Both these observations are viable: David intended to satisfy his lust for Bath-Sheba on the one hand, and to marry a local woman on the other hand.

The sequence could have been as follows: David saw Bath-Sheba (married but childless) and took her to his bed, intending neither to marry nor impregnate her. (David would not have expected the married but childless wife of Uriah to become pregnant, because infertility was seen as an exclusive affliction of women.) But fate played David a nasty trick: Bath-Sheba did become pregnant. Once Bath-Sheba was pregnant, David was unable to convince Uriah to sleep with his wife and deceive him into thinking that the unborn child was his. Therefore, David had Uriah killed and then married Bath-Sheba. In this way he was able to fulfill both his need to satisfy his lust for Bath-Sheba and to marry a Jerusalemite.

The bare facts are that David lusted after Bath-Sheba, connived with Joab to have her husband Uriah (who was his officer) killed, and then married her. This scenario implies that David's act of violating Bath-Sheba was premeditated. Was it?

First of all, according to the biblical account, David inquired about the woman's identity after he saw her bathing. Uriah was one of David's elite officers, from the select order of warriors known as the "Thirty." Surely David would have recognized Uriah's wife, particularly in such a small community as Jebus (City of David), the capital of Jerusalem. Second, it is extremely unlikely that any woman at that time would be bathing her naked body on the rooftop or in the walled courtyard of her house, where she was readily visible. People used their rooftops as an extension of their residences, in full view of their neighbors, not as private space; and courtyards were the domains of animals. Finally, the bath was presumably a private *mikveh*, since the text explains that it was the time of her purification. However, it is most unlikely that the bath was a *mikveh*, because ritual baths follow stringent specifications, requiring *mayim chayim* (living waters) and are built specifically for the purpose of ritual purity; any old bathtub would simply be out of the question, even if it had been filled with rainwater.

In other words, the stories of David's ignorance of Bath-Sheba's identity and his first impression of her must have been concocted by the authors of the Bath-Sheba account to give the sensation that David had been filled with innocent virile lust for a woman who was indecently exposing herself!

Some scholars suggest that Bath-Sheba may have intentionally enticed David with her nakedness—preferring to be the wife of a king than a soldier. This would have made her an accomplice in the adultery. However, this requires Bath-Sheba to have known that David had not gone to war, as he should have; that he would have been available at the precise moment she was bathing; and that only David could have seen her.

None of these situations seem feasible to me. I can only conclude that the author/editor(s) of the Book of Samuel felt that David's involvement in the death of Uriah was so that heinous he felt compelled to revise an old story by inserting a seductive paragraph about Bath-Sheba that could compromise her. At the very least it would introduce her in a most unseemly fashion. He did so by creating a titillating scene of David's lust—kings were allowed such indulgences—and so deflected the crime that ensued. I must admit that the bathing scene was a stroke of genius on the part of the writer, an image so vivid that it has become the most memorable event in the stories about David and Bath-Sheba.

To support my theory that the bathing scene was an insertion by an editor troubled by the actual story, we can turn again to the episode in which Nathan the prophet reprimands David with the words: "Why then have you flouted the command of the Lord and done what displeases Him? You have put Uriah the Hittite to the sword; you took his wife and made her your wife and had him killed by the sword of the Ammonites" (2 Sam. 12:9). No accusation is made against Bath-Sheba, who is simply portrayed as the victim of an all-powerful king.

Bath-Sheba Speaks

Can you imagine my alarm when I realized I was pregnant? Pregnant! How could I be pregnant? I have slept with Uriah these past years, and no fruit has quickened in my womb. When my blood did not come, I hastened to the midwife. "You are pregnant," she said, "and Uriah is on the battlefield."

David had called for me and forced me to his bed. I protested. The king's word is law. I could not deny him.

"As soon as Uriah returns you must tell him what happened. He himself must confront the king that you should not be accused of whoredom," the midwife counseled.

But Uriah never returned. He was killed on the battlefield, and David took me to wife. The child I bore became sick with a fever and died. It was Nathan the prophet who said that the loss of my baby was punishment for David's offense to God for having sent one of his warriors, my Uriah, to his death.

What kind of a man's reasoning could maintain that taking the life of the child I had so yearned for could be punishment for the murderer of my husband? "It was David's son, too," you say. Yes, but David had many sons; this was my only one. And what of the innocent child? Was he to pay with his life for the crime committed by his father?

How can I live with this man? The man who has caused me to mourn, first for my husband and then for my son! True, he dresses me in royal purple and parades my beauty proudly in front of his applauding courtiers and their bowing women. True, too, that I have been blessed with another son, one the king has promised to crown in my presence. But what of David's other sons who covet his throne? Am I to live in fear of their rivalry?

David becomes impatient with my grief. "Forget what has happened. Look, you are the wife of a king, and I have given you another son to comfort you," he exclaims, as though a mother can ever be comforted for the loss of her child. The new one I have called Solomon, that there should be peace during his reign; but also because it can mean "replacement" of the child I have lost.

God, the Merciful One who has seen my suffering, has revealed to me that this son shall be the wisest of all men. He will be the author of 3,000 proverbs. God's name for him is Yedidiah, beloved of Yah.

A Message from Bath-Sheba

You who are reading this need to know that when you read or hear a story, there is usually more than one side to it. If you hear only one side, you cannot know the whole story. For thousands of years you have been reading a story that mentions my name but tells you precious little about me.

But the story we read is not about you, you protest. It is about David, the man who united our tribes and founded a nation that endured as a beacon of light unto all other nations. Your story is incidental to that story.

That is exactly what I mean! In fact, David's success was at the expense of my people, the Jebusites. David usurped the throne of my king and made himself ruler of Jerusalem, just as he removed my husband and made himself lord of Bath-Sheba. Look at it this way: If you had forced yourself into my house, murdered my husband, and taken me to wife, would you be considered a hero or a criminal? Would your council of elders see fit to punish me for the death of my husband by killing my firstborn child?

But, you ask, how then would it have been different had we heard your side of the story also?

I know that my story can be viewed as simply the tale of one woman and one child, an insignificant occurrence, however tragic, in the larger scheme of nation-building. But do my dead son and I not represent the thousands of others who have experienced the same fate? Should the sound of my voice be smothered in order that a perpetrator of violence is viewed as unblemished? We write about heroes and extol their virtues as models for future generations while suppressing their crimes. Does the enforced silence of some absolve others of responsibility? Are the crimes perpetrated against women and children by those we call heroes insignificant? Is this the message we want to give future generations: Succeed in your endeavor and we will overlook the means by which you triumphed?

In other words, I believe that seeing all sides of a story gives it a moral dimension. Had my version, and so many others like it, been included in the stories we tell—particularly those about the fate of women in war and invasion—our values would change; we would be less inclined to dismiss individual failings in order to honor the whole.

For Further Thought

Create a court with judge and jury, and give King David a hearing on his behavior toward Uriah the Hittite. If you think his action warrants punishment, discuss the sentence he receives or should have received.

Do you think King Solomon's legendary wisdom stemmed from his mother's influence? Solomon sat his mother on a throne on his right side after he became king. What advice would Bath-Sheba have given to her son Solomon to guide him in governing his kingdom?

An excellent translation and commentary by Robert Alter provides deep insight into the character of David that further clarifies his relationship with Bath-Sheba: *The David Story, A Translation with Commentary of 1 and 2 Samuel* (New York: W.W. Norton & Company, Inc., 1999), pages 244–265.

David's Secret Demons: Messiah, Murderer, Traitor, King (Grand Rapids, MI: William B. Eerdman's Publishing Company, 2001) is another study of David that attempts to take a critical look at the stories about him in hopes of understanding him better. Author Baruch Halpern includes much material on Bath-Sheba, as well, which sheds light on her part in his story.

Chapter 15
Michal

JUDITH KATES

נוֹדָע בַּשְּׁעָרִים בַּעְלָהּ בְּשִׁבְתּוֹ עִם־זִקְנֵי־אָרֶץ:

"Her husband is prominent in the gates, as he sits among the elders of the land" (Prov. 31:23).

נודע בשערים בעלה, זו מיכל שהצילה לדוד בעלה מן המיתה בשלוח
שאול וישמרו את הבית להמיתו ותאמר חולה הוא. ולבסוף נודע הדבר
אמר לה אביה שקרת בי, אמרה לו כדי להצילך מדם נקי. מה הוא אומר
כי מי שלח ידו במשיח ה' ונקה.

Her husband is prominent in the gates, this is Michal, who saved her husband, David, from death when Saul sent [messengers] who kept watch on the house in order to kill him, but she said, "He is sick" (1 Sam. 19:14). In the end, when the matter became known, her father said to her, "you deceived me." She said to him, "[It was] to save you from [shedding] innocent blood." What did he say [then]? "No one can lay hands on the Lord's anointed with impunity" (1 Sam. 26:9).

—*Midrash ha-Gadol*

Michal's story emerges in fragments interspersed in the tales of kings and warriors in 1 and 2 Samuel. She comes onto the biblical stage as we begin to perceive the rivalry between Saul and David. Saul, Israel's first king, has continued to reign, although rejected by God. In contrast, David, the beautiful, charismatic young man anointed by the prophet Samuel as Saul's successor, has begun to achieve great military success in Saul's army. As in a fairy tale, Saul offers David the hand of his daughter Merab as a reward for fighting "the battles of the Lord" (1 Sam. 18:17), although his real goal is to see his rival slain in battle. In the midst of their tense vying for position, with David claiming to feel unworthy and Saul arbitrarily marrying Merab to another man, we suddenly hear with startling clarity that Saul's other daughter, Michal, "… had fallen in love with David" (1 Sam. 18:20). Saul resolves to use her as a snare for David by offering her in marriage for the bride-price of 100 Philistine foreskins, intending to bring about David's death. Instead, David is wildly successful in battle, counting out 200 Philistine foreskins, and Saul gives him his daughter Michal, "who loves him" (1 Sam. 18:28), in marriage.

Michal plays her most active role when, sometime later, in the episode referred to in our midrash, Saul makes a direct plan to assassinate David in his house. Michal, here identified as "David's wife" (1 Sam. 19:11), not only warns him, but saves his life, letting him down from the window (just as Rachav saves Joshua's spies in Jericho). She deceives the waiting assassins with a household idol (teraphim) that she puts under the bedcovers, topping it off with "a net of goat's hair" (1 Sam. 19:13). This reminds us of her foremothers, Rachel and Rebekah. Rachel deceived her father, Laban, with teraphim, and Rebekah used hairy goatskins to disguise Jacob.

In the first words we hear directly from her, Michal asserts that David is sick in bed. Then she defends herself against her father's accusation of disloyalty by claiming that David had threatened to kill her if she did not help him. This justification seems to work with her enraged, suspicious father. Meanwhile, she has enabled David to escape into the world of action and possibility.

During the long narrative of Saul's decline and ultimate defeat at the hands of the Philistines, and David's rise to military victory and kingship over all of Israel, we hear about Michal in two brief moments. Each time, the narrator presents her as the instrument of political power struggles. While David is roaming the country as leader of a growing band of irregulars, "Saul had given his daughter Michal, David's wife, to Palti son of Laish from Gallim" (1 Sam. 25:43). David clearly understands the message behind this strange treatment of his wife, because his first condition for making a treaty of reconciliation with Abner, Saul's defeated general, is that "… you bring Michal daughter of Saul when you come before me" (2 Sam. 3:13). When he achieves the return of "… my wife Michal, for whom I paid the bride-price of one hundred Philistine foreskins" (2 Sam. 3:14), we hear quite poignantly about the sorrow of the obscure husband, Palti son of Laish, but nothing of Michal's thoughts or feelings.

In our last view of Michal, she is standing apart from the joyous popular celebration as "David and all the House of Israel brought up the Ark of the Lord [to Jerusalem]" (2 Sam. 6:15). This is the culmination of David's military, political, and religious success. Michal, once more called "daughter of Saul," watches from a window again as David dances ecstatically. The text states, "she despised him in her heart" (2 Sam. 6:16). The story that began with a flash of insight into her heart (she "loved" David) now ends with an equally brief notice of what seems to be complete reversal of her feeling.

If Michal could speak and act at all, she could do so only within the confines of the inner chambers. At last she "came out "(2 Sam. 6:20) to denounce David for his revealing self-exposure as he dances with high and low. David's bitter retort turns the sexual innuendo of her speech into a taunt of her isolation and a gloat over her father's defeat. It represents the only direct exchange of words between them and her final silencing. The story ends bleakly with: "And to Michal the daughter of Saul there was no child to the day of her death" (2 Sam. 6:23).[1]

Commentary

Midrash ha-Gadol connects Michal's story to the verse in "Eishet Chayil" that most fully focuses not on the woman, but on her husband. It is the verse in which the *eishet chayil* is praised as the instrument of her husband's renown. This is a perceptive response to the way Michal emerges from the biblical text. Whenever she is mentioned, she is called either "daughter of Saul" or "wife of David." She has no substance as a character apart from her connection to the two rivals, in whose struggle for power she is a crucial weapon. In her moment of greatest activity, to which the midrash alludes, she moves from her position as daughter to triumphant wife. Ironically, that triumph entails abandonment by her husband and return to manipulation by her father. To the end of her life, she is pulled between two definitions of male connection. Reading both the story and the midrash in this way, we might see Michal as the embodiment of women's self-effacement by both biblical and Rabbinic text.

However, a more nuanced reading of the story of this "fragmented woman," in the phrase of scholar Cheryl Exum,[2] opens more possibilities for both strength and tragedy. Michal begins her textual life with vigor, individuality, and even independence. She is the only woman in the Bible who, we are told, "loves" a man. We are used to hearing about men's passionate attachments, such as Isaac for Rebekah and Jacob for Rachel. But among women characters, Michal alone is accorded such a movement of feeling and loyalty to a potential marriage partner. She loves the person who challenges her family's position in a conventional sense, but who represents the surprising, even subversive, choice of the God of Israel. Despite her father's efforts to use her and her feelings against David, she becomes the agent of David's liberation through her intellectual, psychological, and verbal prowess.

In the episode mentioned by our midrash, Michal transforms the limitations of women's restriction to inner domestic space into ingenious tools for David's salvation. The window high up in the wall that encloses her becomes a metaphorical birth canal through which she pushes her endangered young husband. She then exploits the stuff of women's world: blankets, fabrics, even the teraphim to buy the time necessary for his escape. The text implicitly compares her ingenuity, or trickery, to her foremother Rachel. Michal, as a member of the tribe of Benjamin through her father, is a direct descendant of Benjamin's mother, Rachel. Rachel also deceived her father, Laban, in connection with teraphim, while aligning herself with Jacob, her husband, to thwart Laban's potentially lethal anger. Michal enters the company of biblical heroines Rachav, Rachel, Rebekah, and Tamar,

who all use the weapons of the powerless in the service of life and cov-
enantal continuity for the people of Israel. What could be criticized as
trickery or deception appears frequently in the Bible as the only effec-
tive means for subordinated people to achieve goals essential to Jewish
history. Michal also displays the linguistic dexterity of the foremothers. To Saul's angry challenge (couched in a vocabulary that specifically recalls trickery in the Jacob and Rachel story), she responds with
an explanation that fits perfectly into his paranoid expectations of
David. She knows that he will not be surprised at her claim that David
threatened her. She uses that knowledge to protect herself. Moreover,
she relies on his assumptions about her passivity and availability as a
pawn to blind him to the daring reality of her activity.

Our midrash revises this tense scenario. It offers a more harmoni-
ous version of their exchange, in which Michal ingeniously manages to
present her loyalty to her father's "enemy" as a form of *kibud av* (honoring the father). In saving David, she has really saved her father from the
worst crime a true king can commit. She is cast in the same light as the
midrashic understanding of Rachel's deceptive act. That has been explained as a desire to separate her father from his idolatrous practices
(*Bereshit Rabbah* 74:5). Within the scope of the midrash, Michal shields
herself from a painful conflict of loyalties, protects her father's reputation, and launches her husband onto the path of renown. This is what
makes her a praiseworthy *eishet chayil*.

Yet Michal's story cannot be entirely recast in the mode of in-
sider activism. She eventually becomes the pawn and symbol of the
power struggle between David and Saul. We are left to wonder what
happened to the feelings and perspective on life of this daring young
woman. She ends up pushed from one marriage to another according
to the outcome of war and political maneuvering. She may have chosen to love David. But the brutal calculation with which David demands her return when he is consolidating his power over the House
of Saul could not be further removed from personal choice or inner
feeling. The window through which we see her at the end of her story

has now become not the ingenious tool of her independent strategy, but the sign of her separation from David and his triumph.

Her final speech in the biblical text conceals as much as it reveals. Is she angry that David cavalierly left her at the mercy of her increasingly insane father? Has her love turned to jealous rage as she is forced to live with the knowledge of the six other women David has now married for political benefit, each of whom has given birth to a son? After all the time that has passed, does she now think of herself as the sole remaining representative of a royal dignity that David ignores? Is stubborn resistance to the total adulation of David all that remains of her courageous individualism? If we understand her sarcastic denunciation as protest against any or all of these understandings of her fate, we might feel sympathy, even admiration, for her struggle against the constriction of her life. But this remains a futile protest. David triumphs over her in language as he does in action. She may once have dreamed of sharing in the wider realm of kingship as David's partner, but such goals, whether personal, national, or spiritual, have been obliterated. As feminist Bible scholar Ilana Pardes comments, "A female character who tries to fulfill her ambitious dreams, to protest against time's tyranny, runs her head against a wall."[3] The biblical text both silences Michal and undermines her significance when it reduces her identity to "daughter of Saul" and records an absence: "So to her dying day [she] had no children" (2 Sam. 6:23).

Michal Speaks

I have a completely different story to tell. Yes, I loved David. But not because I was the fairy-tale princess, languishing in the palace of my ogre father, the mad king. And not because I was waiting to be rescued by that oh, so handsome, so strong young soldier, the idol of all those singing women. No, I wanted to play my part in the national drama, the transformation of our people into a great kingdom, ruled by God's beloved. (Don't think I didn't know the meaning of David's name—"friend

of" or "loved one of God.") When I saved David, I became God's partner in creating our history. It was all very well for God to send Samuel
to anoint him. That didn't hide him from the knives of the assassins.
God needs humans to carry out divine designs.

I was brought up to know the destiny of royal daughters. My father
expected to use me as he had my sister Merab. But younger daughters
are sometimes indulged, even by stubborn patriarchs. So my father let
me satisfy my appetite for learning. He never bothered to think about
what I was learning. When my brother Jonathan's tutors taught him
Torah, I, too, studied Torah, along with statecraft. Just like Jonathan,
I understood for myself that God's choice had fallen on that unlikely
shepherd from Bethlehem. But anyone who thinks about the stories
of our ancestors knows that our God is the God of surprises. God can
raise up the poor from the dust to set them with the great men of His
people (Ps. 113). (Yes, I appreciated the love poetry David wrote for
God; I didn't need him to write poetry for me.) In a crisis, I could wrap
myself in the spiritual mantle of my mothers Rachel and Rebekah. Then
I could invent schemes to rescue that chosen "younger son," my husband, Israel's true king.

But I couldn't rescue myself. If only David could have seen in me
anything beyond Saul's daughter. He never understood how much
like Jonathan I could be for him—a friend and partner in his search to
do God's will.

How ironic that only much later a few Rabbis, searching our
texts for hints of the ways of God, saw fragments of whom I was. They
preserved the memory of my spiritual life. I may have been silent in
the palace, but I spoke with God. I bound myself with words of Torah,
praying in tefillin. The sages of our people respected this and even
recorded it in their Talmud (*Eruvim* 96a). The Rabbis who praised me
because I insured my husband's renown were shortsighted. Others
knew which verse really belongs to me: "She is clothed with strength
and splendor/ And she rejoices at the last day" (Prov. 31:25). "Clothed
with strength" because I wore tefillin, which are strength (*Berachot* 6a)

and signify my personal path to God. Guided by this verse, they saw the need to read my story differently. Where it says that I had no child to the day I died, they understood that I gave birth—and rejoiced—on the day I died, just like my mother Rachel (*Sanhedrin* 21a). If you look between the lines of David's glorious history and gather up the Rabbinic fragments, you can find my story of strength.

A Message from Michal

I hope my story helps you to see how careful you must be when reading women's stories in the Bible. Do you understand the risks I took, acting as I did while living in my father's palace? I drew strength from a tradition of women being as daring and inventive as could be, given the narrow confines in which we had to work. We have learned that it is possible to exercise power, to act effectively under severe constraints, even when our world considers us merely instruments of "more important" plans. But we have also learned the limitations of female power. While a life of service to important men can be a source of significance for a woman, it can also be the means of her self-effacement.

You must question the assumptions you make about what is valuable in women's lives. The biblical text may be ambiguous about whether or not I ever gave birth to a child, but it clearly equates childlessness and failure. Like me, you need not accept this. You can see in my life path the possibility of another kind of success. We can bring new life into the world not only as mothers, but also as spiritual teachers.

For Further Thought

What satisfactions or benefits does Michal receive from her love for David?

How do you explain Michal's outburst against David when she sees him dancing with the ark?

Nehama Aschkenasy's *Woman at the Window: Biblical Tales of Oppression and Escape* (Detroit: Wayne State University Press, 1998) is an original, well-written book that uses the biblical image of the woman standing in the window looking out at the wider world as a focus for discussion. This image appears prominently in the Michal story, which the author analyzes using metaphors of inner and outer space.

A Feminist Companion to Samuel and Kings, edited by Athalya Brenner (Sheffield, UK: Sheffield Academic Press, 1994), is a collection of essays by American, Israeli, and European scholars, all written from feminist perspectives, on the books of Samuel and Kings. It is part of a series called *The Feminist Companion to the Bible*.

Tikva Frymer-Kensky's *Reading the Women of the Bible: A New Interpretation of Their Stories* (New York: Schocken Books, 2002) includes original interpretations of many women characters divided into the categories of victors, victims, virgins, and voices. It also provides reflections on the general treatment of gender differences in the Hebrew Bible.

Chapter 16
Hatzlelponi

NURIT EINI-PINDYCK

סָדִין עָשְׂתָה וַתִּמְכֹּר וַחֲגוֹר נָתְנָה לַכְּנַעֲנִי:

"She makes cloth and sells it, and offers a girdle to the merchant"
(Prov. 31:24).

סדין עשתה ותמכר, זו הצללפונית והיא אמו שלשמשון, דכתיב בני פרץ
בן יהודה ואלה בני עיטם יזרעאל וישמא וידבש ושם אחותם הצללפוני.
משוכני צרעה ואשתאול. וכתיב התם אלה משפחות הצרעתי, שנגלה עליה
המלאך שני פעמים שלא בפני בעלה וכך אמרה לבעלה לו חפץ ה'
להמיתנו. וחגור נתנה לכנעני, שהיתה טווה ומוכרת בשוק כמה דאת אמר
כנעניה נכבדי ארץ.

She makes cloth and sells it, this is Hatzlelponi,[1] mother of Samson.
It is chronicled that among the descendants of Perez, who is the
son of Judah, are the sons of Etam: Jezreel, Ishma, and Idbash, and
the name of their sister is Hatzlelponi (1 Chron. 4:3). They reside in Zorah and Eshtaol, and it is written, "These were the
families of the Zorathites" (1 Chron. 4:2). The angel [of God]
revealed itself to her twice and not in front of her husband. And
thus she had reasoned with her husband: "Had the Lord meant
to take our lives ..." (Judg. 13:23). "And offers a girdle to the
merchant" (Prov. 31:24). She was weaving and selling in the market to reputable merchants. As it is said, "... whose [Canaanite]
traders the world honored" (Isa. 23:8).
—*Midrash ha-Gadol*

God summons a certain woman to help stir the people of Israel
out of their submissive attitude toward their foreign ruler. The
story contrasts the woman's perceptive qualities with the feeble character of her Danite husband, Manoah, meaning "rest," and presumably of all other men of that time.

The Philistines are oppressing the Israeli tribes of Dan and Judah, whose people are trying to stay at rest and avoid confrontation with the bullying Philistines. Determined to help the passive people of Israel in spite of themselves, God conceives a plan of deliverance, starting with a divine revelation to a woman who has not yet conceived a child. This woman, graciously summoned to create an Israeli national hero, is identified from the period of Judges as the wife of Manoah and the mother of Samson. God's deliberate choice to collaborate with her testifies to her virtue. Her wisdom unfolds through the various tales of God's plan on three different occasions.

God, addressing the childless woman, initiates the first part of the plan. The angel of God appears, announces the arrival of a son, and invites her to participate in the initiation of her son, who will be a nazirite[2] "from the womb on" (Judg. 13:5). In addition to obeying the nazirite dietary rules during her pregnancy, she is expected not to let a razor touch the boy's head. Faithfully, she internalizes God's goal as a guideline to raising her son. "He shall be the first to deliver Israel from the Philistines" (13:5).

She doesn't question God about the incomplete nature of her son's mission. Samson is to raise the people's consciousness of retaliation, but not to lead them to liberation. She is aware that Manoah will be reluctant to endorse any challenge against the Philistines, and she crafts a second tale of God's plan while reporting to Manoah about her encounter with the angel of God. She conceals from her husband both the prohibition against cutting the hair and the boy's destiny to participate in the process of delivering the Israelite people from their enemy. Her wish to protect her son and her commitment to God's plan are translated into a plan to protect the son from his father.

The third tale of God's plan occurs in response to Manoah's petition to God. Manoah wants to be included in an additional revelation of the angel of God to "… instruct us as how to act with the child that is to be born" (13:8). In an embarrassing gesture to Manoah, the angel of God reappears to the woman while she is sitting in the field alone. Only after his wife hurries to summon him does Manoah encounter the angel. It reveals to Manoah less than what he had already learned from his wife's partial account.

Manoah's interest lies in revealing the identity of the angel rather than in learning about God's plan. He stubbornly pursues his lame efforts to decipher the identity of the stranger, while persistently doubting the divine identity. The angel explains its name is Pel'I, which can mean "wondrous" or "unknowable." Then, both Manoah and his wife see the angel of God being elevated in fire. Manoah's immediate response is not remorse for his doubt, but fear for his life: "We shall surely die, for we have seen a divine being" (13:22). The woman's response in this moment of angst is logical and demonstrates her integrity and self-assurance. "But his wife said to him, 'Had the Lord meant to take our lives, He would not have accepted a burnt offering and meal offering from us, nor let us see all these things; and He would not have made such an announcement to us,'" (13:23). Thus the woman's response justifies God's initial trust in her. Unlike her husband, she is a person capable of recognizing God and understanding God's call. She is identified by the Rabbis as Hatzlelponi, whose name is mentioned in the Bible once in 1 Chronicles (4:3) as a descendant of Tamar and Judah.[3]

Commentary

Hatzlelponi is an *eishet chayil* who surpasses her husband in the biblical story and in Rabbinic literature. The poem in Proverbs praises her not as a submissive companion to her husband, but rather as a competent person who functions in the public space as an equal among honorable men. Her integrity stays intact when "she was sitting in the field [alone]" (Judg. 13:9), and "selling in the market [to reputable merchants and traders]" (*Midrash ha-Gadol*).

"She makes cloth and sells it, and offers a girdle [belt] to the Canaanite merchant" (Prov. 31:24). She produces high-quality cloth, makes profit selling products in the market, and trades cleverly with the Canaanites, who are the ones "the world honored" (Isa. 23:8).

Midrash ha-Gadol embraces this praise for the "mother of Samson," in contrast to her husband, whose name is not mentioned in our midrash due to his degrading passivity (marked in his name *Manoah*, meaning "rest"). By not mentioning the man by name (but rather as *her husband*), *Midrash ha-Gadol* recognizes the value in naming women heroines, and it grants a name (Hatzlelponi) to the unnamed woman in the biblical story.

A close reading of our midrash reveals the meaning of her true heroism, which lies in her ability to recognize God's mission as her own. When our midrash mentions that "the angel [of God] revealed itself to her twice and not in front of her husband," it brings to center stage the status of Hatzlelponi as the "chosen" woman. This verbal woman ("in the market") internalizes God's words in a profound understanding, which necessitates no explanation.

In both the biblical story and in Proverbs as the "chosen" woman, Hatzlelponi had a unique response to God's call. With another revelation in mind, we see that she exemplifies the Israelites' devout way of accepting the Ten Commandments while standing at Sinai. It was said that the Israelites responded with "we will faithfully do!" [*na'aseh ve-nishma*, literally, "we shall do and we shall hear"] (Exod. 24:7). The Hebrew text suggests that they committed themselves to "doing" prior to "hearing," in an act of ultimate submission to God. Although God explains to Hatzlelponi the divine plan, we trust that she would have accepted it even without hearing the details. Thus, the story about Samson's birth is a story about a woman who embodies the spirit of the Israelites at Sinai, in contrast to her doubting husband, who negotiates with the angel of God as though they were haggling in the marketplace. The wisdom of such a woman is confirmed by the way she pacifies a weak man. "But his wife said to him, 'Had the Lord meant to take our lives, He would not have accepted a burnt offering and meal offering from us, nor let us see all these things; and He would not have made such an announcement to us'" (Judg. 13:23).

The special connection between God and Hatzlelponi is marked by the deliberate inclusion of the Hebrew letter *heh* in the beginning of the name Hatzlelponi. *Heh* is a letter from God's name, and it was inserted in the names of Avram (Avraham) and Sarai (Sarah) as a spiritual marker to the everlasting covenant established with God.[4]

The biblical tradition embeds intricate messages in names through wordplay. The story of Samson's birth is fully encoded in the name Hatzlelponi. In her name, *tzelel* is the Hebrew word that stands for a response to the sound of God's voice (I Sam. 3:11, Jer. 19:3). The letter *l* in Hatzlelponi is repeated twice. *Poni* in Hatzlelponi is a variant of *panim*, the Hebrew word for "face." *Hatzpen* in Hatzlelponi means "encode, hide." *Peli* in Hatzlelponi means "wonder." *Hatzel* in Hatzlelponi stands for "save." *Tzion* in Hatzlelponi stands for Zion (Israel). As we have seen, the insertion of *h* in Hatzlelponi stands for carrying out God's plan. Therefore the name *Hatzlelponi*, in and of itself, tells the wondrous story of a woman who hears the sound of God's voice via an angel appearing before her face twice. As the angel's name, Pel'I, can be translated as "wondrous" or "unknowable," we understand that this woman will be educating her son to follow God's secret message to save the Israelites. This woman of strength embodies the concept of "the chosen." As women, we sometimes wonder, How can we apply the awareness that we are chosen in a nonjudgmental and respectful way toward people's differences? How can Jews today embrace a divine plan to restore national self-definition in the Promised Land without losing our empathy, ethical values, and human integrity? By the simple use of "cloth" and "belt" in "She makes cloth ... offers a girdle [belt] to the Canaanite merchant" (Prov. 31:24), Hatzlelponi's verse in the poem acknowledges such potential conflicts.

The same sort of items are mentioned in Isaiah to describe other women—the daughters of Zion who walk haughtily in offending and disrespectful ways. The prophecy says that these women will be punished by God for their vanity: "In that day, my Lord will strip off the finery of the anklets ... the turbans, the armlets, and the sashes; ... of the festive robes, the mantles, and the shawls [the cloth] ... And then—instead of perfume, there shall be rot, [and instead of a belt shall be rope]; ... a burn instead of beauty" (Isa. 3:18–24).

In contrast to these disrespectful women, Hatzlelponi commits herself to be "chosen" as a person of integrity and dignity.

Hatzlelponi Speaks

This house on the path to the fields, the one bordering the vegetable garden, is where we women weave. We work as we tell our stories, sometimes with laughter, sometimes with tears. We have finished shearing the wool and preparing the flax. We have already made the cloth we need for our large family for the coming season, and we have still plenty to sell in the market. Resilience is not a new word for us. I trust it is not a new word for you either. So please sit down in my Danite home, refresh yourself with water, and let me introduce myself to you.

My name is Hatzlelponi, and I am a descendent of Perez, son of Tamar and Judah. I assume that my name is novel to you. My paternal grandmother, my *savta*, coined my name from Joseph's additional name: Tzaphenath-paneah (Gen. 41:45). "Your name comes from *hatzpini*, meaning 'conceal' and 'encode,'" she would say. "Hatzlelponi, your name and Joseph's name are like fruits growing from the same tree. Joseph was called Tzaphenath-paneah, meaning 'the one who is skilled in decoding visions encoded in dreams.' Joseph had the gift of deciphering dreams. Your gift, little blessed one, will be equally marvelous."

My *savta* delighted in talking about Joseph. It was an excuse to bring up her favorite man of strength, Judah. "Remember, Hatzlelponi, Judah was the one who saved Joseph. He was the one who said to his brothers: 'Come, let us sell him to the Ishmaelites, but let us not do away with him ourselves. After all, he is our brother, our own flesh' (Gen. 37:27). As a virtuous man, he could never have killed his own brother."

Then she would wait for me to complete the story. I would say, "His brothers agreed. When Midianite traders passed by, they pulled Joseph up out of the pit. They sold Joseph for twenty pieces of silver to the Ishmaelites, who brought Joseph to Egypt" (Gen. 37:27,28). I was then rewarded with my *savta's* praise.

"Hatzlelponi, dear child, you remind me of the wise Tamar. Blessed is the name of the One, and you will grow up to know as much as Tamar did about the laws of the One." Mother's discontent with my conversations with Savta used to puzzle me. Mother would mutter to herself: "This Judah was glad to sell his brother to foreigners." And she would loudly announce: "A Danite man would not have been humiliated by a woman the way this Judah was." The other women joined her in nodding and sometimes in giggling. Mother's clan is linked to Dan, while Father's clan is linked to Judah. You might say that through the story about the wise Tamar, I was exposed to the unfortunate rivalry between these two tribes.

Have you heard Tamar's story? Let me refresh your memory. I tell it as a tribute not only to my beloved storyteller, Savta, and the virtuous Tamar, but to all the women who would have liked their stories to be heard.

Judah marries a foreign woman, who bears three sons. The first son who marries Tamar is evil. He is struck dead by the One before producing a son. Although Judah's second son marries Tamar as our law dictates, in order to produce a son on behalf of his deceased brother, he conspicuously chooses not to impregnate her. He is also struck dead by the One. Judah is distraught at the fate of his two elder sons. Therefore, when his third son becomes a man, he ignores the law and neglects to give his widowed daughter-in-law to his third son.

Tamar, who is living now at her parents' home, is determined to design a plan to activate the law. She inquires about Judah's whereabouts and waits for him on his way to the city of Timnah to do business. While disguised as a harlot, she succeeds in tempting him to have sexual intercourse with her. In return for her "service," Judah promises a kid goat. Tamar insists on getting his seal and cord and his staff as pledges. As you know, these items confirm a person's identity and authority. And, as you can guess, "the harlot" vanished and Judah couldn't retrieve his pledges. Later, when Judah learns that his widowed daughter-in-law is pregnant, he demands that she be burned to avenge the family's honor. In front of all, Tamar displays his personal items, and Judah proclaims that she surpassed him with her devotion to continue the family's name as commanded by the One. He says: "*Tzadka mimeni*" (Gen. 38:26), which means "She is more in the right than I ... ," and that means, "I admit that I am the father."

My passionate *savta* glorified Judah for his words on behalf of a woman and instructed me that he was a strong man for acknowledging a woman's superior judgment.

Are you puzzled as to why I am telling you the story about the woman Tamar in such detail? I have realized over time that there is no one story. My son, Samson, listened to it and it has become part of his story. In his own way Samson has kept Tamar's story alive.

I was telling him a story about a family man.	*He heard a story about a man who married a foreign woman.*
I was telling him a story about a man who could admit making a mistake.	*He heard a story about a man who was shamefully overpowered by a woman.*
I was telling him a story about a man who went to Timnah to do his work.	*He heard a story about a man looking for harlots on his way to Timnah, searching for women rather than work.*
I was telling him a story about a man who wanted to pay with a kid goat as a sign of generosity.	*He heard a story about men giving goat kids in exchange for women.*

| I was telling him a story about a woman who used all means in order to obey God's law. | *He heard a story about the value of trickery, how women desire to deceive men and use sex in order to strip men of their honor and identity.* |

As you can see, Samson's story is different from mine. He went on living his life accordingly and he had his own relationship with the God of my heroine, Tamar. When I first saw the angel of Tamar's God, I knew that my time had come to live up to my name Hatzlelponi. I activated the power in my dear *savta*'s gift to me. How could I not have recognized the angel? Since childhood, I have been participating in the story of all the stories, spoken and unspoken. Women's stories have transformed my life. And my story remains a good story even though my son had to die.

Nobody could have guessed that my son's hair was a divine weapon against the enemy. It had to stay secret in order to protect his life. Who could have imagined that hair could be a gift of power to a man? I concealed it even from Manoah. Tamar's God and I trusted each other, but no one else.

Soon you will meet the rest of the women who reside here, including my unmarried daughters and nieces, my unmarried granddaughters, and my daughters-in-law. You are welcome to join us if you wish. You will find us trying to be compassionate when we have difficulty understanding. We are aware of our power to exclude and to hurt. Healing comes slowly when we talk. We keep talking. We want our stories to live and to carry our names.

A Message from Hatzlelponi

I would like to share with you what I learned from my son: to be open to the world. Not to run away from what is strange and unusual, but to get to know it. He tried to know the foreigners, to live amongst them, and even to adopt their ways. The world was not ready for his vision. I wish I could have been.

I wish I had gotten to know the woman Samson loved, Delilah. From what I know about her, we would have made a powerful team in the marketplace.

Yes, I want to befriend the woman who betrayed my son. Like me, she never understood Samson's love, just as she never understood his desire to change the world by reaching out to foreigners. Like me, she probably didn't believe in the possibility of love across cultures and nations. She chose to prove her loyalty to her people, the Philistines, by delivering my son's secret to them. Yet don't judge her behavior hastily. If you were a Philistine, you would have sung her praise. Remember, Delilah helped destroy the enemy of her people.

I hope you can understand my feelings and that you won't judge me harshly. I say this to you and I say this to the Divine One in the Holy Land.

For Further Thought

Compare Hatzlelponi to other "chosen" women on this list of women of valor: Rebekah, "chosen" by Abraham's servant Eliezer to become Isaac's wife; Yocheved, "chosen" to be the mother of Moses; Serach bat Asher, "chosen" to become immortal, and Esther, "chosen" to save the Jewish people and to become wife of Ahasuerus. How does one apply the consciousness of being "chosen" to a nonjudgmental and respectful attitude toward differences?

Using Hatzlelponi as an example, when in your life has it been important to serve as a leader rather than a follower?

In your family, are there important stories that have passed down through the generations? What new story might you add to the family legacy for your own children, grandchildren, nieces, or nephews?

In Susan Ackerman's *Warrior, Dancer, Seductress, Queen: Women in Judges and Biblical Israel* (New York: Doubleday, 1998), pages 109–117, Hatzlelponi is called by her biblical non-name: Manoah's wife. Ackerman compares Manoah's wife to other women in Judges. She brings Jephthah's daughter and Micah's mother as examples of the search for alternative forms of religious expression as the cult of the God of the Hebrews became more male centered.

Danna Nolan Fewell, in her "Judges" in *Women's Bible Commentary*, edited by Carol A. Newsom and Sharon H. Ringe (Louisville, KY: Westminster John Knox Press, 1998), pages 78–80, calls our attention to women of action such as Samson's mother (Manoah's wife) and Samson's beloved Delilah, who take care of themselves and their own people.

Yaacov Fichman's epic poem "Tzlelponit," in *Women of the Bible: Legends, Poems, Stories, Essays and Concordance* (in Hebrew), edited by Israel Zmora (Davar Press, 1964), pages 366–374, is comprised of three scenes and includes roles for Tzlelponit (his way of naming Hatzlelponi), Manoah, five men from Zorah, and Samson and his Israeli fictional lover, Yael.

Anda Pinkerfeld-Amir wrote a poem called "Like Every Woman," which is included in the collection *Hebrew Feminist Poems from Antiquity to the Present*, edited by Shirley Kaufman, Galit Hasan-Rokem, and Tamar S. Hess (New York: The Feminist Press, 1999), pages 110–111. Consider Hatzlelponi in the light of this poem about a woman who seems like all others but is not. This poem could have been written by Hatzlelponi.

Chapter 17
Elisheba

PENINA ADELMAN

עֹז־וְהָדָר לְבוּשָׁהּ וַתִּשְׂחַק לְיוֹם אַחֲרוֹן:

"She is clothed with strength and splendor; she laughs at the final day" (Prov. 31:25).[1]

עוז והדר לבושה, זו אלישבע שראת ארבע שמחות ביום אחד. יבמה מלך,
אישה כהן גדול, אחיה נשיא, בניה סגני כהונה.

She is clothed with strength and splendor,[2] this is Elisheba, who saw four happy occasions in one day: she became the sister-in-law of a king, the wife of the High Priest, and the sister of a prince, and her sons became deputies of the priesthood.

—*Midrash ha-Gadol*

Aaron took to wife Elisheba, daughter of Amminadab and sister of Nahshon, and she bore him Nadab, and Abihu, Eleazar, and Ithamar" (Exod. 6:23). This is all we hear of Elisheba in the entire Hebrew Bible!

She has an illustrious lineage. Her father is Amminadab, a prince of the tribe of Judah. Her brother, Nahshon, is the first of the Children of Israel who dared jump into the Sea of Reeds. Because of Nahshon's faith, God made the sea part, so that the Israelites could cross safely.

Elisheba does indeed experience at least four joyous occasions, as the midrash points out. She becomes the sister-in-law of Moses when she marries Aaron. She becomes the wife of Aaron, the High Priest. Her son Eleazar becomes a "prince," that is, the head chieftain of the Levites. Her brother, Nahshon, becomes the chief of the tribe of Judah after the revelation at Mount Sinai.

Commentary

In *Midrash ha-Gadol,* many of the women are mentioned in relation to a man or men in their lives. Sarah is an *eishet chayil* because "Her husband puts his confidence in her" (Prov. 31:11). Rebekah is an *eishet chayil* because "She is good to [her husband], never bad, All the days of her life" (31:12). Michal is an *eishet chayil* because "Her husband is prominent in the gates, as he sits among the elders of the land" (31:23).

Each of Elisheba's joyous times celebrates the achievements of the men in her life: her brother-in-law, Moses; her husband, Aaron; her brother, Nahshon; and her sons Eleazar and Ithamar. Is this what the verse "She is clothed with strength and splendor" (Prov. 31:25) means? Are her male relatives her garments and her adornments? Is she basking in their reflected glory the way the moon basks in the light of the sun? Or does she have light of her own?

Perhaps the latter part of Elisheba's assigned verse gives a clue: (literally) "she laughs at the final day" (31:25). At the end of her time on earth, there she will be, having experienced all the fullness and happiness life can bring, as well as the pain and grief, and she will be laughing at it all. For in the end, life is much more than the sum of all the ups and downs one has experienced. Nothing lasts forever; therefore, one might as well enjoy the blissful occasions today, for who knows what tomorrow might bring?

In fact, Elisheba did experience at least one horribly painful event in her lifetime—the sudden death of her two sons Nadab and Abihu. It took place the day after the priests of the Jewish people were consecrated for the first time. Elisheba's husband, Aaron, was offering up sacrifices as directed by Moses. Suddenly, without being commanded to do so, two sons of Aaron and Elisheba offered up their own incense mixture. Immediately, they were devoured by fire from the altar and perished (Lev. 10:1,2). The holy rites of sacrifice as set down by God were not to be trifled with. If the Children of Israel were to remain a cohesive group, they must abide by the rules. This was the lesson of Nadab and Abihu.

Now consider the last half of Elisheba's verse, "She laughs at the final day." She knows that happiness can turn to tragedy in a split second the way it did that day on the altar. Elisheba laughs at life's absurdity and even at her own attempts to understand it.

The phrase "the final day" reverberates with the "four happy occasions in one day" of the first part of the verse. These four occasions did not, of course, happen in one 24-hour day; rather, the "day" in question symbolizes a lifetime. The talmudic tractate *Pirkei Avot* 2:20 supports this interpretation with the following, "Rabbi Tarfon said, 'The day is short, and the work is great, and the laborers are sluggish, and the reward is much, and the Master is urgent.'" Here the "day" in question is also a lifetime.

Elisheba Speaks

You'd probably like to know how I could laugh at my life—at the life we all share for our brief time on this earth. I'm glad you want to know. I used to envy *Sarah Imeinu* (Sarah, Our Mother) for being able to laugh at God, no less. And then there's Serach bat Asher, who lives alongside all of us and knows all too well that there is "A time for weeping and a time for laughing" (Eccles. 3:4). But if you really want to know how I learned to laugh, it was the years working as a midwife with my mother-in-law, Yocheved, and my sister-in-law, Miriam.[3]

You work hard, sometimes all through the night, to urge the baby out of its mother. You feel the baby's struggle to leave the perfect round world, the only one it has known. Why leave the warmth, the food, and the floating sleep? Why go head first into another place it doesn't know at all? Why not stay put?

The mother is sometimes not so sure what this new little life will bring. Will it be happy and relaxed, or tense and uncomfortable?

Eventually the force of God, much greater than that of baby or mother, pushes the child out of the womb to be born! How many times we rejoiced with a mother and then helped find a safe place for her child among sympathetic Egyptians. How many times we wept with a mother when, after a few moments, her baby was dead! Who can explain it? Who can make sense of it?

Yocheved, having emigrated from Canaan here to Egypt, had seen much more death and destruction than I. She taught me that we can help God birth these babies, but we can never know who will live and who will die. It is not for us to know. It is only for us to keep going and have great faith no matter what. We shall never know what it is all for in the end.

Nadab and Abihu were my fussiest ones. I couldn't calm them when they were babies; I couldn't placate them as adults. They would always demand to know why this one received more food than that one; why Aaron and I seemed to favor this one over that one; why they had to look after their other brothers at all. They were never content.

Nadab was always scheming against Abihu to show him up, to get there first. I didn't like the way each of them was turning out. I told Aaron, "No good will come from them."

But he—always seeing the potential for good in all people—said to me, "I am training them for the priesthood. They will learn to fulfill the obligations of the One who is greater than all."

I had my doubts. I had learned from all those years of midwifery, from hundreds and hundreds of babies we helped into this world, that a child's destiny is stamped in their eyes with eternal light, dropped into their mouths like a spoonful of honey, breathed into their nostrils with holy breath, given into their hands with honor, planted under their feet into the sacred ground.

When my two oldest sons, Nadab and Abihu, strode up to the altar in what they may have thought was an imitation of their father, the High Priest, what was in their minds? How long had they been planning their subterfuge? What did they think would happen? Was it *their* glory, or God's glory, they were honoring?

When I saw them struck down, my spirit briefly left me and went to be with them. My boys had come from my womb and now they were returning to the earth's womb. At that moment, I could not weep and I could not laugh.

A Message from Elisheba

Sometimes, when I am trying to figure something out, I write. Here is a poem I composed about a year after my sons died.

Always changing, changing always;
nothing stays the same.
Prepare for the sharp turn,
the deep drop,
the meteoric rise.
A child breathes, stops breathing;
breathes, stops breathing.
The sacred offering is acceptable;
the sacred offering is unacceptable.

I know what God wants from me,
I don't know
I know what I want from myself,
I don't know.
I laugh, question
I weep, question
laugh, weep
laugh, weep
laugh.

For Further Thought

How do you think Aaron made sense of the killing of his sons? Imagine a discussion between Aaron and Elisheba after this tragedy.

Could there have been other work or activities besides being a midwife that would have suited Elisheba? What might they be?

Very little has been written about Elisheba. Ellen Frankel, author of *The Five Books of Miriam* (New York: G.P. Putnam's Sons, 1996), pages 159–161, responds to this void by letting Elisheba speak in her own voice.

Jill Hammer has responded to the lack of material on Elisheba with a midrash of her own, which also portrays Elisheba in her midwife guise. It is called "The Tenth Plague" and can be found in the midrash collection *Sisters at Sinai: New Tales of Biblical Women* (Philadelphia: The Jewish Publication Society, 2004), pages 105–113.

Chapter 18
Serach

ROSIE ROSENZWEIG

פִּיהָ פָּתְחָה בְחָכְמָה וְתוֹרַת־חֶסֶד עַל־לְשׁוֹנָהּ:

"Her mouth is full of wisdom, her tongue with kindly teaching"
(Prov. 31:26).

פיה פתחה בחכמה, זו שרח בת אשר שאמרה ליואב אנכי שלומי אמוני
ישראל, שהיא שקולה כנגד עיר ואם בישראל.

Her mouth is full of wisdom, this is Serach,[1] daughter of Asher who
declared to Joab: "I am one of those who seek the welfare of the
faithful in Israel. But you seek to bring death upon a mother city in
Israel! Why should you destroy the Lord's possession?" (2 Sam.
20:19). Her worth was as much as a city and mother in Israel.
—*Midrash ha-Gadol*

Serach, daughter of Asher, is mentioned briefly by name three
times in the Torah, but she has inspired numerous commentaries
on her role in history. Her grandfather Jacob's heart has just been re-
leased from numbness and disbelief at discovering that his favorite
son, Joseph, is not only alive in Egypt; he is a powerful member of the
ruling class. Resolving to see his son before his death, he sets out for
Egypt and takes along his entire extended family. They are all listed,
including Serach (Gen. 46:17).

Several hundred years later, when the Israelites staying in Shittim
are plagued from within by immorality and from without by enemies, Serach is still alive. Once again a census is taken after the
plague that causes 24,000 deaths before they are to enter the land
of Canaan. She is the only woman mentioned in that census of
Israelites (Num. 26:46).

More than 1,000 years in a later, more extensive census (1 Chron. 7:30), she is listed again as the sister to Asher's four sons.

Commentary

Why is Serach the only woman mentioned in this lineage? Surely there must have been more granddaughters? Although she is listed in the Torah as Asher's daughter, she is not even a blood relative to Jacob. Asher had married her mother, a widow, when Serach was young, in approximately 1543 B.C.E. Malchiel was her birth father. Still, she is consistently listed in the Torah as daughter of Asher, and by inference, Jacob's granddaughter.

Serach was three years old when her mother, Hadurah, married Asher, and Serach became his stepdaughter. Apparently, early on, she won the affection of her step grandfather Jacob and was brought up in his household (*Midrash Avot*). Maimonides deduces that she was always called Serach bat Asher because her stepfather, not her birth father, raised her. Subsequently Serach's mother inherited her first husband's estate, so that Serach received her share of land.[2]

Why did Serach merit such a long life? Rashi writes that she is counted in later population tallies because she is still alive! But to have merited such a long life made the Rabbis curious. A midrash relates that she was chosen as a young, talented maiden by Joseph's brothers to break the news to Jacob that his beloved son Joseph was still alive. She skillfully slipped the words into a gentle song numerous times:

> And Jacob blessed Serach when she spoke these words before him, saying, "My daughter, may death never rule over you, for you have revived my spirit. Only speak to me again like you have spoken to me, for you have made me happy with your words." And she continued to sing these words ["Joseph, my uncle, is alive, and he rules the whole land of Egypt and is not dead."] and Jacob heard and it pleased him and made him happy, and the spirit of God was upon him.[3]

The Angel of Death had no dominion over her and she was one of the few who entered Paradise alive, because "she told Jacob that Joseph is still alive. Jacob said: 'This mouth that informed me that Joseph is still alive will never taste of death.'"[4]

Another midrash states that Serach bat Asher was trusted with the secrets and prized knowledge of the Children of Israel as a result of her wisdom and longevity. She confirmed Moses was the true redeemer of the Israelites because of a code he knew.[5] She also knew exactly where the bones of Joseph had been buried so that the Hebrews could bring them back to the Holy Land, as he had requested.[6]

With all these deeds to choose from, she is cited in *Midrash ha-Gadol* for her part in saving a city. Serach bat Asher is the *isha khochma* (woman of wisdom) who was still alive during the rule of King David hundreds of years after the Exodus. In 2 Samuel 20, we learn that Abel, a city loyal to King David, was under siege because the rebellious Sheba ben Bichri had taken refuge there from King David. David's general Joab, ignorant of the populace's fidelity to David, surrounds the city because of this rebel. According to Rashi, Serach is the *isha khochma* who challenges the general for not knowing the Torah's rules for besieging a city. She negotiates with the people to behead the traitor to save their lives. *Midrash ha-Gadol* gives her due credit for her actions, stating: "Her worth was as much as a city and mother in Israel."

I imagine her at 18, taking the harp and telling Jacob that his son has conquered time and terror and the reversal of fortune. Joseph is still alive, *Od Yosef chai!*

In Serach is everlasting life because she is rooted in wisdom whose heart is compassion. Compassion never dies. It reproduces itself exponentially.

Serach Speaks

Now as I stand at the edge of the Sea of Reeds where my knowledge has brought us, I remember not being so wise when I was younger.

Moses had us set up our camp here, and his incantations have kept the darkness and the Egyptian camp far away. These are the times when I look back on my life because I can't sleep. I remember that when they came and told me what to do and what to say, I had to do it. What did I know as a girl of 18, or was I 20? Who remembers these numbers now? You can't put a real number on time from the world above because it has no meaning. Time was invented for mortal convenience. Knowing the beginning and end of things makes men less anxious. The *Ein Sof*[7] knows … but I digress, as we old ones often do.

Back to the story I want you to know. Then I was beautiful, young, and womanly without any skill in confrontation. After all, you don't argue with the tribal chieftains. But when my uncles told me what to say to my beloved *saba* (grandfather), Jacob, I almost blurted out: "But he's always been alive!" I whispered it to myself anyway, watching shame and embarrassment cover their faces. That happened whenever Joseph's name came up, and I began to suspect why (as if I hadn't suspected before). After all, when I came into their tents I was only three. Even then, playing at their feet, I heard them whispering, raw and ready to blurt out their intrigue.

They ignored me then as a mere baby girl, the way they ignore me now as a budding woman. All they know is that I made their father smile, and being a girl child, I was no threat to them like their younger brother Joseph. When Saba first saw me, I could tell he loved me like a doting father, with no conditions. The whole household of Jacob could never mistreat me because of this first greeting.

Oh, how I missed my father Malchiel. One minute he's playing with me, the next minute he's gone. And Asher tried, he really did try, but his beard was so rough; and he felt so little in his own eyes around his older brothers. They were from Jacob's wives—well, most of them were; but he was from a handmaiden. What could he do but go along with them? Asher was the one who tried to make peace among his stubborn brothers, but even he could not hold his tongue; they were angry with him for telling them that Reuben slept with his stepmother,

Bilhah. They didn't believe him until Reuben confessed and repented. I remember my poor mother weeping when Asher finally told her about his family's troubles. I remember, when Asher tried to cheer her up, he made her smile, so I smiled.

He did try to be a good stepfather, but he was clumsy with a little girl then, because he imitated the bluff and bluster of his brothers. Especially when he tried to feed me olives, which I had never seen before. My grandfather understood this; his beard was white and soft and when he took me in his arms, he let me play with his beard. I was fascinated by it, and soon I was napping on a bed of hair. It was like heaven; actually it is like heaven, now that I know. Every time something upset me, I would go to him and cry in his beard, and he would wipe my tears with it.

At the time my uncles sent me to him, I was going anyway. I was always trying to cheer him up, every since Uncle Joseph went away. My heart broke for his sad face. His brother, my cousin Benjamin, was the same, but he was easier to cheer up. A little song and he was happy again. I learned how powerful songs could be. My *saba* taught me. He even guided me in breaking the news to him about Joseph. I used the harp my uncles gave me, but Saba asked me to repeat the words again and again, singing to him: "Joseph is alive and he rules in Egypt." This brought him so much pleasure. He breathed in each word, and his face got brighter and brighter. The words revived him and allowed him to feel God's *Shekhinah* again. This is how I learned from him to calm a troubled heart with song.

My *saba* taught me so much. Like how to open my heart with silent compassion. He was my first and best teacher. Maybe he knew, too, but he wouldn't tell his sons, except on his deathbed. He even had a private farewell with me, and repeated the blessing of eternal life to me again.

From the mothers, including my own, I learned to be silent at the right time. My mother was silent when Asher was frustrated with his own brothers. She was silent like all the other mothers when their husbands cried out in their sleep, but we all knew that they mumbled about Joseph in their guilty dreams. His mother, Rachel, told me that she sent them those dreams.

Slavery taught me more about silence and more than Saba ever could about compassion.

You want to know why I was counted in each census? Without me, Jacob would still be depressed. Without me, there would have been no Exodus, no journey to the Promised Land. Those uncles—they all thought that wisdom comes from ideas, and lessons, and parchment scrolls—they were so bound by their rules. Compassion leads to wisdom that resides in the heart of silence. If I had dared cry out when I saw my children and my friends buckling under the whip of a Pharaoh, who had forgotten Joseph, do you know what would have happened? Enslavement comes slowly, in baby steps: First they take away one freedom, then another, and another. Before you even realize it, everything is oppression and forced labor. To cry out would mean torture, not death for me, but pain. So I learned to listen and watch and learn from those who knew.

My father, Asher, whom I learned to love, taught me the signs of the redeemer, the one who would deliver us from this living death. He learned the signs from Jacob who learned them from Joseph. My silent knowledge drew many pretenders. I even thought Moses could have been one: After all, magic tricks are easily learned. But I knew, when they told me what he said, that Moses was the redeemer.

After the plagues and the Pharaoh's permission to leave and take booty, Moses wandered about searching for Joseph's casket. Joseph had made our people promise not to leave him in Egypt, but to take him to the Promised Land. I waited until Moses came to me. Maybe that's wisdom, but maybe that's because it's so tiring, when one gets older, to pursue a person. I told him where Joseph was and what the Pharaoh's magicians had done to him. No spell could keep Joseph from the Holy Land, especially when roused like that with God's secret name on Moses' lips.

Now I stand at the water's edge with all these memories and with my many daughters, most of whom have adopted me, for, to them, I appear so old. They want me to speak to them.

And so now we come to this moment of risk.

Stand with me at the water, Daughters of Israel. Before the break with slavery, look at these waters of time and life. Remember the other waters of the river that turned red from blood. Remember how we have been saved. Remember how fragile is our mortal life.

Here is the past in the undercurrent, and the future in the waves rushing across the surface. This is the timeless moment of faith all flowing together in the present.

This is the moment of risk.

Wisdom understands risk as the moment of danger and opportunity. Who could know that my songs would elect me to sing to Jacob? Who could know that the words would come down into my mouth, and so many times at that? In my compassion *for* him, I received compassion *from* him. And that compassion was the birth of wisdom that thrives in the heart.

I have told you my story many times before, but do you know what I will do in the future? Prophecy comes with immortality. The day will come when I will confront King David's officer. Who would have thought, from my timid girlhood, that I would take Joab to task for not knowing Torah and the correct manner to besiege a city? Imagine that he would slaughter a city for one traitor. I was his equal and I stood for the city; my compassion drove me to speak wisely. So many lives were at stake.

Remember that there are many of us who will watch over all of you and who are watching over you now. We take it upon ourselves to intervene and talk through the mouths of strangers or friends to guide you. Try to listen to us throughout your life.

Water is a good thing to part. But beware of idolizing it or making it into a solid paradigm. There are four rabbis who try to enter Paradise, but only one of them, Rabbi Akiva, knows not to call anything by what it appears to be. In the timeless time of Paradise, all becomes thought without materiality. Remember we enter God's mind as we are shown what a miracle looks like. Find the miracles in your life when I leave you. Try not to be too quick to name them at the moment of their birth. Words will come after your heart is open.

A Message from Serach

Risk is taking the leap based on what you've learned to be true.

Angels are watching you always; be ready to believe the one who tells you something important.

Getting old is the path to wisdom; the more you experience, the more compassionate you will be, because you have probably experienced it all.

For Further Thought

A few biblical references spawned a wealth of imaginative midrashim and folk tales about Serach bat Asher. What do you think it was about her that inspired so much creativity?

Serach bat Asher was rewarded with the gift of immortality for one act, reigniting the life force in her grandfather, Jacob, by letting him know through song that his favorite son was still alive. Did this single act merit such a great reward? Why or why not? What does immortality mean to you?

Rabbi Barbara Rosman Penzner has written a clear, concise summary of the main midrashim on Serah bat Asher. It is "Serach bat Asher—the Woman Who Enabled the Exodus," in *The Women's Torah Commentary: New Insights from Women Rabbis on the 54 Weekly Torah Portions*, edited by Rabbi Elyse Goldstein (Woodstock, VT: Jewish Lights Publishing, 2000), pages 112–117.

Marc Bregman, a scholar of rabbinic literature, has delivered a lecture that includes all the well-known midrashim and stories about

Serach bat Asher, as well as some tales from the Israel Folklore Archives in Haifa. For a full transcript of this 1996 lecture given at the University of Arizona, see—http://fp.arizona.edu/judaic/bilgray/bregman/Bregman.htm.

Chapter 19
Wife of Obadiah

ANDREA COHEN-KIENER

צוֹפִיָּה הֲלִיכוֹת בֵּיתָהּ וְלֶחֶם עַצְלוּת לֹא תֹאכֵל:

"She oversees the activities of her household and never eats the bread of idleness" (Prov. 31:27).

צופיה הליכות ביתה, זו אשת עובדיה דכתיב ואשה אחת מנשי בני הנביאים צעקה אל אלישע לאמר, שאמרה אין לי לילך אלא לאלישע. הלכה ואמרה לו רבי לא אתה אחד מבני הנביאים שהחביא עובדיה בעלי במערה, אמר לה הן מה טיבך. אמרה לו בקש עלי רחמים ואתפרנס ממעשי ידי ואל אצטרך לברִיות. באותה שעה בירכה אלישע ונתברכה ונתפרנסה ממעשה ידיה. לכך נאמר ולחם עצלות לא תאכל. ונעשה לה נס בתוך נס.

She oversees the activities of her household, this is the wife of Obadiah. This is what is written: Once a certain woman, the wife of one of the disciples of the prophets, cried out to Elisha, saying, "I have nowhere to turn but to Elisha" (2 Kings 4:1). So she went to him and she said to him, "My lord, were you not yourself one of the Disciples of the Prophets, whom my husband, Obadiah, hid in the caves?" And he said to her, "Yes, what can I do for your good? How can I help you?" She said to him, "Pray for me for mercy that I may be self-sustained from the work of my hands that I need not rely on the habits of creation." In that very instant Elisha blessed her and she became blessed and she became self-sustaining from the work of her hands. That is why it is written, [She] *never eats the bread of idleness*. A miracle was wrought for her inside a miracle.
—*Midrash ha-Gadol*

This oblique and fascinating story brings together not one prior passage from Scripture, but two, both from the period of the Books of the Kings. In them, we have the successive stories of the various kings of the northern and the southern kingdoms, each of them vying for their own kind of power. The prophets of these eras often provided a moral counterpoint to the monarchs.

In the later books of the classical prophets, we are accustomed to hearing the prophetic exhortations and their historical prompts. However, in this earlier narrative material, we have a description of the training process at a sort of prophecy school. We have some information about the leadership of the community, how new recruits were attracted, and their prayer, healing, and music practices. Throughout these narratives, their school is called "Disciples of the Prophets." Their magic and mystery is one of the under-told delights of biblical history.

In 1 Kings 18 there is the story of the wicked King Ahab, who has gone so far astray with his wife, Jezebel, that the Prophet Elijah has declared a drought against him. Indeed, there is a very severe drought in the land. Jezebel, the evil queen, initiates a vendetta against the Disciples of the Prophets and kills off a huge number of them. Some are saved, and Elijah spends part of this period on a 40-day retreat in the wilderness.

The drought is so severe that King Ahab and his trusted majordomo, Obadiah, the steward of the house, go out together to gather up hay so that the animals won't starve. Obadiah and King Ahab go their separate ways to gather fodder, and Obadiah encounters Elijah.

Elijah speaks to Obadiah, saying, "I'm going to see Ahab today." Elijah was well known for provoking King Ahab, as well as appearing and disappearing in startling ways. Obadiah is terrified and says, "When I come and tell Ahab and he does not find you, he will kill me. Yet your servant has revered the Lord from my youth." He continues, "My lord has surely been told what I did when Jezebel was killing the prophets of the Lord, how I hid a hundred of the prophets of the Lord, fifty men to a cave, and provided them with food and drink. And now you say, 'Go tell your lord: Elijah is here.' Why, he will kill me!" Elijah replied, "As the Lord of Hosts lives whom I serve, I will appear before him this very day" (1 Kings 18:13–15).

Obadiah returns to King Ahab to inform him, and we do not hear about him again. In summary, we now have a record of the chief domestic steward of King Ahab providing aid and safety to 100 men of the School of the Prophets, hiding in caves. This occurs at a time of national drought and scarcity, while Elijah himself is on retreat, eating only by miraculous means.

Several chapters later, King Ahab is succeeded by his grandson, Jehoram. The leadership of the Disciples of the Prophets is passed from Elijah to Elisha. Then we hear the story of how "a certain woman, the wife of one of the disciples of the prophets, cried out to Elisha: 'Your servant my husband is dead, and you know how your servant revered the Lord. And now a creditor is coming to seize my two children as slaves'" (2 Kings 4:1). No mention is made here of Obadiah, but three times the single verse uses the Hebrew root for Obadiah's name: o'v'd (servant). The earliest layers of Midrash state that this refers to Obadiah.

This "certain woman" is the wife of Obadiah, now a widow, with the creditor coming to take away her two sons. What creditor is this? This is the son of Ahab who has come to collect for all the food that her husband, Obadiah, stole from the royal storehouses in the time of the famine.

Elisha said to her, "What can I do for you? Tell me, what have you in the house?" She replied, "Your maidservant has nothing at all in the house except a jug of oil." "Go," he said, "and borrow vessels outside, from all your neighbors, empty vessels, as many as you can. Then go in and shut the door behind you and your children, and pour [oil] into all those vessels, removing each one as it is filled" (2 Kings 4:2–4).

"She went away .... They kept bringing [vessels] to her and she kept pouring. When the vessels were full, she said to her son, 'Bring me another vessel.' He answered her, 'There are no more vessels'; and the oil stopped. She came and told the man of God, and he said, 'Go sell the oil and pay your debt, and you and your children can live on the rest'" (2 Kings 4:5–7).

The story continues with Elisha visiting another woman, the Shunammite (see chapter 20). Visitations with women are prominent in the stories of the Disciples of the Prophets. In these biblical texts, we see how people commonly went to the prophets with all sorts of problems and that miracles were wrought regularly. The texts relate instances of people making solid lead float, riding around on whirlwinds, raising people from the dead, communicating by telepathy and curing by the word, commanding fires out of the sky, causing and curing leprosy through speech—among other sorts of miracles.

Commentary

Midrash ha-Gadol connects these stories together immediately and tells them with a slightly different emphasis, assuming that they are all part of one story. In the biblical text the wife of Obadiah says, "I have nothing in my house" when the prophet asks, "What have you?" She goes on to mention "… a jug of oil, one small flask." But in the midrash, Elisha says to her, "How can I help you?" And she says it very directly, "Ask mercy for me that I be sustained by the work of my own hands." What a clear and powerful prayer about exactly what she needs. I see a woman trying to balance the place within herself that needs to be self-sustaining so she can be of service to others. I see her struggling to find that place, praying that she could hold her life together by the work of her hands. The midrash doesn't say exactly what the miracle is. In the biblical text we have the information that she poured forth oil—a beautiful metaphor for her starting from her own home, her own containment, and her own vessels.

This woman has to start with what she has in order to give forth any more, and the prophet is very clear with her. Listen to his verbs: "Go," he says. "Borrow." "Go in and shut the door." She must go in and shut the door behind herself and her children, and pour. This is the teaching. This is the *tikkun*, the healing advice that the prophet gives her. She has everything already. All she needs is to make abundant space for it. She needs to ask for things for herself and for the sake of her children. Then she needs to close the door, making a safe container in which to bring forth the very oil that essentially they already have. It is the blessing of abundance and containment that the prophet gives her: the miracle inside the miracle.

What is the meaning of the rest of the line: "[She] never eats the bread of idleness" (Prov. 31:27)? The wife of Obadiah did not suffer from the illness of the idle rich, even though she belonged to that class. She was a perfect vessel to give and receive. She did not abuse her resources. She sustained herself with great dignity and provided oil for the people coming to Jerusalem. What a wonderful lifestyle for her, one with a great sense of purpose. She struck a healthy balance between wealth and generosity.

The Wife of Obadiah Speaks

Thank you for coming to hear my story. There were times when I have felt truly alone. It is a pleasure now to be seen and heard. I do think that my story has much to teach you.

I had such a blessed life. I know you wouldn't think that. It was hard to lose Obadiah. But there was so much light in our lives together that even in his passing, I was able to accept it. I could still feel him.

I was blessed in the sense that I had the chance to know every kind of richness. My husband looked after the home of the king! We were ostentatious for a while, by Jerusalem standards. We all suffered during the drought, but the prophets were being rounded up and persecuted as well. Obadiah knew all along that he had to help the prophets. He helped them hide and began to bring them provisions. I knew, of course. I helped him. But we never spoke of it. We both felt so sure that no danger would befall us if we were of service. Like his name, like mine.

Those were rich times, too. We had a chance to observe the disciples in retreat. Really they ate very little. We saw the wealth of their communion. They were generous with us. It was surprising to me at first how palpable the wealth of spirit felt. Afterward, it was amazing to me that I had never known that before. I felt so lucky to have known them. And of course, our service to them sustained me in a later time. Being with them always enriched me.

I don't really know how Obadiah died. They told me he fell while in the hills of Judea. I suppose he could have fallen. He may have been pushed. God knows we had enemies in the court after the deed became known.

I tried to keep my face up, but my boys and I were just hollowing out from the inside. The means of the house became sparser. We all appeared sallow from within. We were eating nothing, asking for nothing—trying to keep up appearances. I finally heard a voice ringing in my head: "Go to the prophet. Ask for help."

This was the turning point. What Elisha asked me was, "What do you already have?" He built on that.

I went home and asked all my neighbors to loan me vessels. They were so kind! As if the universe had been waiting for me to ask—the vessels flowed to me from everywhere. The boys and I worked together with a silent steady focus. Amazed but centered. "Abundance—abundance—abundance" kept pouring through my mind as each flask poured and hummed.

We lived for the rest of our lives on that oil. We quietly paid off our debts and became known as one of the way stations for pilgrims to Jerusalem to have a meal and some home hospitality. In my life with Obadiah, I was part of the class that served the kings. Later, we served the prophets. In the end of my life, I served the House of the Presence.

And so it is taught in my name: "She oversees the activities of her household / And never eats the bread of idleness" (Prov. 31: 27).

And since everyone always asks my true name, it is Shachar, which is dawn.

A Message from the Wife of Obadiah

There is a living balance between giving and receiving.

We need to take care of ourselves. I had to go home and close every door. This was not a time for me to worry about others, but myself, my own needs. In doing this, I served my own house and became a servant of God's house. These two houses are intermaintained.

There is a hunger for God that can only be filled by giving. Because the One is as vast as a vacuum and to reach out to it is to be pulled into its expansiveness. The love of God makes us lighter. Our hungers become more appropriate. Our needs become more transparent.

When we can manage our wealth and achievements and power in ways that serve others and ourselves, we are so blessed. We can have any power if we determine to use it for good.

For Further Thought

Express yourself every day.

I "sang" the oil out of the flask. My voiced invited it. I was nourished for many years on the value of that oil, but I was nourished forever by being able to sing out what was inside me. Any time I look inward and sing or hum what is real for me in that moment, I feel like a lubricated channel, a vessel, a stream. Practice creating those openings by expressing yourself every day.

Sing, write, or dance until spirit has had its say through you. Thank the spirit that has filled you and allow the fullness to flow through you for the good of all life.

Chapter 20

Shunammite Woman

ERICA BROWN

קָמוּ בָנֶיהָ וַיְאַשְּׁרוּהָ בַּעְלָהּ וַיְהַלְלָהּ:

"Her children rise and declare her happy; her husband praises her"
(Prov. 31:28).

קמו בניה ויאשרוה, זו שונמית שאמרה לבעלה הנה נא ידעתי כי איש אלהים
קדוש הוא. אמר ר' יוסי בר חנינה מכאן שהאשה מכרת באורחין יתר מן
האיש. קדוש הוא מנא ידעא, רב ושמואל חד אמר סדין שלפשתן הציעה לו
תחתיו ולא ראתה עליו קרי. ואידך אמר שלא ראתה זבוב על שלחנו. עובר
עלינו תמיד, אמר ר' יוסי בר חנינה אמרה לאישה כל המכניס תלמיד חכמים
לתוך ביתו ומאכילו ומשקהו ומהניהו מנכסיו מעלה עליו הכתוב כאלו הקריב
תמידין. נעשה נא עליית קיר קטנה, רב ושמואל חד אמר פרועה היתה
וקירוה וחד אמר אכסדרה היתה וחלקוה לשנים בקיר. בשלמא למאן דאמר
אכסדרה היתה וחלקוה לשנים הינו דכתיב קיר, אלא למאן דאמר פרועה היתה
וקירוה מאי קיר, על שם קירוי. בשלמא למאן דאמר עלייה הינו דכתיב
עליית, אלא למאן דאמר אכסדרה מאי עלייה, מעולה שבבתים. ונעשה לה נס
וילדה ומת הילד והחיה אותו אלישע. ולא נענה חזקיה אלא בשבילה,
דכתיב ויסב פניו אל הקיר ויתפלל אל ה'. מאי קיר, אמר ריש לקיש
שהתפלל מקירות לבו, שנאמר מעי מעי אוחילה קירות לבי הומה לי לבי. ר'
לוי אומר שהתפלל על עסקי קיר. אמר לפניו רבונו שלעולם ומה השונמית
שלא עשתה לפניך אלא קיר אחת קטנה החיית את בנה, אבי
אבא שחיפה את ההיכל כולו בטבלאות שלזהב טהור על אחת כמה וכמה.

Her children declare her happy, this is the Shunammite woman,
who said to her husband, "I am sure that he is a holy man of
God ..." (2 Kings 4:9). Rabbi Yossi bar Hanina said, "From
this [we know] that a woman involves herself with guests more
than a man does." Rabbi Yossi bar Hanina [also] said, "She
said to her husband, 'Whoever takes a student of wisdom into
his house and feeds him and gives him drink and lets him
use his property, about him it is written, It is as if he offered
the daily offering in the Temple.'" "Let us make a small enclosed upper chamber," [said the Shunammite woman to her
husband] (2 Kings 4:9,10). As a result, a miracle occurred and

she gave birth, but the boy died, so Elisha resurrected him ...”

—Midrash ha-Gadol

Elisha, the prophet and disciple of Elijah, visits a place called Shunem from time to time. A wealthy woman lives there and invites Elisha over to dine regularly. She is so impressed by the man's holiness that she convinces her husband to build a special guest room for Elisha, which she furnishes for the needs of a prophet: a bed, a table, a chair, and a lamp. By creating a place for him both to sleep and to study, she hopes he will become a more regular part of their household.

Elisha and his servant, Gehazi, stay there and hope to repay her the kindness. They urge her to suggest a gift and even ask if she is looking for special favors from people of authority. But she replies with a simple statement of self-satisfaction: “I live among my own people.” She is happy with her place in life. When she leaves the room, Gehazi tells the prophet that the Shunammite woman has no son and an aging husband. Elisha calls the woman back and pronounces that she will soon conceive and bear a son. Instead of elation, the Shunammite responds with surprise and asks the prophet not to tease her.

The prophet's words come true. In the predicted season, she has a son. Her son is not named in the story. Neither is she. The child grows up and goes out to see his father in the fields one day. The child cries out in pain: “My head, my head.” The father asks a servant to bring the listless child back to his mother. The child lies on his mother's knees until he dies. In grief, the Shunammite woman places the child upon Elisha's bed. She does not share the news with her husband, but has her donkeys saddled and rushes off to Mount Carmel, where the prophet lives.

Gehazi tries to intervene but the Shunammite woman insists on speaking with the prophet directly. She approaches Elisha and grasps his legs in desperation. The prophet returns with her and goes into his special guest chamber and closes the door behind him, isolating himself with the dead child. He lies on top of the child: "He put his mouth on its mouth, his eyes on its eyes, and his hands on its hands, as he bent over it" (2 Kings 4:34). The body of the child warms up, and he sneezes seven times. Elisha calls the Shunammite woman in and advises her to pick up her revived child. She falls at his feet in gratitude, picks up the child, and leaves the room.

Picking up the child is not a physical act in this narrative. The child is grown and too heavy to bear. The message the prophet leaves the Shunammite woman with is that she must carry the child in the fullest sense: bear him up with love, take responsibility for him, nurture and shape his future.

Commentary

Midrash ha-Gadol uses some irony in its choice of verse in placing the Shunammite woman. Proverbs 31:28 reads, "Her children declare her happy; her husband praises her." An alternative reading is "Her children rise up and call her blessed." The Shunammite woman's child does rise; he rises from the dead. But before he rises he also suffers a death that seems completely unavoidable. This miracle child complains that his head aches. Out in hot mideastern fields, the child's pain is not surprising. We wait for any of the figures in his life to bring a simple glass of water. The father does not help him but sends him to his mother. His mother is passive. She, too, does nothing active to sustain him. The poor boy sits on his mother's knees where he lingers until his life drains out of him.

The Shunammite woman did not ask for this child; she did not believe she could have children. When Elisha asked her for any gift, she did not ask for a child of the prophet. Even when given a child, she seems distant and removed during the child's lifetime. There are several other texts of barrenness in the Hebrew Bible which show linguistic and thematic similarities. Like Sarah, she shows little faith that the prophet's promise can come true. Sarah laughs when she overhears the prediction from the three angels. The Shunammite woman asks not to be deceived by the prophet. Perhaps after decades of trying, she has made peace with her infertility. She does not want to be teased back into that trying time of longing. Other barren matriarchs pray for a child, most notably Hannah. The intensity of her prayer is misread as drunkenness, but she is drunk only with her desire for a child. In Genesis, Rachel tells Jacob that she is purposeless without a child; her life is not worthy. The sense of emptiness or inadequacy that can accompany infertility is nowhere felt in the Shunammite story. She does not ask, does not pray, does not think little of herself for not being a mother. Or if she does, it is concealed from the reader. The biblical text, in portraying multiple responses to barrenness, also implicitly validates the different emotional fields experienced by women who cannot have children.

It is not surprising that when she has a child she seems unengaged by his needs. The text records somewhat flatly that after the conception and birth of the child, "The child grew up." We have no account of how this child grew and what attentions a doting parent displayed. Unlike Sarah and Hannah, the Shunammite woman is not presented as a nursing mother who makes elaborate plans for her child's weaning. The text does not say that she raised a child; the child seems to grow up without her. Where the midrash connects the Shunammite woman to her children's praise, the biblical text connects her to her son's demise.

When the Bible notes the child's death, we feel that the Shunammite woman relinquishes him a little too easily. There is no show of emotion. When she places the dead child upon Elisha's bed, she communicates that the *idea* of a child—in its entirety, from birth to death—had little to do with her. It was the prophet's whim, and now it is the prophet's responsibility. With resonances for the modern reader of Mary Shelley's tragic horror story, *Frankenstein*, Elisha must look upon the creature that he created and that now lies without breath upon the prophet's bed, the very prophet who brought him into the world. The horror is augmented by a small and significant detail. This is the only child in the Hebrew Bible born to a formerly barren woman who was created without divine guidance and support. The other children are acts of God's compassion or mandate; this unnamed child seems the product of a casual afterthought, an impressive thank-you note to follow an act of kindness. We are not surprised that the child has no name. He is, at this point, a child not intended by his mother or by an authentic Creator. We are not surprised that the Shunammite woman has no name. She was blessed with the gift of a child, and she let him go.

Our commentary does not end here. The Shunammite woman is praised in the midrash. For what is she praised, this woman who relinquished a miracle child? She must merit this praise somewhere in the text for the Rabbinic acclaim she received. And she does. Ironically, after the child dies—and only after—does she fight for his life. With speed she races to the prophet and insists that the prophet, and not his disciple, handle the matter. Elisha still pushes her away by using his servant, by not knowing the name of the woman who made him a special room in her house. She grabs his legs as a symbolic gesture of connection. She begs the prophet not to trivialize human need, but to become engaged and take action himself. Elisha alone can save the child, but not without the help of God. Finally Elisha understands that children are not created without divine intent. He prays to God for the first time in our story. But he must do more than pray.

Elisha locks himself in his room with the dead child. He places himself wholly on the child's body. Every orifice and organ of life must be pumped with the human connection that has been sorely missing in this child's early nurturing. All of the body's mechanisms of connection—the mouth, the eyes, and the hands—are warmed between prophet and child. In the simple act of a sneeze, the child displays the sweet innocence of rebirth.

The prophet now advises the woman to pick up the child. He is telling her to earn a name as a mother. He is telling her to give the child a name as a beloved son. Elisha, who was himself guilty of not connecting to the needs of others, asks the Shunammite woman to connect to her son. Both she and the prophet have given new life to this neglected boy.

This child did rise to praise his mother, as the midrash suggests. The child rose literally and figuratively. The Shunammite woman became a true mother only when her child was reborn. In one of the most remarkable biblical articulations of motherhood, the Shunammite woman earns her identity through a fight waged almost too late. Life doesn't always give us second chances at parenting. Elisha's advice to pick up the child is a fine end to this cautionary tale of motherhood. Bear the responsibility for children. Nurture and love them. Pick them up and let them be carried by that love.

The Shunammite Woman Speaks

I sat there helpless. His small arms linked around mine. His legs dangled without energy over my thighs. How I wished at that moment that I knew what God wanted of me. I asked the prophet, I begged him not to fool with me. But he did. He gave me a child when I wasn't ready. I didn't ask him for it. I just wanted the prophet's company, a small share of his sanctity to fill my own house with holiness. I didn't ask to fill my house with the noise of children. I knew that something would go wrong.

Oh, I wanted children desperately when I was a younger woman. My husband and I cried many a night that God did not give us the gift that so many others, some seemingly less deserving, had. When we ate holiday meals with the family I would feel their eyes upon me, wondering what was wrong. Their accusing, blaming eyes gave me no peace. There was nothing we could do. We prayed and prayed and then accepted God's decree and our fate. I worked hard and became known in my area as a woman of means. We had no children, but we had many visitors in our home.

We shared our table with important guests. We honored the prophets and priests in our area. They ate at our table, sang with us, left us with their holy words. Because *my* belly was empty, I tried to fill the belly of the prophet with food. I insisted that he eat with us whenever he visited. I implored him. And even that was not enough for me. I could not make a nursery so I made a special room for the prophet, Elisha. Please understand what would make a woman like me seem desperate to a holy man like the prophet. I had so much love to give. I wanted to add to my family in any way that I could. I had to nurture what I could so I shaped a home for the soul. I imagined my soul was like a womb; I would expand my soul with holiness and feel full and stretched and happy, almost.

My little son was born just as the holy man promised. I did not know how to care for him. He was so small and fragile. I was always afraid I would drop him. My husband was afraid to touch him. He was an old man. I, too, was old. I did not have the energy of the young mothers around me. I sometimes prayed for patience with the child. Each day I would look at him strangely, wondering if he was like other children. "How could he be?" I would say to my husband late at night, after the child was asleep. And then he got sick. God wanted him back. I had told the prophet not to fool with me. I was angry. Very angry. God must have been punishing us for something. Maybe he was punishing the prophet. I don't know. He was not like other children. I asked the prophet not to fool with me. Isn't that what I said?

So I let the little boy just die there on my knees. I was afraid of him. Life wasn't normal any more. There was so much I didn't understand. The holy man hardly came to visit; he never asked after the boy. He didn't stay in that special room we made for him. It all seemed to be a grand mistake. And I let the last breath slip out of my son's body. I watched him breathe, then the small undulations of his bare chest stopped. He died and I sat numb to the strangeness of it all.

I thought I would feel relief that things between my husband and me would go back to normal, that the prophet would come again. But in a flash of my soul I saw that there was something very wrong here. The child was my right. I wanted him back. The prophet gave me a gift and I wanted it back. All the love that I held inside me for so long rushed out to his helpless body. *Please, God, please bring him back. Elisha, bring back my son. I will become his mother, his real mother. I promise.* At that moment I knew what I had to do. I had to put the child in the prophet's room and run. Run as fast as possible, faster than possible. Possibility meant nothing. I had to get the prophet and show him this dead child and tell him that I wanted the child back with all my heart. No, I must demand the child back. I had spent so many hours listening to Elisha. Now it was time for the prophet to listen to me.

A Message from the Shunammite Woman

My message is steeped both in worlds of possibility and impossibility. I am not the typical biblical woman confronting barrenness. My maternal feelings emerged only after the death of my child. You see, maternal instincts are not necessarily felt by all women the same way; nor do all women feel themselves inadequate without children. Our remarkable tradition recognizes this. I find it comforting that there is no singular emotional experience of barrenness in the Hebrew Bible. Sarah, Rebekah, Rachel, Hannah, Hatzlelponi, and me—we each had our own way of handling our pain. We had all lost a child or almost—Sarah, Rachel, Naomi, Bath-Sheba, Elisheba, and me. This has enabled women over the centuries to enter the biblical text with emotional safety and to explore a topic that is typically confronted with silence.

As my story draws to an end, I hope you appreciate the enormity of what is involved in raising a child. Like Elisha's remarkable revival of my boy, we must invest our every breath, our eyes, our mouths, our hands in bringing up children.

My final message to you is perhaps even more profound. We rarely get second chances as parents, certainly not where life and death are concerned. We can't always bring back our children when we haven't nurtured them with our whole selves. God gave me another chance and brought my dead child back to life so that I could finally learn to be a mother. Chances are that we won't always be that lucky.

We will not have the intervention of a prophet to bring back children who are alienated or scorned, abused or neglected. We can't start again as mothers with a clean slate devoid of bad feelings. To our children, we always parent in the present tense. I hope my story reminds us all to pick up our children—as I finally did—every single day.

For Further Thought

Compare the stories of the Shunammite woman and the widow of Tzarephath (chapter 11). Each of them nearly lose a child, but a prophet steps in and brings the child back to life. How are the stories different and similar?

The Shunammite woman seems to have found other ways of mothering that channeled her maternal instinct. What are alternative ways of "mothering"? Which ones do you find satisfying?

Jewish Mothers Tell Their Stories: Acts of Love and Courage, edited by Rachel Josefowitz Siegel, Ellen Cole, and Susan Steinberg-Oren (New York: The Haworth Press, 2000), is a contemporary collection of true accounts by Jewish women that portrays the extensive range of what it means to be a Jewish mother.

In her book *In the Wake of the Goddesses: Women, Culture and the Biblical Transformation of Pagan Myth*, (New York: Fawcett Columbine, 1992), pages 162–167, Tikva Frymer-Kensky provides a thought-provoking chapter called "Our Father and Our Mother," which explores the ways in which God is portrayed as a parental figure in the Bible.

Chapter 21
Ruth

HAVIVA-NER DAVID

רַבּוֹת בָּנוֹת עָשׂוּ חָיִל וְאַתְּ עָלִית עַל־כֻּלָּנָה:

"Many women have done well, but you surpass them all" (Prov. 31:29).

רבות בנות עשו חיל, זו רות שזכת ויצא ממנה דוד ובניו הישרים. אמר ר'
יוחנן מאי רות, שיצא ממנה דוד שרוה להקב"ה בשירות ותשבחות. ואת
עלית על כלנה, שאמר לה בעז בתי היטבת חסדך האחרון מן הראשון.

Many women have done well, this is Ruth, who merited that David and his righteous offspring were to be her descendants. Said Rabbi Yohanan: "Why Ruth? Because David would come from her, whose soul was so full, he would sing to God in songs and praises."
—*Midrash ha-Gadol*

Elimelech, a wealthy leader in Israel, and his wife, Naomi, leave Bethlehem in the Land of Judah because of famine. They go to Moab with their two sons, Mahlon and Chilion. Eventually, Elimelech dies, and the sons marry Moabite women, Orpah and Ruth. Ten years later, the two sons die, too, leaving their wives with no children; and, with no hope of descendants to carry on the line of her husband and sons, Naomi decides to return to Bethlehem.

Naomi advises her two daughters-in-law to return to the homes of their mothers, and at first both refuse; but in the end, Orpah is persuaded by Naomi's argument that she can offer them no future. If they remain in Moab, they will have a future. But Ruth is not convinced; she clings to Naomi and tells her: "… wherever you go, I will go; wherever you lodge, I will lodge; your people shall be my people, and your God my God. Where you die, I will die, and there I will be buried" (Ruth 1:16,17).

At the end of Ruth 1, the two women return to Bethlehem as paupers at the beginning of the barley harvest. Actually, it is only Naomi who is physically returning. Ruth is returning to her deeper, spiritual roots even though it is not her actual homeland. People are excited to see them. After all, it has been many years. But Naomi is bitter and tells them that she left full and has returned empty.

In order to feed herself and Naomi, Ruth goes to glean in the fields of Boaz, Naomi's relation, as according to Jewish Law, one must leave the corners of the fields unharvested for the poor to gather. Boaz notices Ruth and takes an interest in her; he tells his reapers to treat her well, and he invites her to partake of their food at mealtime. She thanks him, and he commends her on her courage and *hesed* (loving-kindness) to have left her home to take care of Naomi.

After some time, Naomi tells Ruth to go to Boaz at night when he will be on the threshing floor and to lie at his feet. Then he can redeem her according to the laws of levirate marriage.[1] Ruth does as Naomi bids and Boaz is moved by her actions. He thanks her for turning to him rather than to a younger kinsman. But he explains that there is a closer relative who should be given first claim on Ruth.

In front of 10 elders, Boaz asks this relative, Ploni Almoni, if he would want to marry Ruth and thus also acquire the land that Elimelech left years before. He refuses. Therefore, Boaz and Ruth are able to marry. They have a son, Obed, father of Jesse, father of King David. In this way, Ruth has done her duty to perpetuate the name of her deceased husband, Mahlon, in Israel. The townswomen tell Naomi that her new grandson "will renew your life and sustain your old age; for he is born of your daughter-in-law, who loves you and is better to you than seven sons" (Ruth 4:15).

Commentary

Deuteronomy 23:4,5 states: "No Ammonite or Moabite shall be admitted into the congregation of the Lord; none of their descendants, even in the tenth generation, shall ever be admitted into the congregation of the Lord, because they did not meet you with food and water on your journey after you left Egypt, and because they hired Balaam son of Beor ... to curse you."

The Talmud in tractate *Yevamot* reacts to this declaration by asking how is it that King David was descended from Ruth, the Moabite convert? After all, she should not have been allowed to convert in the first place because she was a Moabite! The Talmud goes on to interpret the biblical prohibition this way: "Read the verse to mean ... a male Moabite and not a female."

Is this answer satisfying? Could we not find a more meaningful answer in the story of Ruth herself—an answer that could shed light on Ruth's message to us as well?

There is no doubt that in the text of the Book of Ruth, the writer wants to emphasize Ruth's origins. She is constantly referred to as "Ruth the Moabite." Yet, she is also set up as a parallel figure to Abraham, the father of the Jewish nation. "Wherever you go I will go; wherever you lodge I will lodge; your people shall be my people, and your God my God," she tells Naomi in Ruth 1:16,17. This conjures up God's words to Abraham: "Go you from your native land and from your father's house to the land that I will show you" (Gen. 12:1–3). Like Abraham, Ruth leaves her land and her people to go to a place that is unknown to her. Like Abraham, she displays extraordinary courage, vision, and faith.

But there is more to the parallel between Ruth and Abraham than this. Like Abraham, who was known to have opened his tent on all sides to welcome visitors, Ruth exemplifies *hesed* (lovingkindness) that goes above and beyond what would be expected of the average human being. Orpah is the example of ordinary *hesed* in this story. She offers sincerely to stay with Naomi, but when Naomi pushes her to go, she is persuaded. Ruth, on the other hand, will not be swayed. She is determined to remain with Naomi and care for her in her old age. Ruth stays despite the fact that in Judah, as a Moabite among Israelites, this could mean a life of poverty. She will have no hope for a future husband or children. Still, Ruth goes with Naomi.

When they arrive in Bethlehem, she works hard on her feet all day to make sure Naomi does not starve.

The Book of Ruth is telling us that Ruth the Moabite is more akin to Abraham than to her true blood ancestor, Lot, Abraham's nephew. Lot displays a warped sense of *hesed*. He is prepared to sacrifice his own daughters in order to protect strangers when he offers to throw his daughters, instead of his guests, out to the angry Sodomites, to be raped. Ruth, the paradigm of *hesed*, is more a daughter of Abraham than of Lot, the author is telling us. Ruth is not really going to a strange land when she sets out for Judah. She is returning, as the text tells us. Hers is not a physical return, but rather a spiritual one.

In fact, Ruth displays a higher level of *hesed* than Abraham himself. While Abraham is especially welcoming to strangers, his *hesed* at home is not as strong. In Genesis 12:13 he tells his wife, Sarah, to misrepresent herself as his sister. He is worried that the king of Egypt might kill him in order to take Sarah as his wife. He makes Sarah seem sexually available, putting her body in jeopardy, so that his life won't be in jeopardy. Then, later, he is willing to sacrifice his own son. Ruth's *hesed*, on the other hand, has a fuller quality. It is directed to everyone, as her relationship to Naomi demonstrates. Naomi is not a blood relation of Ruth's, but she is also not a stranger. She is something between kin and stranger, telling us that Ruth's *hesed* is nondiscriminating and rises above even that of Abraham himself.

The Book of Ruth transforms the prohibition in Deuteronomy to one based not on ancestry but on character. Moabite men become a symbol for the type of person who is barred from joining the Jewish people. The Gemara, not the Torah, provides this distinction as to why Ruth is allowed to marry Boaz, but the real reason is implied by the text of the Book of Ruth itself. Because of Ruth's character, which is decidedly "un-Moabite" and essentially Hebrew, she is allowed to enter the nation. A spiritual son or daughter of Lot who is with the Moabites in the desert may not enter the assembly of the Lord. However, one who is descended from the Moabites in blood, yet displays that he or she is truly the spiritual heir of Abraham, is accepted with open arms into the Jewish people. Moreover, he or she is honored with the same royal lineage that will eventually bring forth the Messiah, the redeemer.

Ruth Speaks

As far back as I can remember, I did not feel at home among my people. My giving nature did not match what was presented as virtuous in my culture. "Humans are a selfish breed," my father would tell me. "You have to look out for yourself, because no one else will!" But my heart told me there must be another way. So I searched for role models who could show me this other way. And then I met Naomi.

When I first saw Naomi, she was nursing her sick husband, Elimelech. I watched her carry him out of their house to feel the warm sun on his almost translucent skin. This, my heart told me, is the other way that I have been searching for. So I offered my help. I came every day to help Naomi with her husband. She did not want to leave him alone, and her sons needed to look after their livelihoods. She was unable to leave the house until they came home. I would come to stay with Elimelech while she went out to get food or see to other needs outside of the house. It was not easy to convince Naomi to let herself be helped, but really she had no choice, as there were things she needed to attend to outside of the house, even if just for the good of her family.

Soon I brought my childhood friend Orpah along as well, for a bit of company, and because I wanted to expose her to Naomi's ways. Even when Naomi was at home, we stayed and helped her, mostly because we wanted a chance to watch her and listen to her musings.

When Elimelech was not listening, she would tell us of her regrets. "I should never have agreed to leave our home and our people. I knew it was wrong to take advantage of our fortunate position and leave while others starved. If anything, as I told Elimelech, we should go just to gather enough food to bring back with us for the others.

But he assured me we would not be gone long. He said we had to look out for our family first. And this I could understand. But once we settled in Moab, and life was materially good here, not so much of a struggle as it was back home, I knew he would never leave. I thought about going back myself, taking the boys, but then my husband fell ill, and now there is no choice. I could consider leaving him when he was well, but I cannot leave him in this condition. He is my husband, after all."

She nursed him for years until he finally breathed his last breath. By then we were all family. Her sons were grown. It was obvious that we would marry them. I think I was in love with Naomi as much as Mahlon. I was in love with their way of life, what they thought to be most important. They taught me a new word, *hesed*, which was not even in the vocabulary of the culture I came from.

Ten years passed and neither Orpah nor I conceived. This was painful to all of us; and if not for Naomi, I am not sure I would have made it through those years. She showed me how I could transform this desire to nurture and care for a child, which was at the source of my very being, into *hesed*. Our home became an outpost of *hesed* in Moab. No one knew what to make of it. We served food to the poor and cared for the sick, while Mahlon and Chilion were out all day working. They brought home the money, and we poured it into our House of Hesed. But they didn't mind. After all, they were not only the sons of Elimelech, but also the sons of Naomi.

Then came the terrible accident. On their way home from work, bandits attacked Mahlon and Chilion. They were left bleeding on the side of the road, and no one came to help them. They bled to death. After all those years in Naomi's home, I was shocked. How could this happen? What kind of human being would leave two men to bleed to death on the side of a road? And then I remembered that this was how I was raised. And then I knew that I had to leave.

So when Naomi told me to go back to my mother's house, I could think of no fate worse than that. I could not bear the thought of Naomi living on her own. How would she take care of herself in her old age? And how could I bear never hearing from her again? Even more important, how could I stay in this place where there is no *hesed*?

I went with Naomi back to the Land of Judah, despite her pleas that I return home. She was worried about my future. She was right; I knew life would not be easy for me there. Israelites are not supposed to marry Moabites. Mahlon and Chilion did so only because they had no choice. Besides, Naomi allowed it. She said Orpah and I were Israelites at heart. But she warned me that this might not be the way others would see it.

When we first arrived in Bethlehem, I was treated like a stranger. "Ruth the Moabite," they all called me. Then I met Boaz. He noticed me gleaning in his field. He told his reapers to deal kindly with me, and he invited me to eat with them all. He sensed my Israelite heart. He perceived my *hesed*. And when I told this to Naomi, her face lit up. "He sees in you what I did," she said. "He sees that you are a daughter of Abraham. Now go to him, and he will redeem us."

So I did and so he did. My womb was opened after all of those years. And now we have a House of Hesed in Judah: me, Boaz, Naomi, and Obed, our son.

A Message from Ruth

Since I have come from outside the Jewish People, I have had to learn what is central to Jewish identity and tradition.

First, we judge people not by the way they look or the place they come from or the labels others have put on them, and not even by the deeds of their community or family, but by who they are inside and how that manifests itself in their actions in the world. People can defy all labels and categorizations, so it pays to look closely and carefully at everyone rather than to rely on what others tell us about them or even what our first impressions may be. Take the time to look deeply into a person's soul.

Second, people can overcome their national and even personal pasts. A woman can always turn her life around through the acts she performs and the decisions she makes at the immediate moment. I was at a crossroads in my life, and I had to make the decision I knew was right even though it meant leaving home forever.

Third, even in the larger scheme of things, small acts of *hesed* can change the course of history and thus help to repair the world.

Finally, love can, at times, override all rational thinking. Sometimes, listen to your heart instead of your head. Often, it is in these kinds of internal communications that we tap into the spark of the Divine that is in each of us.

Know that when you perform acts of *hesed*, you repair your own soul, the souls of others, and nothing less than the soul of the world.

For Further Thought

What was it about Ruth the Moabite that made her worthy of being the mother of the messianic line, in opposition to the biblical decree that a Moabite should not enter the people of Israel, as described in Deuteronomy 23:4–7?

Boaz was the descendant of Perez, one of the sons of Tamar, a woman whose story is found in Genesis 38. Tamar was also an outsider to the Jewish people. What are links between the story of Ruth and the story of Tamar?

See Judith A. Kates and Gail Twersky Reimer, editors of *Reading Ruth: Contemporary Women Reclaim a Sacred Story* (New York: Ballantine Books, 1994). This exciting compendium of essays on Ruth by imaginative and thoughtful Jewish women writers will stimulate much discussion.

Ilana Pardes' "The Book of Ruth: Idyllic Revisionism" in *Countertraditions in the Bible: A Feminist Approach* (Cambridge, MA: Harvard University Press, 1992), pages 98–117, is a perceptive essay that rereads the Book of Ruth in the light of the story of Rachel and Leah.

Chapter 22a
Vashti

NAOMI GRAETZ

שֶׁקֶר הַחֵן וְהֶבֶל הַיֹּפִי ...

"Grace is deceptive, beauty is illusory ..." (Prov. 31:30).

שקר החן והבל היופי, זו ושתי.

Grace is deceptive, beauty is illusory, this is Vashti.
—*Midrash ha-Gadol*

When King Ahasuerus[1] has reigned for three years, he holds a banquet in his vast gardens for all the people of Shushan. The drinking is according to the law; people are encouraged to drink as much as they can and the king makes sure that nothing is spared for the comfort of his guests.

Queen Vashti, rumored to be the last descendant of King Nebuchadnezzar, prepares a parallel feast for the women in the royal house that belonged to King Ahasuerus. While the men are outside carousing, the women are inside enjoying themselves.

On the seventh day of this feast, when the king has perhaps imbibed a bit too much, he commands his seven chamberlains to bring his property, meaning his wife, Vashti, before him, ordering her to wear the royal turban that will show off her beauty to the people. This he felt was fair, since her beauty was his to possess as well as the royal crown. And she was indeed beautiful, like her name, which some say in Persian means woman of great beauty.

But his beautiful queen refuses to obey his commandment and this upsets him. He does not confront her directly to ask why she has denied his command. Instead, he asks the wise men and the seven princes of Persia and Media, who sit next to him, for their advice: "What shall be done, according to law, to Queen Vashti for failing to obey the command of King Ahasuerus ... ?" (Esther 1:15).

Memucan answers for them all by saying, "Queen Vashti has committed an offense not only against Your Majesty but also against all the officials and against all the peoples in all the provinces of King Ahasuerus. For the queen's behavior will make all wives despise their husbands, as they reflect that King Ahasuerus himself ordered Queen Vashti to be brought before him, but she would not come" (Esther 1:16,17).

"If it please Your Majesty, let a royal edict be issued by you, and let it be written into the laws of Persia and Media ... that Vashti shall never enter the presence of King Ahasuerus. And let Your Majesty bestow her royal estate upon another who is more worthy than she. Then will the judgment executed by Your Majesty resound throughout your realm ...; and all wives will treat their husbands with respect, high and low alike" (Esther 1:19,20).

After his wrath is assuaged, Ahasuerus remembers Vashti briefly, but no longer concerns himself with her, whether she is alive or dead. Instead he listens to his servants who suggest that "... beautiful young virgins fair be sought out for Your Majesty" (Esther 2:2).

Commentary

After reading the biblical story, it is clear that the beautiful heroine—the first half of the pair that makes up the 22nd *eishet chayil*—is someone to emulate. She is brave, defiant, strong, and self-determined. Vashti is a proud, unbending woman, who refuses to obey the drunken husband who sees her as his possession to command to perform for him at will. Rabbinic tradition could have been supportive of Vashti for her stance of independence and personal dignity.

However, the Rabbis have chosen instead to use her grace and beauty as swords against her. "Grace is deceptive, Beauty is illusory," refers to Vashti. "It is for her fear of the Lord that a woman is to be praised," this is Esther. Clearly, *Midrash ha-Gadol* is setting up a binary opposition: whereas Vashti's grace and beauty are deceptive, Esther is praiseworthy and God-fearing. In the midrash, Vashti is identified with *sheker* (deception).

The letter *shin* (ש), the first letter of *sheker*, has three prongs. First, it can be the devil's pitchfork, a comb to brush her beautiful hair, which emphasizes her vanity. Second, like the letter *shin*, which suggests teeth, Vashti can be seen as someone with a bite, a strong voice of her own who has to be put down. Third, *shin* can symbolize the crown of her royalty.

Most *aggadot* (stories and legends) are so negative about Vashti that it is almost impossible to identify with her. The sages deviated from the literal or contextual reading of the text when they turned Vashti into a witchlike, demonic being with no redeeming characteristics. They gave examples of how she stripped the daughters of Israel and made them work naked on Shabbat, no less. They wrote that her husband sent for her on the seventh day after she gave birth, in great joy, since he knew that she was no longer unclean. Yet she was still bleeding and refused to appear before him naked. No wonder she was punished in a similar manner, and sentenced to die on Shabbat. The Rabbis said she refused to obey the king because Daniel was present at the banquet, and she hated him for his terrible prophecies about her ancestor, Nebuchadnezzar. They claimed that she too loved debauchery and that she secluded the women not because of her chastity, but so that they could also "party" and she could control and blackmail them. Some say the angel Gabriel punished her for her sins with leprosy or, alternatively, with having a tail appended to her, which is the real reason why she was embarrassed to obey the king's command, not because of any innate modesty. Vashti's potential for haughtiness was forestalled since she was reviled for having animal characteristics.

Since women who appear in public are considered wanton, why did our sages find it necessary to demonize Vashti, who behaved modestly? Why did they need to turn her into an "other" with whom no one would want to identify? They mocked her and made her into an object of laughter and fear. She became the shrew who had to be tamed and humiliated so that real men could rule.

One reason could be that in the *aggadah*, Vashti was the great-granddaughter of King Nebuchadnezzar and therefore witnessed the Persian conquest of Babylon, ruled by her father, King Belshazzar (*Esther Rabbah* 3:8). When the city fell, the frightened young girl ran to his room and found out her father had been killed. General Darius, the succeeding king, took pity on the young Vashti and gave her hand in marriage to his son, Ahasuerus. This is the source of her later unhappiness with him, because she felt that she had married beneath herself. When Ahasuerus made his famous request of her, Vashti insulted him by reminding him of his lowly status as servant to her father by exclaiming: "You used to be the stable boy of my father's house, and you were used to bringing naked harlots before you. Now that you have ascended the throne you still have not changed your habits" (*Esther Rabbah* 3:14 on Esther 1:12). "But Queen Vashti refused …" So it seems that the Rabbis are getting back at this last descendant of Nebuchadnezzar. Just as Ahasuerus doesn't give Vashti a chance to speak or explain, the Rabbinic tradition only allows us to see the nether side of Vashti.

Vashti Speaks

What hurts me most is that on Purim, there are hardly any little girls who dress up as me. True, there are now some women who wave flags with bells on them in their synagogues, so that my voice is heard as a tinkle, but that is considered a subversive act, not the norm.

Why this conspiracy of the Rabbis to shut my voice out? Didn't they know that I was a secret Jew—that when I didn't appear before Ahasuerus, it was because I believed in the one God and knew that my husband was not my God? I had learned the lessons of modesty from Daniel (the Hebrew prophet who survived the lion's den) when he was in our prison. I went to mock and curse him and came out a convert. Didn't they understand that without me, there would have been no Esther in the palace and that the Jewish people would have been doomed?

They should have thanked me. Instead they mocked me and turned me into a monster. And where am I today? Locked out of the palace, under guard. Everyone thinks I'm dead, but I'm not. I look in my mirror every day and see another wrinkle, not laugh lines, nothing to laugh about yet. All around me are eunuchs, no men to admire me. I have needs, you know. I keep abreast of what's going on in the palace and approve of all that Esther does. I send her letters: It's our secret, giving her advice on how to please my ex-husband—who is a bit of a fool—whom I thought I had under my control—until Haman got ahold of him and put ideas in his head.

Who is going to have the last laugh, I wonder? Will it be Esther and me, or the men? At first I was very jealous of the thought of his having another wife in my stead, but then I realized how lucky I was to be relieved of him. I never wanted children from him; his rank was too lowly. I come from royal stock and he was only a soldier's son. But when my father died, I had no choice; he was my only source of protection. I trusted him for a long time and followed his lead, until he went one step too far and commanded me to appear before him after his extended drinking bout.

He thought I was his prized possession, like our pet leopard, Muni. How dare he summon me and try to degrade me! All the princesses in the world heard about what he wanted. They all knew. They had their eyes on me, wondering how I would respond. I had responsibility to them, not only to myself. If I gave in to the king's demands, there would be total disrespect for women of the Persian kingdom. So I simply refused. I was a queen from royal lineage with a position to uphold. There was no way I would allow myself to be subjected to such an indignity.

I must admit that I miss the life that I used to have. There are limits to the contemplative life of peace and quiet. I miss the intrigue of court and am too dependent on Esther's correspondence with me—but it is all I have, so I make peace with it. At least I am not dead—that is what I want you all to know—not what the Rabbis would like to have you think! They spread rumors that Ahasuerus had me killed after I refused to come

before him. They said I deserved my fate because I would not allow
Ahasuerus to give permission for the building of the Temple, and that
I used to say to him, "Do you seek to build what my ancestors destroyed?"
(*Esther Rabbah* 5: 2). What nonsense! If you read the Bible carefully, it
says that I "shall never enter the presence of King Ahasuerus" (Esther
1:19) again. So all I lost was the dubious privilege of entering the king's
presence (and we all know what that means) and the title of Queen.

And there are some who still consider me to be the lawful queen.
I do have my following, you know. It consists mostly of women who
don't want to be ruled by their husbands. Now that was an idiotic law,
wasn't it? What a farce to use all of Persian law and administration,
and its primitive postal service, to make every man be a master in his
own house. What were they thinking of, those idiots—that every
woman was waiting for me to give a signal to rebel against her husband? Actually, that's not such a bad idea, when I look back. Too bad
I didn't think of it then.

A Message from Vashti

Sheker ha chen ve-hevel ha-yofi (Grace is deceptive, beauty is illusory). When you get up in the morning, don't look at the mirror right
away to see if you look gaunt and thinner than yesterday. Don't get on
the scales to see how much weight you've lost at night. Take a lesson
from me. What is *hevel*? It is usually understood as vanity or lack of
meaning. But it is really the mere breath that separates us from the
living and the nonliving. Beauty is fleeting and fragile—you may think
that beauty gives you advantages over other women and some power,
but in the long run it is transient and doesn't necessarily bring happiness. And when you lose it—if it is all you have going for you—you
will feel that only beauty separates you from being an object of love
and desire, to being unloved and undesirable.

What has given me lasting happiness over the years is my discovery of the one God. I had many discussions with Daniel when he
was locked up in our jails, and from him I learned what is real and

what is not. Although I tried to seduce him at first, he wasn't interested; he said that beauty is vanity and that I should look within myself to see who I really was and what I really wanted from life.

There are two types of beauty. One is external, the other internal. All my life I was known for my external beauty. Rabbi Berekiah went so far as to describe me as a "raven that decks itself with its own feathers and with those of others" (*Esther Rabbah* 3:9). He had a point; I did take advantage of my external beauty. But it is vanity, since you cannot take it with you. If you find some eternal value and seek it out and nurture it, then your beauty will be passed down to generations. Do not allow the allure of jewelry, fashion, makeovers, or perfect hair to influence you to develop only your external beauty. Delve into yourself and find out who you are. And then, next Purim, dress up as me, Queen Vashti. I had a following, lost it, and then was demonized for my ideas.

> Straight and proud I stood.
> Not for me the Selections.
> I had refused
> I had objected
> I would not subject myself,
> Submit to gazing drunken eyes
> Boring into me.
> The path I chose was different.
> Not for me the party clothes
> The giggling,
> The dressing up
> For others.
> I am other
> Anomaly
> Threat to
> Claims of supremacy.
> I, Vashti, bent down.
> Not for me Supplications.
> I bared my head
> For the first
> And last time.
> The party is over
> For me.

For Further Thought

What does it mean "to refuse to come" at someone else's bidding? What qualities does a woman need to have in order to follow her own convictions?

Rabbinic literature is all but unanimous in its disdain for Vashti. Compare her story to that of a similar figure named Lilith, who was also banished, from Adam. For Lilith's story, see *Legends of the Jews*, by Louis Ginzberg (Philadelphia: The Jewish Publication Society, 2003), page 65.

One can see the beginning of the move to reread the story of Vashti from a feminist perspective in Mary Gendler's "The Restoration of Vashti," a chapter in *The Jewish Woman: New Perspectives*, edited by Elizabeth Koltun (New York: Schocken Books, 1976), pages 241–247.

Vanessa Ochs reveals the teachings of Vashti for today in "Vashti: Taking Care of Yourself," a chapter in *Sarah Laughed: Modern Lessons from the Wisdom and Stories of Biblical Women* (New York: McGraw Hill, 2005), pages 165–173.

Chapter 22b
Esther

TAMARA COHEN

אִשָּׁה יִרְאַת־יְהֹוָה הִיא תִתְהַלָּל: ...

"... It is for fear of the Lord that a woman is to be praised" (Prov. 31:30).

אשה יראת ה' היא תתהלל, זו אסתר וישם כתר מלכות בראשה וימליכה
תחת ושתי.

It is for fear of the Lord that a woman is to be praised, this is Esther. "So he set a royal diadem on her head and made her queen instead of Vashti" (Esther 2:17).

—*Midrash ha-Gadol*

The story of Esther, familiar to many from the popular holiday of Purim on which it is read, unfolds in Shushan, the capital of the ancient Persian Empire. It is the third year of Ahasuerus's reign, and he holds a banquet for all his princes and servants. On the seventh day of the banquet, he orders his eunuchs to bring Queen Vashti, wearing her royal crown, to appear before him and all his drunken guests. When Vashti refuses to come, the King not only dismisses her; he issues a decree proclaiming that all wives throughout his kingdom must recognize the sovereignty of their husbands and obey them. With that decree and Vashti's dismissal, the stage is set for a new queen—one who, in the end, will also disobey her husband's rules and so, at least implicitly, overturn this misogynist decree and through her example illustrate its foolishness.

To find a new queen, King Ahasuerus announces a national search for beautiful young virgins. One of the many girls brought to the palace is Esther, also known as Hadassah—a beautiful orphan girl, raised by her cousin Mordecai, who adopted her as his daughter. When Mordecai brings Esther to the court of Ahasuerus, he leaves her with one piece of advice—she is to keep secret her ethnic identity.

In the harem, Esther quickly wins the favor of Hegai, the guardian of the women gathered there. She is provided with maids and special beauty treatments, and after a year of these preparations, her turn to be taken to the king finally arrives. Ahasuerus immediately loves Esther above all the other women of the harem and crowns her in Vashti's stead. Meanwhile, Mordecai has discovered and reported a plot to kill the king. His heroic deed is recorded in Ahasuerus's book of records—a plot twist that will win him a reward at a critical point later in the story.

Sometime after Esther becomes queen, the trouble begins. Mordecai refuses to bow down to Haman, the king's chief minister, and the affronted Haman makes the conflict an ethnic one. He draws lots to pick a day on which to kill the Jews, a people he describes as "... scattered and dispersed among the other peoples in all the provinces of your realm, whose laws are different from those of any other people ..." (Esther 3:8). With the king's permission, Haman decrees that all the Jews throughout the kingdom—men, women, and children—will be killed on the 13th day of the month of Adar.

As soon as word of Haman's plot reaches Mordecai, he tears his clothes and puts on sackcloth and ashes—classic signs of mourning. He also decides that he must enlist Esther to go to Ahasuerus and plead on behalf of their people. When Esther first learns of Mordecai's request, she lets him know that she will be risking death if she goes to the king without being summoned. Mordecai hears this, but warns her that her silence will not protect her, and he suggests that perhaps it was for the very purpose of being in the position to save her people that she achieved her reign. Finally he tells her that help will come from another place if not from her.

Esther launches a plan. She sends Mordecai to gather all the Jews of Shushan to fast for her for three days, and she informs him that she and her maids will be fasting as well. After the three days, she will break the law and go to the king, ready to face the possibility of her death.

On the third day of her fast, Esther dresses herself in royal garb and stands in the inner court of the king's palace. The king sees her, asks her what she wants, and offers her anything—up to half of the kingdom. Esther then asks Ahasuerus and Haman to attend a banquet she has prepared. At this first banquet she invites both her guests to return to a second feast the following day. Haman goes home after the first banquet, filled with pride at having been entertained in the private audience of the king and queen. He passes by Mordecai and becomes enraged when he is not suitably acknowledged by him. Haman's wife, Zeresh, and friends suggest that he build a very tall stake on which to impale Mordecai. Haman has the stake erected.

The tables soon begin to turn. That night, when Ahasuerus has trouble sleeping, his servants read to him from his book of records about Mordecai having saved his life. The king enlists Haman's help in coming up with a suitable reward for a man the king wants to honor. Haman thinks he is coming up with a reward for himself, but the king actually has Mordecai in mind. Haman ends up disgraced as he leads Mordecai, dressed in the king's finest clothes and riding the king's horse, through the center of Shushan. From this first experience of downfall, Haman continues to fall.

At the second of the two banquets arranged by Esther, she dramatically confronts Ahasuerus and Haman with her true identity and with the evil plot of Haman to destroy her people. Ahasuerus grows furious and briefly leaves the scene. Haman pleads with Esther to save his life; and when Ahasuerus reenters the courtyard, he finds Haman falling on Esther's bed. Ahasuerus accuses Haman of trying to rape Esther, and with this, Haman's fate is sealed. He is impaled on the stake he had prepared for Mordecai.

Esther's job is not yet completed, though, because she still has to convince Ahasuerus to overturn the decree against the Jews. Since royal decrees cannot be overturned, the king issues a new decree according to Mordecai's dictation, which grants the Jews permission to defend themselves from all attacks on the 13th of Adar. The Jews rejoice at the news of their salvation. Indeed, when the 13th of Adar arrives, the Jews attack their enemies and kill the 10 sons of Haman and 500 others in Shushan (though they do not take any spoil). Hearing this news, the king asks Esther if she has any further requests. She asks him to grant the Jews of Shushan an extra day to kill their enemies. He grants it, and the Jews kill 300 more people in Shushan and 75,000 throughout the kingdom.

After the recounting of these events, the Megillah introduces the holiday of Purim and its main customs.

Commentary

It is hard to read *Midrash ha-Gadol* on Esther without also keeping in mind the verse it assigns to Vashti, immediately preceding it. Clearly, for the author of the midrash, even more than for the biblical author of the Book of Esther, Esther stands in contrast to Vashti. Here Vashti becomes the symbol of the deceptive nature of *chen* (grace) and the emptiness of *yofi* (beauty), while Esther becomes the apparent opposite, a pious *yirat Adonai* (God-fearing) woman.

This opposition of Esther and Vashti is troubling on many levels. First, it plays into familiar and long-established patterns of pitting women against each other and slotting them into a virgin-whore dichotomy. The opposition is also problematic as it pits Esther, the Jewish, God-fearing queen, against Vashti, the non-Jewish queen, who in the Rabbinic imagination becomes increasingly ugly (for example, she has a tail), evil, and identified with idolatry and the enemies of the Jews. She is also identified as the granddaughter of Nebuchadnezzar, the Babylonian general responsible for exiling the Jews.

This opposition of Esther and Vashti is also not the only obvious reading of the relationship between these characters that arises from the original story. If we take seriously the reading of the Vashti subplot as a foreshadowing of the Esther story, we quickly notice that Esther follows Vashti's lead in implicitly disobeying and over-turning two royal decrees—one against women and the other against the Jews. Read this way, the Megillah's women, Esther and Vashti, are more alike than different, in terms of the roles they play in the story.[1]

Esther and Vashti resist categorization as opposites in the story for another reason as well. Esther herself just doesn't neatly fit into one category of "woman." Despite the ways she has been flattened as a character by years of Purim spiels and pretty costumes, Queen Esther is a complex character.

She is a beauty queen and she is also a smart and God-fearing woman. There is no reason to accept the either/or of Proverbs or of later ages, regardless of the motivations of these forced choices. Early Jewish feminists almost vilified Esther as a symbol of all they were rejecting about idealized Jewish womanhood, while they reveled in their renewed discovery and embrace of Vashti. We have moved be-yond that perhaps necessary step and can now lay claim to the teach-ings of both Esther and Vashti.

Though Proverbs claims that beauty is empty, the Book of Esther has no problem with Esther's beauty. She is beautiful even in the Rabbinic mind, so beautiful that she stirred the hearts of both earthly and heavenly beings (*Esther Rabbah* 6:9). "Beauty" is the same word that, in the context of the midrash, is attributed to Vashti but not to Esther. Proverbs says that *chen* is false, but not the Book of Esther. Neither do the Rabbis in other contexts. So what do we do with the midrash's contrast of *chen* and *yirat Adonai* (God-fearing)?

Perhaps what we can take from the midrash is its insistence that there is a difference between a beauty that is superficial and a beauty that is deep and internally rooted. For the author of the midrash (and the author of Proverbs), it is clear that what makes a woman an *eishet chayil*, a true woman of valor and strength, is not her looks but her ac-tions. And indeed, it is Esther's actions that we must turn to for the best understanding of how she merits being called a God-fearing woman. (I also want to say that Vashti is an *eishet chayil*, but we already know this from reading the previous chapter.)

Though Rabbinic midrashim often embellish the nature of Esther's Jewishness and create out of her a good Jewish woman, according to the plain meaning of text, Esther spends much of the narrative as a closeted Jew who lives in the harem of a gentile king and then becomes his queen. The Rabbis suggest that during her time in the palace Esther is keeping kosher, observing Shabbat, and even going to the *mikveh* after every one of her visits to the king. But the very fact that the Rabbis create these details highlights their absence in the actual text. Esther is not portrayed as an observant Jew in any recognizable way.

But is she God-fearing? In order to assess what makes Esther God-fearing, we might do well to go back to the first time that someone is referred to this way in the Torah, in Genesis 22. Right after Abraham lifts his hand to slay Isaac, an angel of God calls out to him and tells him not to slay his son, because now he knows that Abraham is a fearer of God who would not withhold even his son from God.

What does this moment of high drama—a moment that remains very troubling to many modern readers—have to do with the story of Esther? Esther, unlike Abraham, is not asked to sacrifice her child. She does, though, confront the possibility of sacrificing herself. (Perhaps she is like Isaac, but a knowing Isaac.) She goes through a trial very different from Abraham's trial, but one that can also ultimately be read as proving her to be a God-fearer like him. She does not start out in that place. But somewhere in her conversation with Mordecai and in her acceptance of the reality that her people face, and of the potential role she can play in saving them, she is able to accept putting her life at **risk.. The** sense of the possibility of death is palpable in the text's choice of words. When Esther ends her reply to Mordecai with the words, "... if I am to perish, I shall perish!" (*avad'ti, avad'ti*, Esther 4:16), she doubles the sense of doom aroused when the same Hebrew root first appears in the text of Haman's plan to destroy (*l'abed*) all the Jews.

One crucial way in which Esther's story is different from Abraham's is that she never directly hears the voice of God. In this way the story of Esther is a diaspora story, a story perhaps more relevant to our own experience than is Abraham and Isaac's story. If Esther is going to become a woman of faith, she is going to do so in a textual world where God plays no explicit role. The only voice Esther hears, according to the Megillah, is the voice of her uncle, which is not enough to prepare her to risk her life. Esther, like Abraham, gets three days to prepare for her moment of potential sacrifice. But she does something very different with her three days. First, she asks for them directly. Second, she asks the community of the Jews of Shushan to join her in fasting.

This proclamation of a communal fast has been seen as the closest the Megillah gets to religion or God. If we read this as a religious moment in the text, it tells us—particularly when examined in contrast with Abraham's three days—that Esther's spirituality is both a solitary experience and an experience in which community plays a very significant role. She does not explicitly express a personal plea to God but she does express a plea for communal, ritual support. This suggests the potential importance of community in at least this diasporic expression of spirituality. It is also important because it counters many prevailing images of women's spirituality, and Jewish women's spirituality more specifically, as personal and private rather than communal. Here Esther manages to find a way to create an expression of spirituality that resists categorization, just as her character does more generally: Hers is a spirituality neither wholly personal nor fully public.

Furthermore, if we read Esther's actions as an expression of her faith and experience of God, they offer an interesting model. Hers is not a faith of sitting, waiting, and praying, nor is it a faith of simply doing. She needs the three days of fasting and then she acts decisively and courageously, on her own, without the explicit voice of God telling her what to do. In this sense she is like Moses, and like many prophets, for whom reluctance is an important step that ultimately leads to acceptance of mission.

For these reasons I think we can rejoice in the fact that the midrash has recognized Esther as a woman who teaches us something new about what it means to live with *yirat Adonai*—to live with a sense of divine awe. For Esther it meant recognizing her role as a redeemer of her people. It meant accepting a partnership with a God not directly seen or heard. It meant finding a balance between asking for the support of individuals and community and asking for time and space for personal spiritual practice. It also meant having a partner, in this case Mordecai, to help push along the process of spiritual development or awakening. I also see Esther's *yirat Adonai* as what makes it possible for her to be a religious innovator, who calls for a public fast that has made its way into the Jewish calendar and is still observed today (though only for one day).

There is one thing that *yirat Adonai* does not mean for Esther, which this modern reader wishes it could have meant: the development of a sharp sense of justice that would have demanded a different, less bloody end to the Megillah.

Esther Speaks

The first thing you will notice of course is the way they always try to pit us against one another. She, Vashti, the old queen—she was beautiful but her beauty was all lies. But I am Esther—"God-fearing," they call me—and for that, not my beauty, I am to be praised. It is true I am a believer. But don't think I got here all on faith. And Vashti, she's one of my teachers. Has been since the moment I learned of her refusal that night so long ago. So let me tell you a few things I've learned about beauty during my life in this palace. Then, once you've come to know me a bit better, you'll start to understand what all of this has to do with God.

My beauty is something I had to acquire slowly. Sure, I always saw how others looked at me and sometimes I liked it and sometimes it made me uncomfortable or confused and sometimes I just ignored it. But it wasn't mine. As you know I grew up without a mother or father and without any sisters or brothers either. It was only Mordecai and me.

He was good to me. We had many good times playing together in the fields on the outskirts of Shushan. I liked to climb trees and swim and fish—and Mordecai, he was never as fast a runner as I was, and he was pretty afraid of heights, but he kept good watch over me. We used to play for hours, and sometimes he would tell me stories about a Jerusalem he'd never seen. One thing we never talked about was what it meant—our being different from most of our neighbors. I knew we belonged to a people called the Jews, but Mordecai didn't like when I asked questions about what that meant. I could tell by the way his faced changed whenever I brought it up.

Things started to get harder when I turned 11 and my body began to change. I noticed Mordecai looking at me differently. Others on the streets, too, but the hardest for me was Mordecai. That look of nervousness he used to get when I asked him about the Jews—now it was on his face whenever he saw me. Then he started telling me I shouldn't be climbing trees anymore. He told me I had to start dressing differently and be sure to cover my legs, my elbows, even my hair. We started to bicker all the time. I was becoming a woman, and he had no idea what to do with that. Neither did I exactly. I guess we were both struggling against it in different ways, and we both had different ideas about what my transition to womanhood could and should mean. But instead of supporting each other we just fought, constantly.

It all came to a head the morning after Queen Vashti was kicked out of the palace. That "no" of hers traveled faster than any messenger on horseback or any homing pigeon could have brought a king's decree to the farthest reaches of the kingdom. For the first time in my life I felt I was part of something bigger than myself, a group called women. And suddenly we had won.

Because, you have to understand, Vashti was the most beautiful woman in all of Persia. Vashti was the one that every little girl—well, not me—but most every little girl in the kingdom wanted to be like when she grew up. And now suddenly Vashti was letting us in on a secret. Even if you were the most beautiful woman in all of Persia, even if you were queen and you could clearly mesmerize 1,000 knights and princes with one sway of your hips, you didn't have to. So that morning I decided to do something I'd never done before. I ran past the markers where I usually stopped. I ran the entire stretch around Shushan's walls in under two hours, by far the fastest I had ever made it. When I looked at the sun and realized what I had accomplished, I wanted to share it with Mordecai right away. So I kept running all the way home.

And then, crash. Mordecai was waiting for me with his own plan—born out of the same moment of Vashti's "no." I was to go to the palace. He suddenly believed it was the only way to save both of us. First I told him he was killing me. Then, after three days of not eating, I had a dream. At least I think it was a dream. What I know for sure is that I met God.

She was like a mixture of Vashti and my mother, though of course my mother died when I was two months old, so I don't really know what she looked like. But she looked like the warm smell of milk would look if it were God. And she wore the most amazing golden crown studded with rubies and diamonds and sapphires. She didn't say anything to me; I didn't say anything to her, but I knew she wanted me to go to the palace.. And suddenly I trusted her. It was like she was holding all of us in her hands and, in order to keep holding, she needed me in that palace. I woke from the dream with an unfamiliar name on my lips. Hadassah. I wasn't sure what it meant but I knew it was mine.

So there I was learning to put on makeup and shape my eyebrows and though having all these beautiful women around me was quite unexpectedly satisfying, I wasn't sure if this was what God had had in mind. I was smartening up, though. I was realizing that maybe I didn't have to fight growing up so much because there wasn't just one way to do it. I think being around all those different women was teaching me something. Every day I saw how varied women's bodies were, and I saw how many kinds of beauty the world is filled up with and how many different kinds of loving, too. Then one afternoon Hegai called me over to tell me it was my turn to go to the king. It was right then, in my confusion at the news, that God came to me again.

But this time I couldn't see her. It was more like a feeling in my body that started at my shoulders and slowly radiated up and down and across my shoulders, so that suddenly, I swear, I was taller than I had been in the morning. I knew I was ready. I also knew that I was going to stay pretty hidden myself, at least for a while. The king had a bad reputation for taking the wrong advice, drinking too much, and, of course, not respecting women. I would greet him with caution, but I would not share too much of myself until I could get a good sense of him. I would keep my Hebrew name to myself. Maybe Mordecai had been right after all.

You know what happened next. I became queen. Mordecai thought that made him something special, too, so he decided to stop bowing to Haman. That was all Haman needed. Suddenly I was queen of a kingdom planning to exterminate the Jews. They even picked a day for it. When I heard the other women talking, I knew I had to do something, but I had no idea what. Things had settled into such a routine, and I hadn't seen or thought about God in so long, I had almost forgotten about Her all together. I could barely even remember that I had ever had a Hebrew name.

When I first saw Mordecai at the gates of the palace, when I saw his face covered in ash, I just wanted to clean him up and send him new clothes. I wanted to send him away like he had sent me away. But then I started listening to him. And I looked at his face. And under the ash I saw a pride I had never seen before. Standing up to Haman had been good for him. He was scared but he wasn't hiding any more. He wasn't ashamed to sit there, right out on the ivory steps of the royal palace, and be an eyesore that refused to go away.

That's when I realized how much hiding had been hurting me, too. I needed to be who I was and be seen for who I was. I needed to show my face. As much as Vashti had needed not to be seen that night, that's how much I needed to be seen. And before I could be seen by the king, I needed to be seen by my people. I realized that I would only find the strength to risk recognizing my connection to them if they would first acknowledge me and my importance to them.

Do you know what I did? I asked the Jews to fast for three days, and those three days included the first day of Passover. The biggest risk I took was asking for that fast. I knew that a celebration of freedom would be an empty celebration if it was going to be observed by people sitting shivah for themselves. I knew many would question my author-ity, not wanting to listen to the pretty female face in the palace (an |intermarried woman, no less) on an issue of religious observance. But I asked anyway. And the people—they were so in need of hope that they complied.

It would be so much easier if my story ended there, but of course it doesn't. I had kept my secret for so long, I had dreaded this mo-ment for so long, and then I found the strength to take the risk. Soon the king knew about the plot. He was furious. Haman was falling all over me begging me for mercy. And then suddenly this man whose hands were grasping my ankles one second was dead on the stake the next.

I had revealed myself. I was back in touch with a sense of utter awe at the workings of God's world, a sense of awe at how much God was not up above me but right there in me, in my decision to act, in the community's decision to be with me in prayer and fasting. And then I faltered. We both did—Mordechai and I.

For then Mordechai showed up with that ring.

Suddenly he was living in Haman's house and wearing the king's ring, and he wanted me to go ask the king for more—for the right for the Jews to defend themselves. I did not even think to ask about the line between self-defense and aggression. I lost my voice.

Honestly, though, when I asked, I had no idea the rage I was un-leashing. I hadn't been out of the palace for a very long time. I didn't know what it had felt like to be a Jew out there in the provinces over the past year. Seventy-five thousand dead in one day—that much rage and fear—I could never have imagined it. Still the blood is on my hands, our hands.

That's why it feels kind of right to me that they memorialized me with a fast day—that's the one they named after me, not the day of merriment and celebration. Because even though I'm proud of what I did to save my people, and I too want to join the feasts of celebration, I have grown very suspicious of masquerade. I want us to look in the mirror and not be afraid to see who we are. When it is beauty we see, we should celebrate; and when it's power gone awry, we have to name that, too.

A Message from Esther

Live with your eyes wide open. Prepare yourself always to hear the voice that calls you to fulfill your mission. You are on this earth for a purpose, at least one. Meaning may not come like mine came in the Megillah version of things—urgent and clear in the voice of Mordecai, a life-or-death choice, my people's fate in the balance. It will probably not come that way.

But there is always a decree somewhere against somebody. There is always someone's fate in the balance: a whole people, one child, an entire species, a river.

So when you hear the knock at your door, when you become aware of a voice asking you to follow—before you answer, stop. First, remind yourself that you are not the only one in the universe hearing the call. The entire future does not rest on your shoulders alone.

Then let yourself hear it again. Maybe this voice *is* yours to answer. How will you know? It can take a long time to grow quiet enough to really listen. I gave myself three days. Give yourself more time. Be silent. Pray. Ask others to pray with you. Don't hide what you are going through. Find a partner to push you if you need to be pushed.

Remember also, that it is very likely that when you take a step forward you will at some point find yourself falling back. Life doesn't move only in one direction. When you enter a place of power, don't stay stationary in it. Keep asking questions.

Finally, live with awe. Stand back and let your mouth fill with praise for the beauty around you as naturally as it fills with air. Step forward and speak the truth when it needs to be spoken. Take action when it needs to be taken. Dare to believe that God needs you as a partner on this earth.

And let me tell you something. If you find a way to do these things, in the moments that you do, you will find yourself sitting up a bit taller in your chair. Because royalty isn't something that happens to you when an earthly king finds you beautiful. Royalty is something that comes to rest inside you when you honor its seed within you. Yes, it can slip away just as easily as a crown can tarnish if you stray from justice. Yes, there will always be more risk if you involve yourself in a solution rather than joining a problem. But there will also be more reward. This is what I know so far.

For Further Thought

Have your thoughts about Esther and Vashti changed over the course of your life? How?

Do you consider Esther to be God-fearing? What does that mean to you?

What part of the Esther story (in the Book of Esther) do you like best and what part do you find most troubling?

Gail Twersky Reimer chronicles the different perspectives on Esther in "Eschewing Esther/Embracing Esther: The Changing Representation of Biblical Heroines," a chapter in *Talking Back: Images of Jewish Women in American Popular Culture*, edited by Joyce Antler (Hanover, NH: Brandeis University Press, 1998), pages 207–219.

Rabbi Susan Schnur deals with Esther as a controversial figure for Jewish women in "Our [Meaning Women's] Book-of-Esther Problem," in *Best Contemporary Jewish Writing*, edited by Michael Lerner (San Francisco: Jossey-Bass, 2001), pages 205–212.

Epilogue
The Rest of the Women

תְּנוּ־לָהּ מִפְּרִי יָדֶיהָ וִיהַלְלוּהָ בַשְּׁעָרִים מַעֲשֶׂיהָ:

"Extol her for the fruit of her hand, and let her works praise her in the gates" (Prov. 31:31).

תנו לה מפרי ידיה, לרבות שאר כל הנשים הצדיקות והכשרות שבעולם. ד"א תנו לה מפרי ידיה, זו כנסת ישראל שנקראו כולם צדיקים, שנאמר ועמך כולם צדיקים. תנו רבנן גדולה הבטחה שהבטיח הקב"ה לנשים הצדיקות יתר מן האנשים. דכתיב נשים שאננות קומנה שמענה קולי בנות בוטחות האזנה אמרתי. אמר ליה רב לרבי חייא האני נשי במאי זכאן לעלמא דאתי, אמר ליה באקרויי בנוהי בבי כנשתא ובאמנויי בדרבנן ומנטרין לגבריהו עד דאתו מבי מדרשא ומשריאן בני בי רב בבתיהי. תנו רבנן כל הנושא אשה כשרה כאלו קיים כל התורה כולה מעלף עד תיו, שכך שלמה משבחה בפרשת אשת חיל מאלף עד תיו. תחלתה אשת חיל וסופה אשה יראת ה' היא תתהלל, וכל כך בבעלי תורה אנשי חיל יראי אלהים. ובזכותן מזכיר הקב"ה לישראל חסדו ואמתו, שנאמר זכר חסדו ואמונתו לבית ישראל. וכן הוא אומר כה תאמר לבית יעקב, אלו הנשים. ותגיד לבני ישראל, אלו האנשים.

Extol her for the fruit of her hand, this is the rest of the righteous and proper women of the world. Another interpretation: *Extol her for the fruit of her hand*, this is the Community of Israel, all of whom are called righteous, as it is said, "And your people, all of them righteous ... are ... My handiwork in which I glory" (Isa. 60:21). The Rabbis taught, God, Blessed be He, promised a greater promise to righteous women than to men. As it is written, "You carefree women, / Attend, hear my words! / You confident ladies, / Give ear to my speech "(Isa. 32:9). Rav said to Rabbi Chiya, "Why do women merit eternal life?" Rabbi Chiya said, "Because they bring their children to the synagogue to learn Scripture and they send their husbands to the study hall to learn and because they wait for their husbands until they come home from study hall." The Rabbis taught that everyone who marries a proper woman, it is as if he brought the whole Torah into being, from *alef* to *tav*, just as Solomon sang praises in the portion on "Eishet Chayil," from *alef* to *tav*. The beginning of the poem is "What a rare find is a capable wife!" and the end is "It is for her fear of the Lord / That a woman is to be praised" (Prov. 31:10–31), and how much this is true for those who embody the Torah, "capable men who fear God, trustworthy men" (Exod. 18:21). And by the merit of the women, God, Blessed be He, remembers Israel in lovingkindness and truth, as it is said, "He was mindful of His steadfast love and faithfulness toward the house of Israel" (Ps. 98:3). "Thus you shall say to the house of Jacob ..." (Exod. 19:3), these are the women. "and declare to the Children of Israel" (19:3), these are the men.

—*Midrash ha-Gadol*

The Rest of the Women Speak

How thoughtful the Rabbis were in interpreting this verse as they do! It shows how much they must have respected their mothers, sisters, wives, and daughters to mention all the rest of us righteous women of the world in closing. Of course, it did go without saying that they valued the way we spoke Torah, as it was always on our tongues. They learned from us, too, and they often told us that, and yet something kept them from writing our words down. We have some ideas, and probably you do too, as to why that was. And still is, we see.

How unfortunate that there are not enough letters in the alef-bet to include the myriads of *nashei chayil* (women of valor) on earth! We end this book with a challenge:

Who can find the rest of us women, numerous as the stars of heaven and the sands on the seashore? Who can find the ones whom the writers of *Midrash ha-Gadol* have chosen not to name, the ones whose stories may pose a threat to men, the ones who never become wives at all, the ones whose legacies are not portrayed in stories?

This list of 22—23, including Vashti—is only a beginning. It is up to you to add to it. Think of women whose hands have produced fruit that has been unnoticed or unappreciated, misunderstood, or misconstrued for so long that it has rotted. Think of women who work hard every day in their kitchens, studios, offices; on the road; and on the land. It is up to you to bring their stories to the gates, to the public arena, to the written page, and into your own lives. Expand the list with stories of the many unsung *neshei chayil* as you invite more and more women from the Bible, from all of Jewish history, and from the entire world, to speak. Whoever adds to this list is to be praised!

Contributors

PENINA ADELMAN lives in Boston, where she is a resident scholar at the Women's Studies Research Center at Brandeis University. Her first book, *Miriam's Well*, helped launch the Rosh Hodesh movement, which today involves thousands of American Jewish women. She is the author of *The Bible from Alef to Tav*, a finalist for the 1999 National Jewish Picture Book Award, and co-author of *The JGirl's Guide, The Young Jewish Woman's Handbook for Coming of Age*.

SUSAN BERRIN is the editor of *Sh'ma: A Journal of Jewish Responsibility*, a monthly journal addressing cutting-edge issues facing North American Jewry. She is also the editor of two landmark Jewish anthologies, *Celebrating the New Moon: A Rosh Chodesh Anthology* and *A Heart of Wisdom: Making the Jewish Journey from Midlife through the Elder Years*. She lectures frequently about Rosh Chodesh, as well as Jewish midlife and elder issues. Susan lives with her three children in Newton, Massachusetts.

ERICA BROWN is the scholar-in-residence for The Jewish Federation of Greater Washington and director of its Jewish Leadership Institute. She formerly served as scholar-in-residence for the Federation of Boston. Erica did her undergraduate studies at Yeshiva University and continued her graduate work at the University of London and Harvard University. She was a Jerusalem Fellow and is a faculty member of the Wexner Heritage Foundation. She has been teaching Jewish adult education for 16 years and has lectured widely in the United States, London, and Israel, in addition to extensive writing in journals of education and Jewish studies. She has chapters in *Jewish Legal Writings by Women, Torah of the Mothers*, and *Wisdom from All of My Teachers*, and writes a weekly Internet essay on the Torah portion of the week. Erica is the author of the forthcoming book, *The Sacred Canvas: The Hebrew Bible in the Eyes of the Artist*. She lives in Silver Spring, Maryland, with her husband and four children.

TAMARA COHEN is a Jewish feminist writer, activist, and educator. She is the director of Lesbian, Gay, Bisexual, and Transgender Affairs at the University of Florida and the monthly spiritual leader of the Greater Washington Connecticut Coalition for Jewish Life. Tamara recently directed a national survey of Jewish women and feminism for Ma'yan: The Jewish Women's Project. Tamara continues to work with Jewish women in the Former Soviet Union through Project Kesher. She serves on the boards of Joshua Venture and Brit Tzedek V'Shalom and is the editor of the feminist haggadah *The Journey Continues*, as well as an author of numerous articles on Jewish women's spirituality.

ANDREA COHEN-KIENER is the director of the InterReligious Eco-Justice Network, a faith-based initiative in environmental theology and practice, and the spiritual leader of Congregation P'nai Or of Central Connecticut. She has degrees in Hebrew literature, secondary education, and pastoral counseling. Andrea was ordained as a rabbi in July 2000 by the Alliance for Jewish Renewal. She lectures frequently on issues in congregational worship, Jewish feminism, ecology, communication, and spirituality. She is the translator of *Conscious Community: A Guide to Inner Work*, by Reb Kalonymus Kalman Shapira, and coauthor of *For All Who Call: A Guide to Enhancing Prayer Instruction*.

NURIT EINI-PINDYCK, MFA, MA, is an artist who is a resident scholar at the Brandeis University Women's Studies Research Center. Her work is interdisciplinary, draws on cultural studies, and incorporates text, sound, performance, and audience participation. Her interactive art installations have included *Remember: A Woman's Perspective on the Holocaust* (Brandeis University, 1999) and *House of Gender: A Feminist Jewish Woman Confronting Biblical and Talmudic Texts* (Tufts University, 2001, and Brandeis University, WSRC Studio, 2002). She is currently expanding her repertoire of women's narratives in a collaborative work about the transformative power in the telling of women's narratives.

NAOMI GRAETZ teaches English at Ben Gurion University of the Negev and lectures widely on the subject of women in the Bible and midrash. She is the author of *Silence Is Deadly: Judaism Confronts Wifebeating; S/He Created Them: Feminist Retellings of Biblical Stories; The Rabbi's Wife Plays at Murder;* and *Unlocking the Garden: A Feminist Jewish Look at the Bible, Midrash and God.*

JUDITH KATES, PhD, is a professor of Jewish women's studies at Hebrew College, Newton, Massachusetts. Her teaching and writing focus on classical Jewish texts, especially Bible and midrash. She received a PhD in comparative literature from Harvard University, where she also taught literature for 11 years. Currently, she is a member of the core faculty of the new Rabbinical School at Hebrew College and she teaches Bible and Rabbinics for adults in the Jewish community. She is coeditor with Gail Twersky Reimer of *Reading Ruth: Contemporary Women Reclaim a Sacred Story* and of *Beginning Anew: A Woman's Companion to the High Holy Days.* In 1998 Dr. Kates received the Keter Torah Award for outstanding educators from the Bureau of Jewish Education of Greater Boston.

IRIT KOREN uses her study of the intersection of gender and religion as an exegetical lens through which she approaches and explicates Jewish texts and society. She is currently writing her doctoral dissertation in gender studies at Bar Ilan University on the ways in which religious women resist and challenge the Orthodox wedding ritual. Koren's first book, *Closet within a Closet: Stories of Orthodox Homosexuals,* was published by the Israeli publisher Yediot Aharonot in 2003. Koren teaches courses on Judaism and feminism at the College of Tel Aviv–Jaffa.

MARSHA PRAVDER MIRKIN, PhD, a clinical psychologist, is a resident scholar at Brandeis University Women's Studies Research Center and on the faculty of the Social Science Department at Lasell College, Newton, Massachusetts. Dr. Mirkin provides workshops and teaches about psychological insights into Torah. Her most recent book, *The Women Who Danced by the Sea: Finding Ourselves in the Stories of Our Biblical Foremothers*, explores how biblical characters give us insights into our relationships with ourselves, others, and the Divine. She is the editor of four books and has written numerous articles and book chapters. Her writing interests include psychological interpretations of Torah as well as the social and political contexts of psychotherapy.

HAVIVA NER-DAVID is a writer, teacher, and student who is completing her doctorate at Bar Ilan University—writing about *niddah*—as well as studying for Orthodox *semikhah* (ordination). Her book, *Life on the Fringes: A Feminist Journey towards Traditional Rabbinic Ordination*, goes back and forth between her exploration of halakhic texts dealing with issues of women and Judaism and her personal experiences trying to harmonize the Jewish tradition and feminism. Haviva is active in a number of Jewish women's causes, such as Women of the Wall, a group struggling for the right to pray as a women's *tefillah* (prayer) group at the Kotel (Western Wall). She also counsels couples on *niddah* observance. She lives in Jerusalem with her husband and five children.

ROSIE ROSENZWEIG is an author and poet who is a resident scholar at the Women's Studies Research Center at Brandeis University. She has written *A Jewish Mother in Shangri-la*, about her journey to Asia to meet her son's Buddhist gurus. An ordained meditation teacher, she founded *Mitbonnenim*, a meditation group at Brandeis. She is currently working on a book on the process of creativity.

STEPHANIE NEWMAN SAMUELS teaches TANAKH (Jewish Bible) to middle school students at the Maimonides School in Brookline, Massachusetts. In addition to her teaching, she also mentors novice teachers through the Rabbi Joseph B. Soloveitchik Institute's Teacher Training Program. She holds an MA in medieval Jewish history from New York University and a BA in English literature and education from Barnard College. She resides in Newton, Massachusetts, with her husband and three sons.

LEAH SHAKDIEL was born in 1951 in Jerusalem to a family of modern Orthodox pioneers. She moved to Yeruham, a small development town in the Negev, in 1978 with a group committed to *halakhah* (Jewish law and observance), social responsibility, peace, and ecology. She has a BA from Bar Ilan University in English and French literatures. In 1988 she became Israel's first female member of Yeruham's municipal religious council, following a successful struggle that ended with a landmark Supreme Court decision. As a School for Educational Leadership fellow from 1994–1996, she developed a model for feminist pedagogy for Israel. She currently teaches in Be'er (A Well), a Torah study program for young religious women in Yeruham and in Sapir College near Sderot. She is married and has three children.

RUTH H. SOHN teaches Jewish Studies in Los Angeles at the Milken Community High School and in various settings for adult students. Her articles, biblical commentary, midrashim, and poetry have appeared in books, periodicals, and prayer books, including *Reading Ruth: Contemporary Women Reclaim a Sacred Story*, edited by Judith A. Kates and Gail Twersky Reimer, and *Kol Haneshama*, the Reconstructionist prayer book. Ruth was ordained at Hebrew Union College-Jewish Institute of Religion in 1982. She worked as a Hillel rabbi at Columbia University and Boston University for 10 years before moving to Los Angeles, where she lives with her husband and three children.

SAVINA J. TEUBAL is the author of the groundbreaking works *Sarah the Priestess: The First Matriarch of Genesis* and *Ancient Sisterhood:*

The Lost Tradition of Hagar and Sarah and has contributed many articles and essays to books and magazines on women in the Bible. She is the cofounder of the organization Sarah's Tent: Revitalizing Jewish Community through Shared Sacred Experience, ongoing since 1995.

Savina is also the creator of the original *Simchat Hochmah* (Joy of Wisdom), a ritual that celebrates the transition from adult to elder. Savina wrote the lyrics, with Debbie Friedman, to the now popular "L'chi Lach," the theme song of her *Simchat Hochmah*.

Notes

Introduction

1. This concept, called "intertextuality," is discussed at length in Daniel Boyarin, *Intertextuality and the Reading of Midrash* (Bloomington, IN: Indiana University Press, 1994).

2. There are other later versions of the midrash on "Eishet Chayil." One is called *Midrash Mishlei* (Midrash on Proverbs), probably edited after the final editing of the Babylonian Talmud, the most significant editions in print being a Constantinople version from 1517, a Venice version from 1547, and a Prague version from 1613. The other is called *Midrash Eishet Chayil* (Midrash Woman of Valor,) a collection based on *Midrash HaGadol*, also Yemenite, from 1428. They include other women such as Zipporah (wife of Moses), Tamar (consort of Judah), Bruriah (respected teacher in the Talmud and wife of Rabbi Meir), and Rachel, wife of Rabbi Akiba. Yael Levine Katz wrote her dissertation, "Midreshei Eshet Hayil" (PhD diss., University of Bar-Ilan, 1992), on these midrashim.

3. Arlene Agus, "This Month Is for You" in Elizabeth Koltun, ed., *The Jewish Woman: New Perspectives* (New York: Schocken, 1976), 84-93.

4. Penina Adelman, "A Drink from Miriam's Cup: Invention of Tradition among Jewish Women" in Maurie Sacks, ed., *Active Voices: Women in Jewish Culture* (Chicago: University of Illinois Press, 1995), 109-124.

5. See Richard Handler and Jocelyn Linnekin, "Tradition, Genuine or Spurious," *Journal of American Folklore* 97, no. 385 (1984): 287; and Allan Handon, "The Making of the Maori: Culture Invention and Its Logic," *American Anthropologist* 91 (1989), 895.

Chapter 1   Wife of Noah

1. Author's translation.

2. Tillie Olsen, *Silences* (New York: Dell Publishing, 1978; The Feminist Press, 2003), 35.

Chapter 3   Rebekah

1. For more on Lilith, see Louis Ginzberg's *Legends of the Jews* (Philadelphia: The Jewish Publication Society, 1938), 1:65.

Chapter 5   Rachel

1. Athalya Brenner, ed., "Female Social Behavior: Two Descriptive Patterns within 'The Birth of a Hero' Paradigm," in *The Feminist Companion to the Bible* (Sheffield, UK: Sheffield Academic Press, 1993), 203–221.
2. Ibid.
3. Rabbi Yitzchak Arma, in Nechama Leibovitz, *Commentaries on Genesis* [in Hebrew] (Jerusalem: World Zionist Organization, 1967), 223.

Chapter 6   Batya

1. A reference to God's outstretched arm mentioned several times in the Maggid section of the Haggadah.
2. I would like to thank Dr. Steven Copeland, professor of Jewish Thought and Education at Hebrew College, Brookline, MA, for an imaginative discussion on the theme of redemption and these three scarcely-mentioned women.
3. Louis Ginzberg, *Legends of the Jews* (Philadelphia: The Jewish Publication Society, 1938), 2:271, n. 61.

Chapter 8   Miriam

1. According to Rashi, when Zipporah hears that some of the men will gain prophetic status, she exclaims that she pities their wives because the husbands will separate them just as Moses separated from her. Miriam overhears Zipporah's statement and recognizes that Zipporah is being treated poorly. Also in *Beha'aloscha* 738, in the Babylonian Talmud, Zipporah tells Miriam that she feels sorry for the wives of the newly appointed elders because the elders will separate from them. And in *Habbukuk* 3:7 it says that it's likely that Kushite means from Kushan, another word for Midean, pointing to Zipporah as the Kushite woman.
2. I would like to thank Alan Shapiro for this idea.
3. For more on the legend of Miriam's Well, see Eliahu Kitov, *The Book of our Heritage* (New York: Feldheim, 1978), 2:157–162.

Chapter 9   Hannah

1. Author's translation.
2. "Compassion" here is *rachamim* in Hebrew, which is from the same root as *rechem*.

Chapter 10   Yael

1. Also spelled "Jael."

Chapter 11   Widow from Tzarephath

1. Author's translation.
2. It is noteworthy that the father-and-son trial in Genesis 22 (Abraham and Isaac) is preceded by a parallel mother-and-son trial in Genesis 21 (Hagar and Ishamel). These two chapters are thus assigned as reading for the first and second days of Rosh Hashanah (Jewish New Year), respectively. For more on this, see Gail Twersky Reimer and Judith A. Kates, eds., *Beginning Anew: A Woman's Companion to the High Holidays*, (New York: Simon & Schuster, 1997), 32–34, 44–54. Moreover, the absence of Sarah from this sequence gave rise to later constructs of her Pietà, in midrash, modern literature, and art. See David Sperber and Anat Chen, "'But the Weeping of the Mother will be for Evermore,' The Appearance of Sarah in the Akedah Narrative in Israeli Art" [in Hebrew] (Israel: Bar Ilan University, 1997). See also Rachel Ofer, "No Games of Hide-and-Seek with Moms" [in Hebrew], *Kolech* 57, Rosh Hashanah 5763.
3. Author's translation.
4. Author's translation.
5. Author's translation.
6. *Pirkei d'Rabbi Eliezer* 32, *Yalkut Shim'oni* 209.
7. Only after I chose to write about the Zarephit did I realize that her verse in Proverbs 31 is the one we daughters chose for our mother's gravestone. I have written this in memory of Esther Koral Shakdiel (1910–1992), who was widowed when I, her youngest, was five years old. Only after I had finished writing the entire chapter did I realize that I had painted the Zarephit's portrait here after my mother and her various strengths, including her decision not to remarry.
8. The sages of the Talmud understood that the Zarephit was the mother of Jonah the prophet.

Chapter 13   Rachav

1. Also spelled "Rahab."
2. The Red Sea is a misnomer. The Hebrew, *Yam Suf*, means Sea of Reeds.

A typographical error in the English translation rendered it Red Sea and that mistake has continued until today.

Chapter 15   Michal

1. Author's translation.
2. Cheryl Exum, *Fragmented Women: Feminist (Sub)versions of Biblical Narratives* (Valley Forge, PA: Trinity Press International, 1993).
3. Ilana Pardes, *Countertraditions in the Bible: A Feminist Approach* (Cambridge, MA: Harvard University Press, 1992), 77.

Chapter 16   Hatzlelponi

1. Also spelled Hazlelponi. I assume the name of the woman to be Hatzlelponi, based on the grammatical construct of the name in 1 Chronicles 4:3. The illuminating factor is the missing dot in the letter *"tzadi"* (*tz*). It excludes the alternative readings of the name as Tzlelpon, Tzlelponi, or Tzlelponit. According to these alternative readings, the "ha" in "Hatzlelponi" is actually the Hebrew definite article (the). This treatment of the name seems at first glance to be consistent with other cases, such as the Shunammite ("the one from Shunem" in 2 Kings 4:36). A closer look shows that the difference between haShunammite (meaning the Shunammite) and Hazlelponi lies in this small dot that signals the appearance of the definite article in Hebrew and appears in haShunammite, but not in Hatzlelponi.
2. One who is dedicated to God and who doesn't cut his hair or drink alcohol.
3. The story about Tamar and Judah appears in Genesis 38 and takes place when Joseph is in Egypt, following the incident in which his brothers sold him to foreign traders. Tamar was Judah's widowed daughter-in-law, and she tricked him into having sexual intercourse with her while disguised as a harlot. Being a widow with no children, Tamar schemed a way to force Judah to perform the law of levirate marriage. According to this biblical law stated in Deuteronomy 25:5–10, a relative (the *levir*) of the deceased husband (primarily a brother) has the duty to marry the childless widow (the levirate) and impregnate her. The firstborn son from this union is considered the son of the deceased brother, thus keeping the deceased's name alive. The son is entitled to the lot that the deceased man would have inherited. In the biblical patriarchal structure this law served as a social and economic protection to women in ensuring their place in their marital clan. From this one sexual encounter between Judah and Tamar, Tamar gave birth to twin sons, Perez and Zerah. Hatzlelponi and King David were both among the descendents of Perez.
4. "And you shall no longer be called Abram, but your name shall be Abrah-am, for I make you a father of a multitude of nations" (Gen. 17:5). "And God said to Abraham: As for your wife Sarai, you shall not call her Sarai, but her name shall be Sara-h. ... She shall give rise to nations" (Gen. 17:15,16).

Chapter 17   Elisheba

1. Author's translation.

2. According to Yael Levin, who wrote her doctoral thesis on this midrash on "Eishet Chayil," it was common for only the first part of a line to be mentioned. The assumption was that anyone studying the midrash automatically knew the entire line, so it was not necessary to quote the whole thing. It was a kind of shorthand for those who knew the Bible by heart, standard for any literate Jew of the postbiblical era.

3. In *Sotah* 11b and *Sifre* on Numbers 78, there is a midrash that states that one of the midwives mentioned in Exodus 1:15 was Elisheba.

Chapter 18   Serach

1. Also spelled "Serah."

2. *The Stone Edition Chumash* (New York: Mesorah Publications, Ltd., 1998), 883.

3. *Targum* Yonasan.

4. J.D. Eisenstein, *Otzar ha-Midrashim* (Israel, 1929), 50.

5. *Yalkut Shimoni* on Genesis 12:64.

6. *Yalkut Shimoni* on Deuteronomy 34.

7. A name of God meaning "without end, limitless, infinite."

Chapter 21   Ruth

1. Levirate marriage is the practice of the brother of a deceased man who had no children marrying the widow of the deceased so that the name of the deceased will be carried on.

Chapter 22a   Queen Vashti

1. There is speculation that Ahasuerus was actually Xerxes (485–465 B.C.E.), King of Persia.

Chapter 22b   Esther

1. See Arthur Waskow, *Seasons of Our Joy* (Boston: Beacon Press, 1982), for an early articulation of this reading of the stories intertwining feminist and Jewish themes, or "jokes," as Waskow puts it.

Midrash ha-Gadol

מדרש הגדול

מדרש הגדול
חיי שרה, כ״ה:א

אשת חיל מי ימצא זו אשתו שלנח שהיתה מצדקת את בעלה כשאמר לו הקב״ה כי אתך ראיתי צדיק לפני. ורחוק מפנינים מכרה, שהיתה היא וכלותיה מעשיהן רחוקין ממעשה דור המבול. — בטח בה לב בעלה, זו שרה שהיה לבו שלאברהם בטוח בה שאמר לה אמרי לי אחי הוא. ושלל לא יחסר, שהיתה מכנסת את האורחין תחת כנפי השכינה. — גמלתהו טוב ולא רע, זו רבקה. וכי מה גמול גמלה ליצחק, שבשעה ששלח אברהם את עבדו ואמרו נקרא לנער ונשאלה את פיה, מנהגו שלעולם אדם משיא את בתו לאחד אפלו השיאה לעבד מתביישת היא לומר כלום, אבל רבקה כשאמרו לה התלכי עם האיש הזה ותאמר אלך. ד״א שהיו מעשיה דומין למעשה שרה, דכתיב ויביאה יצחק האהלה שרה אמו. — דרשה צמר ופשתים, זו לאה שראתה ברוח הקדש שעתיד לצאת ממנה בן שהוא מתיר דבר אסור בישראל. ואיזה, זה לוי. בישראל כתיב לא תלבש שעטנז ובאהרן כתיב ועשו את האפד שהב תכלת וארגמן ותולעת שני ושש. והיתה מתחמדת לינשא ליעקב ושדלה באחותה ויכלה. — היתה כאניות סוחר, זו רחל שאמרה ליעקב הבה לי בנים ואם אין מתה אנכי. אמר לה יעקב התחת אלהים אנכי. ואין תחת אלא לשון ביוש, כעניין שנאמר חתו ובשו. אמר לו הקב״ה לא דייך שלא בקשת רחמים על הצדקת הזו אלא שבייישתה, חייך שאני זוכרה ונותן לה בן ואינו נקרא על שמך. הדא היא ויזכר אלהים את רחל ולא אמר את יעקב. — ותקם בעוד לילה, זו בתיה בת פרעה שראתה ברוח הקדש שעתיד מושיען שלישראל להתגדל על ידיה והיתה משכמת ומערבת היא ונערותיה להטייל על היאור וכיון שבא משה לידה נתן לה הקב״ה מה שביקשה ושמחה הרבה, דכתיב ותפתח ותראהו את הילד. — זממה שדה ותקחהו, זו יוכבד שעל ידיה נקראו ישראל כרמו שלהקב״ה, שנאמר כי כרם ה׳ צבאות בית ישראל. ולמה נקרא שמה יוכבד, שהיו פניה דומין לזיו הכבוד. — חגרה בעוז מתניה, זו מרים שאמרה לאביה כשגירש את אמה קשים גזירותיך משלפרעה. הוא גזר על הזכרים ואתה גזרתה על הזכרים ועל הנקיבות, הוא רשע ספק גזירותיו מתקיימין ספק אין מתקיימין ואתה צדיק ותגזר ואמר ויקם לך. ולא עוד אלא שראיתי שעתיד לצאת ממך מי שמושיע את ישראל. מיד החזיר אשתו וכיון שילדה משה והשליכתו ליאר טפחה לה אמה על פניה

ואמרה לה היכן נבואתיך, מיד ותתצב אחותו מרחק, שעמדה בנבואתה. —
טעמה כי טוב סחרה, זו חנה שטעמה טעם תפלה, שנאמר ואשפך את
נפשי. לא יכבה בלילה נרה, ונר אלהים טרם יכבה ושמואל שוכב בהיכל
ה'. — ידיה שלחה בכישור, זו יעל שבא סיסרא לידה שנאמר וסיסרא נס
ברגליו. ותפתח את נוד החלב ותשקהו. לידע אם דעתו נכונה עליו אם
לאו. שתה ונשתכר תבעה לדבר עבירה, מיד ותתקע היתד ברקתו. וכתיב
ידה ליתד תשלחנה וימינה להלמות עמלים. לפי כך נתברכה באהלי תורה
בבתי כנסיות ובבתי מדרשות, שנאמר תברך מנשים יעל. — כפה פרשה
לעני, זו צרפית שאמר לה אליהו תני לי מעט מים. ומה שכר נטלה על כך,
כד הקמח לא תכלה וצפחת השמן לא תחסר. — וידיה שלחה לאביון, זו
נעמי שהכניסה את רות תחת כנפי השכינה, דכתיב ותרא כי מתאמצת היא
ללכת אתה ותחדל לדבר אליה. — לא תירא לביתה משלג, זו רחב
שהחביאה את המרגלים. ומי היו ר' יוסי אומר זה כלב ופינחס. ויש אומרין
פרץ וזרח היו כשבקשה מהן אות אמר לה זרח את תקות חוט השני הזה
תקשרי בחלון, זה שנבדקתי בו במעי אמי, דכתיב ותקשר על ידו שני. לפי
כך זכתה ויצאו ממנה עשרה כהנים. ואלו הן חלקיה ירמיה שריה מחסיה
ברוך נריה חנמאל שלום בוזי יחזקאל. ויש אומרין אף חולדה הנביאה,
דכתיב אשת שלום בן תקוה בן חרחס ולהלן הוא אומר את תקות חוט
השני. — מרבדים עשתה לה, זו שבע שראת ברוח הקדש שעתיד
לצאת ממנה בן שהוא אומר שלשת אלפים משל דכתיב ויחכם מכל האדם. —
נודע בשערים בעלה, זו מיכל שהצילה לדוד בעלה מן המיתה בשלוח
שאול וישמרו את הבית להמיתו ותאמר חולה הוא. ולבסוף נודע הדבר
אמר לה אביה שקרת בי, אמרה לו כדי להצילך מדם נקי. מה הוא אומר
כי מי שלח ידו במשיח ה' ונקה. — סדין עשתה ותמכר, זו הצללפונית
והיא אמו שלשמשון, דכתיב בני פרץ בן יהודה ואלה בני עיטם יזרעאל
וישמא וידבש ושם אחותם הצללפוני. משוכני צרעה ואשתאול. וכתיב התם
אלה משפחות הצרעתי, שנגלה עליה המלאך שני פעמים שלא בפני בעלה
וכך אמרה לבעלה לו חפץ ה' להמיתנו. וחגור נתנה לכנעני, שהיתה
טווה ומוכרת בשוק כמה דאת אמר כנעניה נכבדי ארץ. — עוז והדר לבושה,
זו אלישבע שראת ארבע שמחות ביום אחד. יבמה מלך, אישה כהן גדול,
אחיה נשיא, בניה סגני כהונה. — פיה פתחה בחכמה, זו שרח בת אשר
שאמרה ליואב אנכי שלומי אמוני ישראל, שהיא שקולה כנגד עיר ואם
בישראל. — צופיה הליכות ביתה, זו אשת עובדיה דכתיב ואשה אחת מנשי
בני הנביאים צעקה אל אלישע לאמר, שאמרה אין לי לילך אלא לאלישע.
הלכה ואמרה לו רבי לא אתה מבני הנביאים שהחביא עובדיה בעלי
במערה, אמר לה הין מה טיבך. אמרה לו בקש עלי רחמים ואתפרנס ממעשי
ידי ואל אצטרך לבריות. באותה שעה בירכה אלישע ונתברכה ונתפרנסה
ממעשה ידיה. לכך נאמר ולחם עצלות לא תאכל. ונעשה לה נס בתוך נס. —

קמו בניה ויאשרוה, זו שונמית שאמרה לבעלה הנה נא ידעתי כי איש אלהים
קדוש הוא. אמר ר' יוסי בר חנינה מכאן שהאשה מכרת באורחין יתר מן
האיש. קדוש הוא מנא ידעא, רב ושמואל חד אמר סדין שלפשתן הציעה לו
תחתיו ולא ראתה עליו קרי. ואידך אמר שלא ראתה זבוב על שלחנו. עובר
עלינו תמיד, אמר ר' יוסי בר חנינה אמרה לאישה כל המכניס תלמיד חכמים
לתוך ביתו ומאכילו ומשקהו ומהניהו מנכסיו מעלה עליו הכתוב כאלו הקריב
תמידין. נעשה נא עליית קיר קטנה, רב ושמואל חד אמר פרועה היתה
וקירוה וחד אמר אכסדרה היתה וחלקוה לשנים בקיר. בשלמא למאן דאמר
אכסדרה היתה וחלקוה לשנים הינו דכתיב קיר, אלא למאן דאמר פרועה היתה
וקירוה מאי קיר, על שם קירוי. בשלמא למאן דאמר עלייה הינו דכתיב
עליית, אלא למאן דאמר אכסדרה מאי עלייה, מעולה שבבתים. ונעשה לה נס
וילדה ומת הילד והחיה אותו אלישע. ולא נענה חזקיה אלא בשבילה,
דכתיב ויסב פניו אל הקיר ויתפלל אל ה'. מאי קיר, אמר ריש לקיש
שהתפלל מקירות לבו, שנאמר מעי מעי אוחילה קירות לבי הומה לי לבי. ר'
לוי אומר שהתפלל על עסקי קיר. אמר לפניו רבונו שלעולם ומה השונמית
שלא עשתה לפניך אלא קיר אחת קטנה לאלישע החייתה את בנה, אבי אבא
שחיפה את ההיכל כולו בטבלאות שלזהב טהור על אחת כמה וכמה. — רבות
בנות עשו חיל, זו רות שזכת ויצא ממנה דוד ובניו הישרים. אמר ר'
יוחנן מאי רות, שיצא ממנה דוד שרוה להקב"ה בשירות ותשבחות. ואת
עלית על כלנה, שאמר לה בעז בתי היטבת חסדך האחרון מן הראשון. —
שקר החן והבל היופי, זו ושתי. — אשה יראת ה' היא תתהלל, זו אסתר
וישם כתר מלכות בראשה וימליכה תחת ושתי. — תנו לה מפרי ידיה,
לרבות שאר כל הנשים הצדיקות והכשרות שבעולם. ד"א תנו לה מפרי
ידיה, זו כנסת ישראל שנקראו כולם צדיקים, שנאמר ועמך כולם צדיקים.
תנו רבנן גדולה הבטחה שהבטיח הקב"ה לנשים הצדיקות יתר מן
האנשים. דכתיב נשים שאננות קומנה שמענה קולי בנות בוטחות האזנה
אמרתי. אמר ליה רב לרבי חייא האני נשי במאי זכאן לעלמא דאתי, אמר
ליה באקרויי בנוהי בבי כנשתא ובאמנויי בדרבנן ומנטרין לגבריהו עד
דאתו מבי מדרשא ומשריאן בני בי רב בבתיהי. תנו רבנן כל הנושא
אשה כשרה כאלו קיים כל התורה כולה מעלף עד תיו, שכך שלמה משבחה
בפרשת אשת חיל מאלף עד תיו. תחלתה אשת חיל וסופה אשה יראת ה'
היא תתהלל, וכל כך בבעלי תורה אנשי חיל יראי אלהים. ובזכותן מזכיר
הקב"ה לישראל חסדו ואמתו, שנאמר זכר חסדו ואמונתו לבית ישראל.
וכן הוא אומר כה תאמר לבית יעקב, אלו הנשים. ותגיד לבני ישראל, אלו
האנשים.

Midrash ha-Gadol: Commentary on Hayyei Sarah, Genesis 23:1[*]

A *woman of valor, who can find?* This is the wife of Noah, who caused her husband to be righteous, as God said, "... for you alone have I found righteous before Me in this generation" (Gen. 7:1). *Her worth is far beyond that of rubies.* Her deeds and those of her daughter-in-law were far beyond the deeds of the generation of the flood. — *The heart of her husband trusts in her.* This is Sarah, in whom the heart of Abraham trusted, as he said to her, "... say ... He is my brother" (Gen. 20:13). "And lacks no good thing," for she used to invite in guests under the wings of the *Shekhinah.* — *She is good to him, never bad,* this is Rebekah. And what kind of good did she do for Isaac? At the time that Abraham sent his servant, and they said, "Let's call the young girl and make a request of her" (Gen. 24:57); now it was customary in the world that when a man would wed his daughter to someone, even if it were a servant he was wedding her to, she would be embarrassed to say anything. But when Rebekah was asked, "Will you go with this man?" ... she said, "I will" (24:58). Another thing: Rebekah's deeds were like Sarah's, as it is written, "Isaac then brought her to the tent of his mother Sarah ..." (24:67). — *She looks for wool and flax,* this is Leah who saw through the holy spirit that in the future would come from her a son who would allow a thing which is forbidden in Israel. And who is it? It's Levi. In Israel it is written, "Do not wear *shatnez* [a mixture of materials such as wool and flax]" (Deut. 22:11). And it is written about Aaron, "Make the ephod [priestly garment of woolen cloth] of gold, blue, purple, scarlet and linen. And she (Leah) really desired to marry Jacob and so she coaxed Rachel [to help her marry him] and she succeeded" (Exod. 28:8). — *She is like a merchant fleet*, this is Rachel, who said to Jacob: "Give me children, or I shall die!" (Gen. 30:1). Jacob responded, "Can I take the place of God ... ?" (Gen. 30:2). This is nothing but a language of shame, as it is said, "they were afraid and ashamed" (Isa. 37:27). The Holy One, Blessed be He, said to him, "Isn't it enough that you didn't pray for mercy for that righteous woman, but you embarrass her, too? By your life, I shall remember her and give her a child, but he will not have your name." Thus it is written: "Now God remembered Rachel" (Gen. 30:22) and Jacob is not mentioned. — *She rises while it is still night*, this is Batya, daughter of Pharaoh, who foresaw by the Holy Spirit that in the future the savior of Israel would be raised by her. In the evenings and mornings she and her handmaids used to stroll by the Nile. When Moses came her way, God had given her what she had requested. She rejoiced a great deal, as it is written, "When she opened [the basket], she saw that it was a child, a boy crying" (Exod. 2:6). — *She sets her mind on an estate*, this is Yocheved, because of whom Israel was called vineyard of the Holy One, Blessed be He; as it is said, "For the vineyard of the Lord of Hosts is the House of Israel" (Isa. 5:7). And why was she called Yocheved? Because her face was like Ziv HaKavod (Majestic Splendor). — *She girds herself with strength*, this is Miriam who said to her father when he divorced her mother, "Your decrees are harder than Pharaoh's. He decreed against the boys and you have decreed against the boys and the girls. He is evil and so there is a doubt about whether his decrees will come to be or not. 'You will decree and it will be fulfilled' (Job 22:28). Not only that, but I have seen that in the future there will come from you one who saves Israel." Immediately he remarried his wife, and since she gave birth to Moses and had to throw him into the Nile, her mother slapped her [Miriam] across the face and said to her, "Now where is your prophecy?" Immediately "... his sister stationed herself at a distance" (Exod. 2:4). She stood by her prophecy. — *She sees that her business thrives,* this is Hannah, who tasted the taste of prayer, as it is said, "... I have been pouring out my heart to the Lord" (1 Sam. 1:15). *Her lamp never goes out at night.* "The lamp of God had not yet gone out, and Samuel was sleeping in the temple of the Lord ... " (1 Sam. 3:3). — *She sets her hand to the distaff,* this is Yael and how Sisera came to be in her hands. As it says, "Sisera fled on foot to the tent of Yael ... She opened a skin of milk and gave him some to drink" (Judg. 4:17–19), to see if his mind was right or not. In his drunken stupor, he wanted her. "... she drove the pin through his temple" (4:21). Deborah later sings of this act in a poem, saying: "Her left hand reached for the tent pin, Her right for the workmen's hammer." (5:26). Thus she is blessed amongst the tents of Torah, in synagogues and study halls. As it is written: "Most blessed of women be Yael, wife of Heber the Kenite, most blessed of women in tents" (5:24). — *She spreads out her hand to the poor,* this is the Tzarephit, the woman from Tzarephath, to whom Elijah said, "Please bring me a little water" (1 Kings 17:10). And what was the reward that she took for this? "The flour jar shall not be finished and the oil cruse shall not be lacking" (1 Kings 17:14). — *Her hands are stretched out to the needy,* this is Naomi, who brought Ruth beneath the wings of *Shekhinah* (indwelling presence of God), as it is written, "When [Naomi] saw how determined she was to go with her, she ceased to argue with her" (Ruth 1:18). — *She is not worried for her household because of snow, for her whole household is dressed in crimson,* this is Rachav, who took in the spies. Who were they? Rabbi Yosi says Caleb and Pinchas. Others say Perez and Zerah. When she requested a sign from them, Zerah said to her, "... you tie this length of crimson cord to the window ..." (Josh. 2:18), this is the scarlet thread which was tied to my hand in the womb to prove my birthright, as it is written, "... the midwife tied a crimson thread on that hand ..." (Gen. 38:28). Therefore Rachav merited having 10 priests as descendants: Hilkiah, Jeremiah, Seraiah, Mehasiah, Baruch, Neriah, Hanamel, Shalom, Buzi, Yehezkel. Others say also Huldah the prophetess, as it is said: "the wife of Shallum son of Tikvah son of Harchas" (2 Kings 22:14), and regarding Rachav it is written: *tikvat chut ha-shani*—"the scarlet thread." — *She makes covers for herself*, this is Bath-Sheba, who foresaw by the Holy Spirit that in the future she would bear a son who would say 3,000 parables, as it is written, "He [Solomon] was the wisest of all men: …" (1 Kings 5:11). — *Her husband is prominent in the gates*, this is Michal, who saved her husband, David, from death when Saul sent [messengers] who kept watch on the house in order to kill him, but she said, "He is sick" (1 Sam. 19:14). In the end, when the matter became known, her father said to her, "you deceived me." She said to him, "[It was] to save you from [shedding] innocent blood." What did he say [then]? "No one can lay hands on the Lord's anointed with impunity" (1 Sam. 26:9). — *She makes cloth and sells it*, this is Hatzlelponi, mother of Samson. It is chronicled that among the descendents of Perez, who is the son of Judah, are the sons of Etam: Jezreel, Ishma, and Idbash, and the name of their sister is Hatzlelponi (1 Chron. 4:3). They reside in Zorah and Eshtaol, and it is written, "These were the families of the Zorathites" (1 Chron. 4:2). The angel [of God] revealed itself to her twice and not in front of her husband. And thus she had reasoned with her husband: "Had the Lord meant to take our lives …" (Judg. 13:23). "And offers a girdle to the merchant" (Prov. 31:24). She was weaving and selling in the market to reputable merchants. As it is said, "… whose [Canaanite] traders the world honored" (Isa. 23:8). — *She is clothed with strength and splendor*, this is Elisheba, who saw four happy occasions in one day: she became the sister-in-law of a king, the wife of the High Priest, and the sister of a prince, and her sons became deputies of the priesthood. — *Her mouth is full of wisdom*, this is Serach, daughter of Asher who declared to Joab: "I am one of those who seek the welfare of the faithful in Israel. But you seek to bring death upon a mother city in Israel! Why should you destroy the Lord's possession?" (2 Sam. 20:19). Her worth was as much as a city and mother in Israel. — *She oversees the activities of her household*, this is the wife of Obadiah. This is what is written: Once a certain woman, the wife of one of the disciples of the prophets, cried out to Elisha, saying, "I have nowhere to turn but to Elisha" (2 Kings 4:1). So she went to him and she said to him, "My lord, were you not yourself one of the Disciples of the Prophets, whom my husband, Obadiah, hid in the caves?" And he said to her, "Yes, what can I do for your good? How can I help you?" She said to him, "Pray for me for mercy that I may be self-sustained from the work of my hands that I need not rely on the habits of creation." In that very instant Elisha blessed her and she became blessed and she became self-sustaining from the work of her hands. That is why it is written, [She] *never eats the bread of idleness.* A miracle was wrought for her inside a miracle. — *Her children declare her happy,* this is the Shunammite woman, who said to her husband, "I am sure that he is a holy man of God ..." (2 Kings 4:9). Rabbi Yossi bar Hanina said, "From this [we know] that a woman involves herself with guests more than a man does." Rabbi Yossi bar Hanina [also] said, "She said to her husband, 'Whoever takes a student of wisdom into his house and feeds him and gives him drink and lets him use his property, about him it is written, It is as if he offered the daily offering in the Temple.'" "Let us make a small enclosed upper chamber," [said the Shunammite woman to her husband] (2 Kings 4:9,10). As a result, a miracle occurred and she gave birth, but the boy died, so Elisha resurrected him ..." — *Many women have done well,* this is Ruth, who merited that David and his righteous offspring were to be her descendants. Said Rabbi Yohanan: "Why Ruth? Because David would come from her, whose soul was so full, he would sing to God in songs and praises." — *Grace is deceptive, beauty is illusory,* this is Vashti. — *It is for fear of the Lord that a woman is to be praised,* this is Esther. "So he set a royal diadem on her head and made her queen instead of Vashti" (Esther 2:17). — *Extol her for the fruit of her hand,* this is the rest of the righteous and proper women of the world. Another interpretation: *Extol her for the fruit of her hand,* this is the Community of Israel, all of whom are called righteous, as it is said, "And your people, all of them righteous ... are ... My handiwork in which I glory" (Isa. 60:21). The Rabbis taught, God,

Blessed be He, promised a greater promise to righteous women than to men. As it is written, "You carefree women, / Attend, hear my words! / You confident ladies, / Give ear to my speech "(Isa. 32:9). Rav said to Rabbi Chiya, "Why do women merit eternal life?" Rabbi Chiya said, "Because they bring their children to the synagogue to learn Scripture and they send their husbands to the study hall to learn and because they wait for their husbands until they come home from study hall." The Rabbis taught that everyone who marries a proper woman, it is as if he brought the whole Torah into being, from *alef* to *tav*, just as Solomon sang praises in the portion on "Eishet Chayil," from *alef* to *tav*. The beginning of the poem is "What a rare find is a capable wife!" and the end is "It is for her fear of the Lord / That a woman is to be praised" (Prov. 31:10–31), and how much this is true for those who embody the Torah, "capable men who fear God, trustworthy men" (Exod. 18:21). And by the merit of the women, God, Blessed be He, remembers Israel in lovingkindness and truth, as it is said, "He was mindful of His stead-fast love and faithfulness toward the house of Israel" (Ps. 98:3). "Thus you shall say to the house of Jacob …" (Exod. 19:3), these are the women. "and declare to the Children of Israel" (19:3), these are the men.

    *   Edited with notes and sources by Mordecai Margaliot (Jerusalem: Mosad HaRav Kook). Translated by Penina Adelman and many of the contributors.

Index of Scriptural Passages

Prophets

Subject Index

CPSIA information can be obtained
at www.ICGtesting.com
Printed in the USA
LVHW111719150319
610814LV00002B/199/P

9 780827 608238